Yard & Garden Projects

EASY, STEP-BY-STEP PLANS AND DESIGNS
FOR BEAUTIFUL OUTDOOR SPACES

TIME
LIFE
BOOKS

ALEXANDRIA, VIRGINIA

Yard & Garden Projects

Introduction

Transforming your yard and garden into the beautiful low-maintenance landscape of your dreams is easy when you proceed step by step. Start with a surefire investment, a simple bed of colorful annuals or drifts of pastel perennials in an unused corner of your yard. As you experiment with the outdoor spaces you've got and discover your gardening tastes, you will develop projects perfectly suited to set off your home.

Practical information is your first steppingstone on the pathway to a glorious garden. Use this book as your personal gardening teacher; you'll learn exactly how to assess your site, how to select quality plants, how deep to dig each planting hole, and where to make each pruning cut.

After you master the basic techniques, you will want to move on to the fun of design. Easy-to-follow design ideas and planting tips in this book will simplify garden planning and show you how to improve your outdoor areas, making them comfortable and more enjoyable for family and guests to use. The projects presented here focus on design principles that lead to gardening success. They also show how to handle problem areas, such as landscaping for a wet site or deep shade.

When you're ready for bigger challenges, you'll see how to install a new lawn or patio, renovate your entryway, or build raised beds. And you do not need a green thumb, building expertise, or exotic tools to accomplish these goals—only the confidence that you can achieve your landscaping dreams by mapping out a plan and following it, one project at a time.

Getting Started

Deciding to establish a new garden is an exciting step in creating a beautiful landscape. You'll get the most rewarding results when you start the right way: by investigating your site, drawing a garden map, selecting appropriate plants, and gathering the right tools for the job.

The process of turning your ideas into reality starts with learning about your site conditions: the soil characteristics, the amounts of sun and shade, and the drainage. Perhaps you already know which plants you want to grow, and you need to find the spot that will best meet their needs. Or maybe you know exactly where you want the garden to be, and you'll choose plants that will thrive in growing conditions available there. Either way, taking the time to learn about the soil and light characteristics of your site with the simple tests explained in this chapter will help you make informed decisions about the garden's exact placement and plants.

Making a garden map is another important planning step. A map will give you an overview of your property, making it easy to see the space and the existing features. A map is also a great place to record the information you've learned about your property's growing conditions. When you get down to planning individual planting areas, you'll have all the information you need at a glance.

Of course, even the best-laid plans aren't much help if you don't have the necessary tools for digging and planting. In this section, you'll also find the basics of choosing the right tools for each task and caring for them properly so that they will last for many years. Once you have your tools and plans in hand, you'll be well on your way to creating your own dream garden. ❧

Making a Garden Map

Even if you are starting with one small garden, it will still be worth your while to make a simple map of your entire property. Having an overall plan will help guide your decisions about where and what to plant next. A map is also an excellent place to record garden information such as soil test results and sun and shade patterns.

Don't think you have to be an artist to make a garden map: a rough sketch is fine, as long as you can read it. Graph paper is a handy tool for creating a basic map. You can begin by measuring the outer dimensions of your property, then transfer them to paper, using a scale that will let you fit your whole map on one sheet and still allow room for details. When you sketch in your house, indicate doors and windows so that you can consider views from and of your house when you plan your gardens. To indicate trees, use an "x" to mark the trunk and a dotted line to show the outer reaches of branches, called the dripline.

When you've finished drawing existing features, redraw the map, if necessary, to clarify the outlines. Even for a small property, it can be helpful to create a separate key for features rather than labeling everything directly on the map.

When you are ready to plan a new garden, make photocopies of your base map or use tracing paper overlays so you won't have to redraw the original map. You may want to try different approaches on paper until you are satisfied with shape and size. Then, transfer your ideas to the site. Use garden hoses, or stakes and string, to mark the outline of new plantings and adjust as desired. Mark the final outline on a new map copy or overlay. If you would like to draw in plants, or try different designs within your garden outline, redraw the garden outline alone on a separate piece of graph paper at a larger scale, such as 1 square per 1 foot on the ground. ❧

HAVE ON HAND:

▶ Tape measure

▶ Pencil

▶ Eraser

▶ Graph paper

▶ Clipboard

Measure the outer dimensions of your property. Draw the outline of your property to scale on a large piece of graph paper.

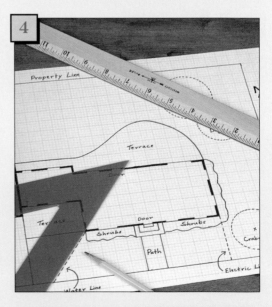

Mark the location of any rights-of-way, buried utility lines, wells, septic tanks and fields, and other underground features.

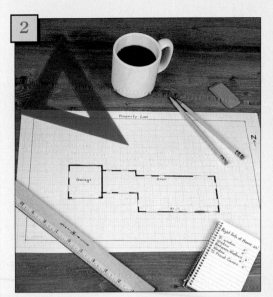

Draw in the outline of your house, marking openings for doors and windows. Also outline your garage and other outbuildings.

Sketch in other existing features, including decks, paved surfaces, trees, shrubs, hedges, fences, and garden beds.

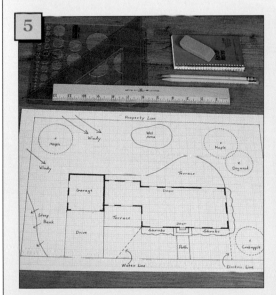

Sketch in any obvious site characteristics or problem areas, such as wet spots, steep slopes, and windy and rocky areas.

The final result is your base map. To try out new garden ideas, use photocopies or tracing paper laid over the base map.

HERE'S HOW

SETTING PLANTING PRIORITIES

Whether you're renovating an existing garden or starting from scratch, it can be tough to decide where to start. Here are some pointers to help you plan your garden priorities:

Stage 1: Work on areas you see all the time along the house and driveway. Start setting garden boundaries by planting trees, shrubs, and hedges and installing fences. Remove unwanted plantings and features. Control weeds, especially in unplanted areas. Begin a garden notebook.

Stage 2: Install any major garden projects, including decks, patios, paths, and paving. (This will avoid your damaging established plantings later on.) Gradually extend plantings away from the house. Continue to control weeds in unplanted areas.

Stage 3: Add details to existing plantings, such as edging strips to prevent lawn grass from creeping into beds. Plant vines and climbers along walls and fences. Create a continuous bed to link individual shrubs and trees, and underplant them with ground covers for easy maintenance. Add special touches, such as benches, as time and money permit.

Determining Sun and Shade

To get the best results in your garden, take time to observe the site you're considering. A spot that looks sunny and open in April or May might be heavily shaded by deciduous trees or shrubs in midsummer. Areas that seem cool and shady in fall or spring may actually get strong sun in midsummer, as the sun changes position. If you base your garden on conditions you observe at just one time, you may select plants that aren't entirely suited to their location.

Observe sun and shade patterns in your yard over the course of one entire growing season (roughly

April through September). Create a set of sun and shade maps to aid your future garden planning. They will allow you to tell at a glance how much light a particular site will receive at any time.

Most gardeners divide sun and shade into three categories: full sun, partial shade, and full shade. Full sun sites receive at least 6 hours of sunlight between 10 a.m. and 6 p.m. A partial shade (or partial sun) site gets less than 6 hours of direct sun during that time, or dappled sunlight all day. Full shade sites receive no direct sunlight.

If your site gets full sun in spring and partial shade in summer and fall, consider spring bulbs for early color and hostas, ferns, and other shade-lovers for interest later on. Where spring shade is followed by summer sun, combine early-blooming wildflowers with sun-loving annuals and perennials for a colorful, long-season display. 🌸

HAVE ON HAND:

▶ Base map

▶ Copies or overlays

▶ Pencil

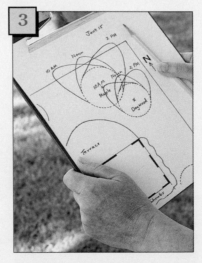

Use your property base map, indicating all permanent features. Make copies or use overlays.

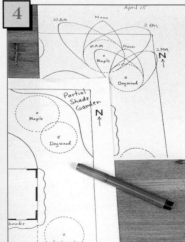

On a sunny day, observe your garden midmorning, noon, and mid-afternoon. Draw in shaded areas.

Repeat Step 2 every other month during growing season, drawing sun and shade patterns. Date maps.

When considering a site for a new garden, refer to maps or overlays to determine appropriate plants.

Understanding Drainage

Checking soil drainage is a critical step in learning about a prospective planting site. Drainage refers to the movement of water over the soil surface, below the surface, and between individual soil particles.

Surface drainage depends largely on the steepness of ground slope. On a gentle slope, water may soak in and excess run off. On a steep slope (especially if the soil is clay), water may run off before it can be absorbed. Flat sites absorb all the water they can, but excess will puddle on top until water already in the soil drains away. In most cases, gently sloping or flat spots will be fine for a garden.

Drainage below the surface depends on conditions below the topsoil layer. If the upper 8 inches of soil feels loose and crumbly, but water collects on the surface after heavy rains, there may be a compacted layer (called hardpan) below the topsoil. Hardpan keeps water in topsoil from draining through the subsoil. Or you may have water coming up from an underground spring. Subsurface drainage problems are usually hard to fix. You might either choose plants that thrive in wet conditions or build raised beds to provide better drainage.

The third aspect of drainage is the way water moves between soil particles. Sand particles stay loose, allowing water to drain quickly. In sandy soil, water may drain through faster than roots can absorb it. Clay particles can pack together tightly and become waterlogged, drowning plant roots. Loamy soils hold enough water while letting excess drain away. ✿

HAVE ON HAND:

▶ Trowel

▶ Water

SIMPLE TEST. *Dig a hole about 1 foot deep and 6 inches wide. Fill the hole with water; let it drain.*

Add water to refill hole. If it takes more than 8 hours for the water to soak in, your soil is poorly drained.

SPOTTING PROBLEMS. *If you strike a dense layer before digging 2 feet deep, you have hardpan.*

If soil does not drain, use plants that will thrive in wet soil, or build one or more raised beds.

Working with Garden Tools

CHOOSING TOOLS

When you shop for garden tools, don't be overwhelmed by the wide array of equipment available. You only need a few basic tools to get started. A spade and spading fork for digging, a metal garden rake for smoothing, and a trowel for close work around plants are musts. Other basics include pruning shears for trimming and a shovel for moving soil and mulch.

Buying good-quality tools will save the cost and hassle of buying replacements later. Bargains tend to break quickly, make your job harder and litter your storage area with unusable tools.

Check all parts of digging tools: the blade, the handle, and the connection between the two. A high-carbon or stainless steel blade will last longer than regular steel. Forged blades, made from thick metal, are stronger and more durable than stamped blades, which are cut from a metal sheet and have a fold where joined to the handle.

High-quality tools usually have wooden or plastic-coated steel handles. Ash and hickory are the most durable and desirable woods for handles. Avoid buying tools with painted handles; the paint may cover knots or flaws in the wood. Long, straight handles provide more leverage for digging, while shorter, "D"-grip handles offer more control and prying power. Choose the length that feels most comfortable for your height.

Look for tools with "solid-socket" or "solid-strap" construction. Both have metal extending from the blade to cover part of the handle. One-piece construction makes them very strong. Cheaper "tang-and-ferrule" construction is made with a thin metal extension from the blade-top into the handle. A metal collar surrounds the base of the handle, secured by a rivet or bolt. This type of construction is less expensive but also less durable than either solid-socket or solid-strap.

A footrest makes it easier to push a blade into soil and protects your leg if your foot slips off the blade.

Solid-socket/solid-strap construction means a sturdy, durable connection between blade and handle.

Check wooden handles. The "grain" should run straight down the handle, with no knots or cracks.

If your soil is rocky or hard to dig, choose a spading fork with thick tines; thin ones will quickly bend.

CLEANING TOOLS

After a day in the garden, you may be tempted to toss your tools into the garage and head inside for a cool drink. But it's worth taking a few minutes to clean your tools after each use to keep them in top shape. With regular maintenance, they will repay your investment with many years of service.

At the end of each gardening session, remove damp soil on blades so rust won't develop. Never use a metal tool to scrape soil from another tool; you'll damage both. A stiff utility brush should do the job. Or keep a bucket of sand near your tool storage, so you can plunge the blades into the sand to clean off the soil. Once metal parts are clean, coat them with a thin layer of light machine or mineral oil or spray with a lubricant to prevent rust from developing.

Handle care is important for your own comfort. A clean, smooth handle is much more pleasant to hold and is less likely to cause blisters. When necessary, sand handles lightly to smooth out rough spots. A coat of varnish, tung oil, or other sealer will help protect the wood. Replace damaged handles as soon as possible.

Brush wood scraps and clean dried sap from pruning tools (use steel wool, if needed). Oil all metal parts lightly. Check and tighten the blades as needed. 🌺

HAVE ON HAND:

- ▶ Wooden scraper
- ▶ Water
- ▶ Dry cloth
- ▶ Wire brush
- ▶ Motor oil on rag
- ▶ Sandpaper
- ▶ Sealer

Scrape off soil clinging to blades or tines of digging tools with a wooden or plastic scraper.

If you can't remove all the soil with the scraper, rinse it off with water, then dry the tool thoroughly.

Use a wire brush to remove rust on any metal parts, then wipe metal with an oily rag to prevent rust.

Wipe handles with a dry cloth to clean off clinging soil. Sand and seal handles to keep them smooth.

KEEPING TOOLS SHARP

A clean, sharp tool can make almost any garden job a pleasure. Sharpening your tools often will keep them in top shape, so they're always ready when you need them. A sharp blade can also be safer for you and your plants, since it will cut easily and cleanly through plants or soil; dull blades tend to slip and crush or tear stems.

The goal of any sharpening job is to create an edge that is both sharp and durable. You'll want to keep the existing angle of the cutting edge (known as the bevel), but remove nicks and improve the keenness of the edge. Before sharpening, check the existing bevel of the blade. Most spades, shovels, and hoes have a single bevel, with one flat side and one angled side. Always sharpen single-bevel tools on the angled side only; otherwise, you will create a weak cutting edge that is susceptible to damage.

A mill bastard file is the sharpening tool of choice for most home gardeners. Holding the file at a shallow angle to the blade will create the thin, sharp edge desirable for cutting and weeding tools. A steeper angle will produce a longer-lasting edge more suitable for digging tools.

File until you feel a slight buildup of metal, called a "burr," on the back side of the blade. When the burr extends all along the blade edge, turn the blade over and rub the file flat across the blade to remove the burr. 🌼

HAVE ON HAND:

▶ Protective gloves

▶ Flat file for flat-bladed tools

▶ Curved file for curved-bladed tools

▶ Oily rag

Wear gloves. Secure spade, inside of blade facing you. Hold file to match bevel angle, toward blade edge.

Push file away from blade, while sweeping it from one side of blade to the other. Use the length of file.

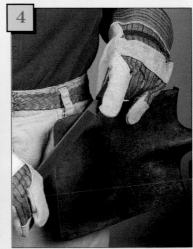

Give nicks a few extra strokes with the file to smooth them out, for an even, uniform edge.

Turn blade over. Hold file flat against blade, draw back and forth to remove "burr." Wipe with oily rag.

STORING TOOLS

When you are ready to dig, plant, or prune, you want to gather your tools and start. Preparing a proper storage area for your tool collection will help ensure that your tools are ready for use and easy to find.

You don't need much room to store a basic tool collection; a corner of your garage will be fine. As your collection expands, you may want to construct a separate storage shed or toolhouse. Wherever you choose, the site should be dry to prevent metal tools from rusting, and also well lighted so that it's easy to see what you are looking for.

A well-planned storage area has racks or hanging spaces for tools and shelves or cupboards for supplies. For long-handled tools, you can make a simple rack by nailing a 2 x 4-inch strip to the wall, about 4 feet above the ground, and attaching several broom holders (available in most hardware stores). A pegboard is handy for hanging small tools. If desired, you can outline the shape of each tool in paint on the pegboard. You'll be able to see at a glance where each tool belongs and if any are missing. Choose a storage system that is comfortable and convenient for you—don't be tempted to dump your tools in a corner and deal with them later.

Don't forget to bring in other garden equipment for the winter. Drain hoses, then coil loosely and hang indoors. Wash and dry garden stakes and store them inside. 🌼

HAVE ON HAND:

▶ Motor oil on rag

▶ Fine-grit sandpaper

▶ Varnish or tung oil

▶ Files

▶ Steel wool or wire brush

Scrape or wash off soil from metal parts; dry thoroughly. Wipe metal parts with oily rag to prevent rust.

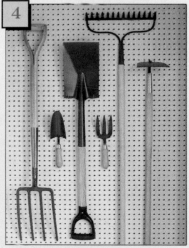

Wipe off handles. Sand rough spots; seal with varnish or tung oil. Replace damaged handles.

Sharpen tools before putting them away in fall, so they'll be ready to use when you need them in spring.

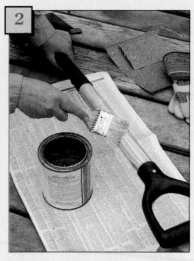

Hang tools in a dry place. Remove rust spots that develop with steel wool or a wire brush, and oil again.

Winterizing Outdoor Power Equipment

When your lawn mower, weed trimmer, leaf blower, and other outdoor gas-powered tools are to be stored for more than two months, spend a little time preparing them so that they will be ready when you need to use them again. While you're at it, manual and electric tools will also benefit from your attention before being stored.

Clean dirt and debris from your equipment by washing waterproof parts with warm, soapy water and a soft cloth. Wipe off dust that has accumulated on air intake vents, and remove and clean filters if your tools have them. Before storing any battery-operated tools, fully charge batteries. Then unplug battery chargers, wipe them clean with a damp cloth, and store them in plastic bags once they are completely dry. Your large tools will take up less room in your storage area if you are able to remove or fold down the handles.

Clean and dry the blades of manual reel mowers or lawn edgers; then, to prevent rust, wipe them with a rag that has been lightly sprinkled with household oil. Before putting garden hoses away, drain them. Water left inside will expand as it freezes, which may result in cracked hoses.

GAS-POWERED MOWER

The hour or so it takes to winterize your lawn mower will go a long way toward extending its engine's life, and the same procedures will benefit all other gas-powered tools. Fuel system parts such as tanks, hoses, filters, and carburetors should all be cleaned before storage.

Begin by draining the fuel tank. Put leftover gas in a closed container and dispose of it properly. When the fuel tank is empty, try to start the engine. This should clear the fuel lines and carburetor of any remaining fuel. Use a damp cloth to wipe away oil and dirt that have accumulated on the outside of your mower, paying special attention to air intake vents. If possible, lay it on its side, scrape, then use a strong spray of water to remove any dried grass from the blade and under the deck. This is a good time to inspect the blade for large nicks and to install a new one if needed.

Drain the oil in your mower before you store it for the winter, being careful to dispose of the old oil in an environmentally safe manner. Changing the spark plug as described at right is another way to ensure a fast spring start-up. Finally, cover your mower with a blanket, canvas tarp, or plastic drop cloth to keep it clean. ✳

HAVE ON HAND:

- ▶ Spark plug wrench or adjustable wrench
- ▶ Tablespoon
- ▶ Fresh engine oil (two-stroke oil for two-stroke engines)
- ▶ Disposable paper or plastic cup
- ▶ Two clean rags
- ▶ New spark plug
- ▶ Canvas tarp or plastic drop cloth

Before changing a spark plug, turn ignition off. Disconnect spark plug, and unscrew it with a wrench.

Place 1 tablespoon oil in paper cup; pour it into the spark plug hole. Plug hole with a clean rag.

Slowly pull the starter handle to distribute the clean oil; allow it to recoil, and slowly pull it again.

Install the new spark plug. For safety, leave the ignition cable disconnected until the tool is used again.

Testing Your Soil

JAR TEST

Soil is the key to creating a healthy, beautiful garden. Its makeup can vary widely from place to place on your property, so use this simple test more than once to find out what kinds of soil you have in each garden site.

A jar test will determine your soil's texture. Texture refers to the soil's sand, silt, and clay content. Sand particles are large; clay particles are tiny. Silt particles are between sand and clay in size.

HAVE ON HAND:

▶ Clean 1-quart glass jar with lid

▶ Air-dried soil, no sticks, stones, or leaves

▶ Nonsudsing dishwasher detergent

▶ Water

▶ Grease pencil or masking tape

The relative amount of each in your soil affects many traits, including drainage and fertility. Soils high in sand feel gritty and are loose and easy to dig. They drain quickly and don't hold nutrients well, so need frequent watering and fertilizing. Soils high in clay are sticky when wet and hard to dig when dry. They hold more nutrients and water than sand, but they can become waterlogged. Silt particles are between sand and clay in size, have a powdery feel, and hold fair amounts of nutrients and water, letting the excess drain away.

Soil that contains approximately 40 percent silt, 40 percent sand, and 20 percent clay is known as loam. Loam provides ideal conditions for a wide range of plants. Sites high in clay or sand, however, will need amending. Both can be improved with compost or other organic matter which will loosen clay soil and will improve water and nutrient retention in sandy soil. ✿

Add 1 cup soil, 1 teaspoon detergent to jar. Fill ⅔ with water, close tightly. Shake hard for 2 minutes.

Set jar on a level surface. After 1 minute, mark the level of settled soil on the jar. This is the sand level.

After 2 hours, mark the new soil level; this is the silt layer. After 2 days, mark the final clay layer.

Compare the depth of each layer to the total depth of settled soil to determine the percentage of each.

pH TEST

Your soil's pH, or relative acidity or alkalinity, influences the nutrients available to plant roots. Know the conditions you're starting with, and you will make good decisions before planting.

Soil pH is measured on a scale of 1.0 to 14.0, with 7.0 considered neutral. A value less than 7.0 indicates acid (or "sour") soil, while a value higher than 7.0 means your soil is alkaline (or "sweet"). Most garden plants grow well when the pH is 6.0 to 7.0.

If your soil's pH is not ideal, you have two options:

choose plants that are naturally adapted to the existing pH, or add amendments to adjust it. You can do a simple pH test at home with a kit available at your local plant nursery, but before amending your soil, have it tested professionally, either by a private laboratory or your state Cooperative Extension Service. Most tests are inexpensive, and you'll get a detailed report on your soil's nutrient content and pH level. The results may also include specific recommendations for amendments to add for the plants you want to grow.

If you decide to plant for your conditions, azaleas and rhododendrons require acid soil, for example, while baby's breath and lilacs can tolerate alkaline conditions. If you want to grow the widest range of garden plants, add amendments such as lime (to raise pH) or sulfur (to lower pH). Compost or other organic matter can also help adjust pH to a suitable level.

HAVE ON HAND:

▶ Air-dried soil, no sticks, stones, or leaves

▶ Soil test kit

▶ Distilled water

Place 1 tablespoon of soil in container. Add distilled water, stir until mix is consistency of a milkshake.

Let sit for 1 to 2 hours. Add more water, if needed, to keep the mixture at the right consistency.

Lay a strip of litmus paper on mixture and let it sit for 1 minute. Remove, rinse with distilled water.

Compare the color of your test strip to the chart supplied with soil test kit to determine pH.

Cultivating Your Soil

SIMPLE DIGGING

When you are creating a garden for annuals, a simple dig will cultivate enough surface soil to provide good growing conditions for these shallow-rooted plants. If your soil is on the sandy side and fertile, a simple dig will be sufficient for perennial, rose, and shrub plantings.

You can dig your soil any time of the year that it isn't frozen or too wet. To test soil moisture, use a trowel to dig up a handful of soil. Squeeze the soil, then open your hand. If the soil crumbles right away, or when you tap the ball lightly, it is fine to dig. If the soil stays in a ball, wait a few days and test again. If the weather has been dry for several weeks, water the area thoroughly a few days before planting to soften the soil and make digging easier.

Before you dig your garden, remove any vegetation growing there. Simply digging or tilling grass and weeds into the soil will not get rid of them; the plants will quickly resprout. Slice just under the soil surface with a spade to sever plants from their roots. The roots will break down easily, adding organic matter to the soil. Some weeds, such as dandelions, will resprout right from the roots, so remove them as far down as possible. Pick out and dispose of strong-looking, white roots creeping horizontally through the soil. Don't compost them; they may resprout and spread through your compost pile. 🌾

HAVE ON HAND:

▶ Stakes

▶ String

▶ Spade

▶ Shovel or spading fork

▶ Rake

Mark area with stakes and string. Use spade to slice off top 2 to 3 inches of turf to remove weeds.

Start at a corner of bed; insert full shovel blade into the soil. Pull the handle toward you to loosen soil.

Twist shovel to turn soil over. Repeat steps, working backward to loosen the soil in the entire bed.

Use metal rake to smooth surface. Remove rocks and other debris before planting.

DOUBLE DIGGING

Double digging helps you provide the best possible growing conditions for deep-rooted plants such as perennials, roses, and shrubs. This technique loosens the top 18 to 24 inches of soil. Deep digging takes extra time and energy, but it helps plants thrive by providing an extra-deep zone of loosened soil. Plant roots can spread easily to search out water and nutrients. By double digging, you work organic matter deeper into the root zone to improve soil structure and fertility. This also improves drainage by breaking up the compacted subsurface layers.

Before starting a double dig, follow the same preparations as for a simple dig: squeeze a handful of soil to make sure it isn't too wet (it should crumble when you open your hand), then remove existing grass and weeds. Pick out thick, white roots as you dig; it's okay to leave fine, branching grass roots.

To avoid stepping on and compacting the loosened soil, walk on broad boards laid over the area to distribute your weight evenly. Remove the boards when you are finished. Or lay broad, flat steppingstones and then plant around them. Later on, you will be able to reach plants for maintenance without stepping directly on the soil.

After digging, your soil surface will be several inches higher than it was before. Let the soil settle for a week before planting. ❧

HAVE ON HAND:

▶ Stakes

▶ String

▶ Spade

▶ Tarp or wheelbarrow

▶ Shovel or spading fork

▶ Compost

Mark outline of bed with stakes and string. Use spade to slice just below surface to remove growth.

Working along back edge, dig trench 1 foot wide and at least as deep. Pile soil on tarp or wheelbarrow.

Loosen soil in bottom of trench; add 2 inches of compost. Dig another trench next to the first one.

Fill first trench with soil from new one. Repeat until entire bed is dug. Fill last trench with reserved soil.

Improving Your Soil

If you have less than ideal soil, you can condition it before planting. The steps you need to take depend on the special characteristics of the site (see Testing Your Soil, page 20, and Understanding Drainage, page 13), but even loam will benefit from the addition of compost.

For soil that is particularly sandy or clayey, work in organic matter, such as compost (see Here's How), to improve its structure and drainage. Where soil pH is lower than 6.2, add lime (sold as garden lime or ground limestone) to raise the pH to around 6.5 to 7.0, which is ideal for a wide range of garden plants. Elemental sulfur (sold as garden sulfur) will lower soil pH; use it on soil with a pH higher than 7.0.

If most plants in your garden grow well without regular fertilizing, your soil probably has an adequate balance of nutrients. But if your plants grow poorly without supplemental fertilizer, test your soil to check the nutrient content. Check your local garden center for kits, or ask them to recommend a soil testing laboratory. Review the test results and add fertilizers as needed to prepare a new bed.

Correct drainage problems before planting, unless you intend to grow only moisture-loving plants. First, identify the cause of the problem. If the surface soil is fairly loose but you hit a dense, compacted subsurface layer when you dig, called hardpan, deep cultivation will break it up (see Double Digging, page 23). For soil too hard or rocky to dig deeply, build a raised bed, which will add 8 to 10 inches of soil on top of the ground to give plants rooting room. To hold the soil in place, frame the bed with landscape timbers or rocks. Raised beds are useful for wet sites, since the plants will be growing in a layer of well-drained soil, rather than in the water-logged earth. 🌺

HAVE ON HAND:

▶ Soil test kit

▶ Compost or other organic matter

▶ Lime

▶ Sulfur

▶ Organic fertilizers

▶ Spade, shovel, or spading fork

▶ Rocks or landscape timbers

SOIL pH. *Test with kit. Add lime or sulfur as indicated in the test results; dig into the top 1 foot of soil.*

SOIL HIGH IN CLAY OR SAND. *Dig or till a 1- to 2-inch layer of compost or other organic matter into the top 8 inches of soil.*

Raise the pH of acid soil by 0.5 by digging in 4 pounds of lime per 100 square feet. Test again every 3 to 4 years.

Lower the pH of alkaline soil by 0.5 by digging in ½ pound of sulfur per 100 square feet. Test again every 2 to 3 years.

COMPACTED SOIL. Improve drainage by digging deeply to loosen top 12 to 18 inches of soil. Avoid stepping on loosened soil.

WET OR ROCKY SOIL. Build raised beds. Use rocks or timbers as framing. Make sides 10 to 12 inches high. Fill with well-drained soil.

HERE'S HOW
MAKE YOUR OWN COMPOST

Make your own soil amendment by composting garden trimmings and kitchen scraps. Choose a garden spot that's out of the way. You can have a freestanding pile or enclose it in a homemade or commercial bin. You'll need enough room for a pile at least 3 feet long, wide, and tall, the size necessary to generate sufficient heat.

To build the pile, layer roughly equal amounts of high-carbon and high-nitrogen materials. High-carbon materials tend to be brownish and dry; they include fallen leaves and straw. High-nitrogen materials tend to be greenish and wet; think of fresh grass clippings and vegetable peelings.

As the materials accumulate, water the pile occasionally to keep it moist but not wet. When the pile is about 3 cubic feet in size, use a pitchfork to stir up the materials. Turn the pile once or twice a week after that. The compost will be ready to use in 2 to 4 months, when it is dark and crumbly and the original materials are mostly unrecognizable.

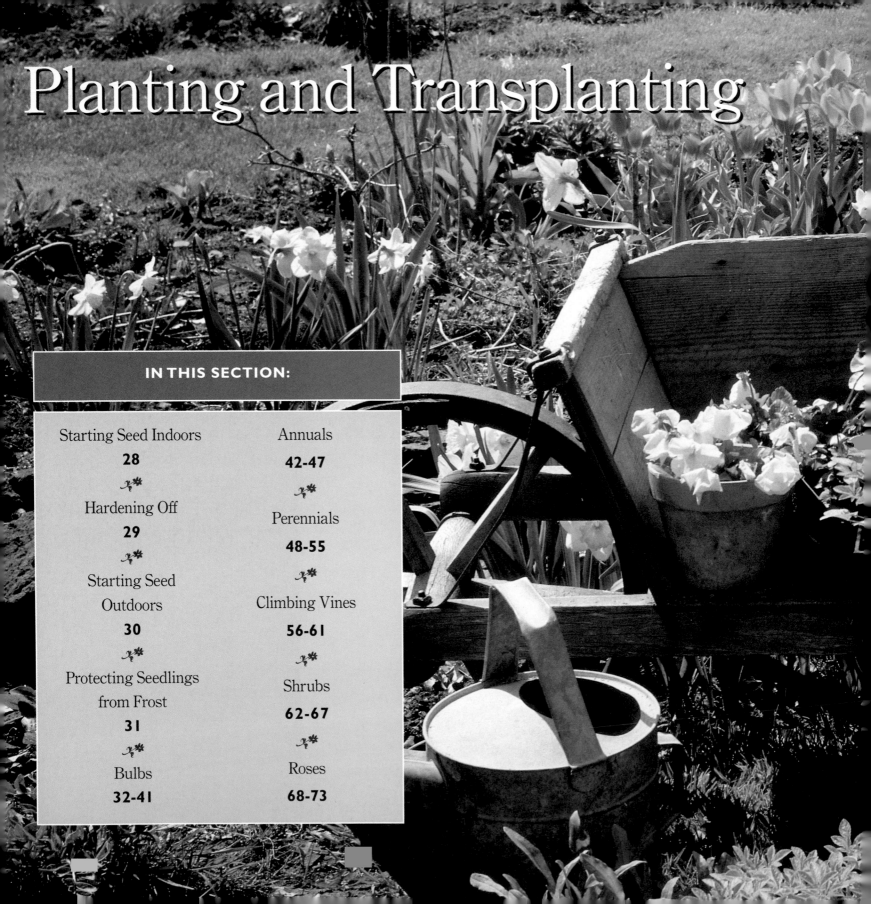

Planting and Transplanting

You've developed a wonderful garden plan and prepared the perfect planting site. Now it's time to get your garden growing. First you need the plants—either grown from seed, bought from a nursery or garden center, ordered by mail, or ready to be transplanted from other parts of your yard. Then you need to know the proper planting techniques to get your plants off to a healthy and vigorous start.

Plant shopping for a new garden is fun, but it's important to take a plant list with you—and stick to it. (Otherwise, consider creating a special "trial" bed, where you can grow your unplanned acquisitions until you find a good spot for them in the garden.) And, it is essential for you to inspect all new plants for pests and diseases before you buy them. Don't pay for the privilege of bringing problems home to your healthy garden.

Of course, you have the option of raising your own plants. Most annuals are easy to grow from seed, even for beginning gardeners. Perennials don't take much more skill, but they do demand more patience, since they can take two years or more to reach flowering size. When you are starting out, it's easier to purchase plants for your first garden, then experiment with seed sowing for future plantings.

In this section, you'll learn the basics of starting, growing, and buying top-quality plants and getting them settled into your garden. You'll also find guides that highlight plants for special purposes. With all of this at your fingertips, you're virtually guaranteed a great garden! 🌸

Starting Seed Indoors

With a few basic materials and a bit of patience, you can grow dozens of new plants for the price of a single seed packet.

Your planting containers should be at least 2 inches deep, with holes in the bottom for drainage. Fill your pots with moistened commercial seed-starting mix. Avoid using garden soil; it will pack down in the pots, discouraging healthy root growth, and may contain weed seeds or diseases that can harm new seedlings. After sowing seeds, place a plastic bag around the pots, using pencils or other supports to make a tent, and place under fluorescent lights or in bright but indirect sunlight (direct sun will overheat, or even cook, seedlings). When seedlings are ½ to 1 inch tall, remove the bag. Fertilize seedlings with fish emulsion or other liquid organic fertilizer.

When seedlings have two or three pairs of "true" leaves (not the first leaves on the plant, which form inside the seed), transplant to individual pots. Carefully slide seedlings out of container. Separate seedlings by holding leaves with the fingers of one hand while gently loosening roots with a pencil. Transplant to a 3-inch pot filled with moistened potting soil. With a pencil, make a hole for the roots and set them in. Gently firm the soil around roots with your fingers. Water and set in a bright place until the plants are ready for the garden.

HAVE ON HAND:

- ▶ 4-inch pot
- ▶ Commercial seed-starting mix
- ▶ Seeds
- ▶ Shallow pan
- ▶ Water
- ▶ Plastic bag

Fill 4-inch pot with moistened soil mix to within ½ inch of the rim. Smooth surface with your finger.

Scatter small- and medium-sized seeds evenly over surface. Place large seeds about ½ inch apart.

Cover seeds with more mix, according to seed packet instructions. Lightly firm the surface.

Set in pan with 1 inch of water for 1 hour. Drain. Set pot in plastic bag. Place in warm, bright spot.

Hardening Off

Seedlings grown indoors lead a pampered life, with regular watering, even temperatures, and protection from wind. In the garden, though, they will need to adapt to less than perfect growing conditions. You can ease this transition from indoors to out through a process called "hardening off."

Hardening off means exposing seedlings to gradually longer periods of outdoor conditions, until they are tough enough to withstand wind and weather without damage. It's a critical step for getting home-grown seedlings off to a good start in the garden. It's also useful if you've purchased transplants from a greenhouse or garden center in early to mid-spring, when the plants may have been kept indoors to protect them from cold.

To decide when to start hardening off, calculate the proper transplanting time for your plants. The seed packet may give you some guidance, such as "plant after danger of frost has passed." If you buy transplants, ask the supplier when you can set them in the garden. If you are unsure of the last frost date in your area, check with a local garden center.

Mark the transplanting date on a calendar, then count back 1 to 2 weeks for the date to begin hardening off. If you aren't home during the day, set seedlings out in the early evening; bring them indoors at night. Over weekends, leave them out for a half day each day, then for a full day on Monday. Water them thoroughly in the morning, so they won't dry out before you return home.

A porch or patio sheltered from strong sun and wind is a great place to harden off seedlings. Other possible spots include under shrubs and trees, or on the north side of your house.

A week before transplanting, set seedlings out for 1 hour the first day in partly shady, sheltered spot.

About 2 weeks before transplanting, allow the top ¼ to ½ inch of soil to dry out between waterings.

Water often to keep plants from drying out. After a whole day out, they are ready to transplant.

Over the next few days, leave the seedlings out for longer periods, an extra hour or two each time.

Starting Seed Outdoors

Some annuals are so easy to grow that you can sow their seeds directly into the garden. You can also raise many perennials and bulbs from outdoor-sown seeds, although they tend to grow more slowly than annuals. You should sow these bulbs and perennials in a special "nursery bed," an out-of-the-way spot where the seedlings can grow and develop. After a year or two, they will be big enough to transplant to a permanent spot in the garden.

To prepare your site for planting, first loosen the soil with a simple or double digging (see Cultivating Your Soil, page 22). Lay broad boards to avoid stepping on the bed after digging; otherwise, you will compact the soil and make it harder for the roots of your seedlings to spread.

The best time to sow depends on where you live and the seeds you're planting. Check the seed packet or catalog for recommended planting times. You'll often see a reference to the "last frost date" in the recommendations. This refers to the average date of the last spring frost for your area. If you don't know your last frost date, check with a local garden center.

Once seedlings emerge, you may have to thin them out to prevent crowding. Snip less sturdy seedlings at ground level with garden scissors, as pulling them out may injure the roots of the remaining ones. Clip as many seedlings as necessary to leave the rest at the spacing recommended in the seed packet instructions. 🌺

HAVE ON HAND:

▶ Garden rake

▶ Seeds

▶ Water

▶ Scissors

Rake the prepared soil just before planting to smooth the surface. Remove any roots and debris.

Scatter small- and medium-sized seeds thinly and evenly. Rake lightly to scratch the seeds into the soil.

Place large seeds individually, at the depth and spacing indicated on the seed packet. Cover with soil.

Lightly firm the soil with palm of hand. Water gently with fine mist; keep moist until seedlings appear.

Protecting Seedlings from Frost

The one thing you can predict about the spring weather is that it will be unpredictable. One day will be sunny and summer-like; the next may bring the return of winter-like cold. Hardening off your seedlings helps them tolerate these extreme temperature changes. But if a sudden cold snap brings nighttime frost, even hardened-off seedlings will need extra protection.

Once you've set out transplants, pay close attention to daily weather forecasts to see if frost is predicted so you can take measures to protect your seedlings.

Fortunately, frost protection doesn't require fancy or expensive materials. You can use a variety of items found around the house, including plastic milk jugs (either quart or gallon), cardboard boxes, and newspapers. Or you can buy floating row covers—lightweight, polyester material available at garden centers or through mail-order garden suppliers. All of these protectors cover the plants and hold in the heat radiating up from the soil. To retain as much heat as possible, make sure the cover reaches to the ground on all sides of the plant or bed. Watering thoroughly before covering the plants may help too, since moist soil holds and releases more heat than dry soil.

Place covers over plants in late afternoon to early evening. Remove them the next morning.

HAVE ON HAND:

- ▶ Plastic milk jugs
- ▶ Scissors
- ▶ Stones
- ▶ Cardboard boxes
- ▶ Newspaper
- ▶ Floating row covers
- ▶ Boards

SINGLE PLANT. *Cut off the bottom of a plastic milk jug. Place jug over the plant.*

GROUPS. *Set cardboard boxes over transplants. Place stones around edges to keep them in place.*

SEEDBEDS. *Lay sheets of newspaper over seedbeds. Weight down edges with soil or rocks.*

WHOLE BEDS. *Protect beds with floating row covers. Use boards, stones, or soil to hold down edges.*

Bulbs

SPRING

Planting spring-flowering bulbs is truly an act of faith. It seems impossible that the tiny bulbs are capable of producing beautiful flowers and lush foliage. They also require patience and planning on your part, since they need to be planted months ahead of when they'll bloom. It's hard to think about daffodils and tulips in August and September, when there is so much else going on in the garden. But after a long winter, you'll be glad you made the effort when you see masses of cheerful and colorful bulbs emerging to greet the spring.

It's easy to tuck these versatile plants into all parts of your garden. Plant tulips and daffodils at the back of your perennial borders, so emerging perennials can cover up ripening bulb foliage. Combine spring bulbs with early blooming annuals, such as forget-me-nots and pansies, for a spectacular spring show. Or use later-flowering annuals to fill the spaces left when spring bulbs die back to the ground in early summer. Spring bulbs also work well interplanted with ground covers such as common periwinkle. The bulbs provide seasonal color while the ground cover provides an attractive foundation. Container plantings let you enjoy spring bulbs either outdoors or in. 🌾

FOR SHADE

Shady gardens don't have to be green and boring; you can add sparkle with colorful, shade-appreciating annuals. There are a number of annual plants that prefer some shade, such as the dappled sun and shade created by a high tree canopy. Fragrant, old-fashioned flowering tobacco is one. It appreciates partial shade so much that its flowers will fade if it is placed in full sun.

Also for partial shade areas, flowering annuals such as impatiens and wishbone flowers will brighten beds and borders all season long. A more varied look can be obtained by adding coleus or caladium (a bulb often treated as an annual) and other shade-loving foliage plants to your garden. Their unusual leaf colors, variegated leaf patterns, and plant forms can add variety and contrast to an edging of flowers and provide a backdrop for more vivid bloomers.

Container gardens filled with shade-loving annuals also make excellent accents for shady gardens—and you don't even have to do any digging. In addition, these portable gardens can be moved and rearranged as the season progresses so that they always get the right amount of shade and provide you with the best display. 🌿

Selecting Healthy Annuals

To get the best possible annuals for your flower garden, you need to be a smart shopper. By taking a few minutes to look carefully at potential purchases, you can make sure that you're getting healthy, top-quality plants that will thrive when you get them home.

Start by shopping at a reputable nursery or garden center. The facility should be clean and organized, without weeds or dead plants lying around. The plants themselves should be clearly labeled, so you can be sure you're getting the ones you want. And they should be well watered, not dry or wilted. Most annuals can recover from wilting once or twice, but repeated wilting can lead to stunted growth later on.

It's also critical to check plants for pests and diseases before you buy them. After all, you don't want to bring problems home to your healthy garden. Common pests of annuals include aphids, spider mites, and whiteflies. Always inspect the leaves (both sides) and the stems, especially near the shoot tips, for signs of damage. Aphids feed on stems, leaves, buds, and flowers, causing yellowing or distorted growth. The leaves of aphid-infested plants often feel sticky, from the sugary "honeydew"

excreted by the pests as they feed. Spider mites are tiny pests that tend to feed on the undersides of leaves, producing a yellow or brown stippling on the upper leaf surfaces. You may also see tiny webs on the undersides of the leaves. Whiteflies are easy to see; just look for these small, bright white pests to fly up when you shake or brush a plant. Whiteflies usually feed on the undersides of leaves, producing stunted growth and yellowed leaves. You'll also want to avoid buying any annuals with powdery white or fuzzy gray patches on the flowers or foliage (symptoms of powdery mildew and botrytis blight).

When shopping for flowering annuals, avoid the temptation of buying plants that are in full bloom. It's fine if there are one or two flowers per plant, especially if you need to be sure you're getting a certain color. But plants not yet flowering will recover most quickly from transplanting; they can put their energy into producing new roots rather than flowers. When they start blooming, usually within 2 to 3 weeks of transplanting, the plants will have a well-established root system that can support a generous display of flowers throughout the season. ❧

When selecting plants, choose compact, bushy, vigorous-looking plants, with top growth that is in proportion to the size of the container.

Choose plants with firm, evenly-colored leaves and stems. Avoid annuals with yellow, discolored, or limp foliage.

Check the bottom of the container for visible roots. Avoid buying annuals that have circling or matted roots, which are likely to be dried out.

On flowering annuals, choose plants with only leaves or just a few open blooms, rather than those in full flower.

Look closely at stems and at both sides of a few leaves. They should be free of holes, speckling, webbing, and other signs of insect problems.

Inspect shoot tips and buds for aphids, tiny green, black, or reddish pests, that cluster on stems. Don't buy infested plants.

HERE'S HOW

CONTROLLING SELF-SOWERS

Self-sowing annuals—those that sprout from seed from the previous year's plants—can be a bane or a boon in your garden. If you enjoy creating carefully planned annual displays or color theme gardens, self-sown plants of varying colors may pop up here and there and alter your design. If you enjoy an informal look to your beds and borders and don't mind a variety of colors and heights mingling together, allowing annuals to self-sow can provide playful and surprising results.

While it's possible for almost any annual to self-sow, exactly which ones will reseed for you depends on your particular garden conditions. A few that reseed readily in most areas include bachelor's buttons, cleome, cosmos, garden balsam, morning glory, sweet alyssum, four-o'clocks, flowering tobacco, moss rose, and nasturtiums.

To prevent annuals from self-sowing, pinch or cut off the flowers as soon as they fade and start to set seed. (This also encourages more blossoms.) Otherwise, simply allow plants to produce and drop their seed as they will.

Planting Annuals

Once you have healthy, homegrown, or purchased seedlings in hand, it's time to get your garden growing. First, make sure your annuals are properly adjusted to outdoor conditions (see Hardening Off, page 29), and danger of frost has passed. Next, you'll need a site with fertile, prepared soil (see Cultivating Your Soil, page 22).

Choose a cool, cloudy day for planting. Early evening is also a good time. Hot sun can cause transplants to wilt quickly, stressing the plants and slowing down the development of new roots. Water your annuals thoroughly before planting to minimize wilting.

Pinch off any flowers that have formed on the plants. Removing the flowers will encourage your plants to put energy into root growth, where it is truly needed. Within a few weeks, annuals treated this way will be growing and blooming vigorously, supported by a strong, spreading root system.

Take annuals out of their containers and plant them one at a time, so the roots won't be exposed to drying sun and wind. If they are growing in peat pots or pellets, simply tear off the upper rim and bottom and use a knife to cut a few slits in the sides. Space plants according to the directions on the seed packet or label. If you can't find specific recommendations, space holes at a distance of half the plant's ultimate height. Though your planting might look sparse at first, your annuals will quickly fill in the space, growing stronger and healthier than crowded plants would.

Keep annuals well watered for the first few weeks after transplanting, until the plants are well established and are producing new growth. Mulching with chopped leaves, shredded bark, or other organic material will help to keep the soil moist, as well as discourage weed seeds from sprouting around your plants. 🌸

HAVE ON HAND:

▶ Trowel

▶ Water

▶ Fish emulsion or seaweed extract

▶ Mulch

Water your hardened-off annuals thoroughly. Pinch off any open flowers to help channel energy to roots.

Fill in around the plant's roots with soil. Gently but firmly tamp down the soil around the stem with your fingers.

Use a trowel to dig individual holes in prepared soil. Space holes 6 to 12 inches apart, depending on your plant's mature height.

Remove plant from its pot or pack. Set it in the hole with the stem base, or crown, at the same depth that it was in the container.

When you are finished planting, water your annuals thoroughly. Fertilize with fish emulsion or seaweed extract.

Apply a 1- to 2-inch layer of mulch over the soil. Keep mulch at least 2 inches away from the base of the plant's stem.

HERE'S HOW

QUICK COLOR TOUCH-UPS

Flower beds are a traditional and popular way to display annual plants, but you don't have to stop there. Annuals also make ideal fillers around perennial plants, especially in new gardens where the perennials have not yet filled in. You also can plant annuals in the bare spots created when spring-flowering bulbs die back to the ground in early summer. (Dig planting holes to the side of the bulb clump, to avoid digging up or cutting into the bulbs.)

Annuals are a natural choice for container plantings, too. Growing them in pots and planters allows you to bring beautiful flowers and fragrance close to the house, brightening up decks, patios, steps, and porches. Tuck potted annuals into beds and borders to fill in gaps that have developed by mid- to late summer.

Perennials

FOR SUN

Think of perennials, and images of peonies, poppies, and phlox probably come to mind. These and other classic perennials are the stars of the sunny garden. Full-sun sites provide perfect conditions for the widest range of flowering and foliage perennials, giving you plenty of plants to choose from.

To add interest along a wall or fence, for example, plan a perennial border filled with a variety of heights and colors, such as mat-forming pinks, mounding asters, and spiky, tall irises. Or make an attractive landscape accent by creating a free-form "island" bed in part of your lawn. In either garden style, the general rule is to put the tallest plants in the back (or middle, for an island bed) and work down to the lowest plants around the edges. But it's also interesting to bring a few medium and tall plants toward the edge, to avoid creating a stair-step effect.

Full-sun sites need some special attention, however. Soil will probably dry out quickly, so you'll likely have to water more often. Working compost or other organic matter into the soil before planting will keep more moisture where the roots need it. And applying mulch over the soil after planting will help the roots stay cool and moist. ❧

FOR SHADE

On a hot summer day, few things are more welcome than a shady glade filled with lush foliage and pale flowers. Most properties have at least one spot ideal for perennials that can't take the heat. In that area, start the season with spring-blooming perennials, such as the dainty flower sprays of barrenworts or the curious-looking hooded blooms of Jack-in-the-pulpit. For later interest, add a variety of ferns for their lovely leaves. Hostas also offer fabulous foliage, in shades of green, gold, and dusty blue, often edged or striped with cream or white. Their purple, lavender, or white summer flowers are an added bonus.

Shady spots often tend to be on the moist side, since they are more sheltered from drying sun and wind. If your shady site has evenly moist soil, you will want to include plants that thrive in those conditions, including ferns, astilbes and primroses. If your site tends to be dry (possibly due to the thirsty roots of nearby trees and shrubs), work compost or other organic matter into the soil as you dig. Water regularly for the first month or two after planting to help your new shade-loving selections get established. Then, water only as needed during spells of dry weather. ❦

Selecting Healthy Perennials

Successful perennial gardens begin with healthy, vigorous plants. You'll want to check each potential purchase carefully to make sure you are getting the best-quality plants for your money.

Shop at a reputable supplier. Ask gardening friends and neighbors about their good and bad experiences with perennial plant sources, and find out which places they recommend. Nurseries and garden centers with display gardens are helpful, since you can see how the plants will perform in your particular area. If the perennials are thriving there, chances are good that they are well adapted to your area's climate and weather conditions.

Clearly labeled displays and plants are more than just a bonus, they are critical if you are looking for perennials with particular colors, heights, or habits. You want to buy your plants while they are still young and leafy, since full-grown perennials will be slow to become established in your garden after planting. Useful labels will tell you what color the flowers should be and what height the plant should reach when mature.

Mid-spring is the ideal time to start shopping for perennials. By then, the plants will have started growing, but they will still be young enough to adjust easily to your garden and produce a good display the same year. Toward the end of the season plants may be on sale, but the selection will be greatly reduced and the plants may have overgrown their containers. Big plants in small pots tend to dry out quickly and may have wilted often, stressing the plant and leading to poor growth after planting.

Healthy perennials will have lush, unblemished foliage. Yellowed or discolored leaves may indicate a nutrient deficiency or disease. (Some perennials do have unusual foliage color or markings, so it's important to check the label or ask the supplier if you're not sure whether or not there's a problem.) When you inspect the plants for signs of pest problems, make sure you look at the undersides of the leaves—pests often hide there. Do not buy perennials with visible pests or signs of pest or disease damage, even at a reduced price.

If you buy from a mail-order nursery, your plants will either be coming out of dormancy (spring) or going into it (fall). Woody shrubs and trees are also perennials and are usually shipped bare-root. They may not look impressive at first but will survive if handled properly (see Here's How, page 53).

Shop at a reputable nursery or garden center. Look for clean, weed-free displays and well-labeled plants.

Inspect leaves for holes, speckling, insect webbing, discoloration, malformation, and other signs of pest and disease problems.

Choose perennials that are bushy and vigorous, with top growth that's in proportion to the size of the container they are in.

Look for plants that have leaves only, or a few buds at most. Plants in full bloom will not have energy for rooting.

Make sure stems are firm and evenly colored, especially where they enter the soil; discolored stems, such as those shown here, may have rot.

Slide the perennial out of its pot so you can get a good look at the rootball. Avoid buying plants with matted or circling roots.

HERE'S HOW

SMART SHOPPING

Buying perennials can be an expensive proposition, especially if you need enough to fill a new garden. But with a few smart shopping strategies, you can get healthy, good-looking plants without breaking your budget.

Whenever possible, plan your garden a few months to a year before you are actually ready to plant, then begin shopping right away. Purchase full-looking pots, with large plants that have multiple stems. These bigger perennials will be more expensive, but you'll need only a few of each. When you get home, divide the clumps and plant the divisions in an out-of-the-way bed where they can grow and develop. By the time you are ready to transplant them to your new garden, you will have three or more good-sized perennials for the price of one.

If you want to get a new garden started immediately, consider buying small plants in 4- to 6-inch pots. They will catch up to larger plants within a year or two, and you'll have saved yourself some money in the meantime. If the garden looks a little sparse after planting, tuck in some annuals to fill the gaps while the perennials get established.

Planting Perennials

Perennials are likely to live in the same place for several years, so it's important to get them off to a great start with proper planting. First, prepare a fertile planting site (see Cultivating Your Soil, page 22). Once the site is ready, gather your plants and materials.

You can plant container-grown perennials any time the ground isn't frozen; spring and fall are ideal, since there tends to be adequate rainfall and temperatures are moderate. Hot sun can quickly cause new plants to wilt, so plant on a cool, cloudy day or in the early evening.

Watering your pots before planting will help the perennials handle trans-

planting with minimal stress. To make sure the soil is thoroughly moistened, irrigate until water runs out the bottom of the pot. Or, if the soil is very dry, set the pot in a container of water for an hour before planting to make sure the plants absorb all the water they can hold. While the perennials are still in their containers, set them out on the prepared soil, according to your garden design. Space them based on their mature spread, so that the edges of the plants will just touch when they are full grown. For example, if the plants have a 1-foot spread, space them 10 to 12 inches apart. (To find the mature spread, check the plant label or refer to an encyclopedia of perennial plants.) Make any needed adjustments to the plant arrangement before digging the planting holes.

Take the perennials out of their containers one at a time and plant them immediately, to avoid exposing the roots to drying sun and wind. Keep the plants well watered for the first few weeks after transplanting, until they are established and producing new growth. Mulch with shredded bark, chopped leaves, or other organic material to keep the soil evenly moist, encourage good root growth, and discourage weeds. 🌾

HAVE ON HAND:

▶ Water

▶ Trowel or shovel

▶ Fish emulsion or seaweed extract

▶ Mulch

Preferably on an overcast day in spring or fall, thoroughly water perennial containers and arrange the plants in your garden.

Backfill the soil around the roots. Use your fingertips to gently but firmly press down the soil around the stem.

Dig planting holes in prepared soil with a trowel or shovel. Space holes according to mature spread of each plant.

Gently slide plant out of its pot; loosen roots with your fingers. Set plant in hole carefully, so that stem base is at the same level as in the pot.

After planting the bed, water the soil thoroughly. Fertilize the entire planting with fish emulsion or seaweed extract.

Spread a 2-inch layer of mulch over the soil. Keep mulch at least 2 inches away from the base of the stem of each plant to prevent rot.

HERE'S HOW

PLANTING BARE-ROOT PERENNIALS

If you buy perennials through a mail-order nursery catalog, they may arrive bare-root—with packing but no soil around the roots. Bare-root perennials will adapt well in your garden if you give them special care at planting time. First, remove the packing material, then prune off any broken or damaged roots. Soak the remaining roots in lukewarm water for an hour or two before planting. Dig planting holes before removing the perennials from the water. Make the holes large enough to hold the roots comfortably without bending them. Then replace some soil in the center of each hole to create a cone. The top of the cone should be just even with the soil surface.

Plant bare-root perennials one at a time, setting the plant on the peak of the cone and spreading the roots out evenly over the sides. Fill in around the roots with soil, and firm the soil around the base of the plant. After planting, water thoroughly, fertilize with fish emulsion or seaweed extract, and mulch. Keep the soil evenly moist for the first 4 to 6 weeks, until plants become established and produce new growth.

Protecting Tender Perennials

Perennials are plants that live longer than two years. Not all perennials, however, can survive a harsh winter outdoors. Tender perennials, those requiring special protection from northern winters include zonal geraniums, wax begonias, impatiens, coleus, heliotrope, and browallia.

Many gardeners grow these plants as annuals, buying new ones each spring and pulling them out during fall cleanup. But you can bring your favorite tender perennials indoors in the fall and plant them in your garden again in spring. You'll get a better flower or foliage display more quickly, since overwintered plants tend to be larger than newly purchased transplants.

Three weeks before you bring a plant indoors, treat it preventively for aphids and whiteflies by spraying with insecticidal soap. Repeat a few times before digging plant up. Destroy plants that show signs of pest damage such as distorted growth, speckling, or yellowing.

During the winter, grow tender perennials in a warm, sunny window or under fluorescent plant lights. Water as needed to keep the soil evenly moist. Fertilize with a liquid organic fertilizer, such as fish emulsion. In late spring, when the danger of frost has passed, gradually move plants back outdoors (see Hardening Off, page 29). When your plants are again adjusted to the outdoors, plant them in the garden. 🌿

HAVE ON HAND:

▶ Insecticidal soap

▶ Trowel

▶ Pots, 6 to 8 inch

▶ Potting soil

▶ Water

▶ Pruning shears

▶ Fish emulsion

In early fall, dig up small clumps of plants; plant in 6- to 8-inch pots filled with potting soil; water well.

For plants too large to move, take cuttings from stem tips in late summer to grow indoors over winter.

In late summer, determine which plants to overwinter indoors. Pick those that are the most healthy.

Cut stems back by half. Feed with fish emulsion. Set in shade; bring indoors before the first frost.

Transplanting Perennials

Even the best-planned perennial garden needs a bit of fine-tuning now and then. Perhaps two flowers next to each other don't harmonize well, or two plants that would make great companions are at separate ends of the garden. Fortunately, it's easy to move most perennial plants. You can adjust your plantings until you are satisfied with the results.

The best time to transplant perennials is when they are dormant or just beginning new growth. For most, early spring is ideal. Perennials that bloom in spring adapt well to transplanting either after flowering or in the fall. If you must move your perennials during the growing season, cut their foliage back by ½ to ⅔ to reduce moisture loss, and water them regularly. Prepare the new planting site before digging perennials, so you can replant them immediately without their root systems drying out.

Of course, there are some perennials that don't take kindly to transplanting. Peonies, for example, may take a year or two to adjust to their new site and bloom after being moved. Those that are tap-rooted, with a single, vertical root, such as butterfly weed and gas plant, can also be tricky. If you must transplant them, dig deeply around the crown to secure as much of the main root as possible. Don't move Oriental poppies when their foliage is visible. Keep the soil moist after planting to encourage root growth. 🌸

HAVE ON HAND:

▶ Spade or trowel

▶ Spading fork or hand fork

▶ Water

▶ Mulch

Use a spade or trowel to cut a circle around plant, 6 inches or more away from stems and as deep.

Pry clump out of soil with a hand fork or spading fork. Keep as much soil around roots as possible.

Place clump in planting hole, with crown at level of soil surface. Fill hole around roots with soil.

Firm soil around crown. Water thoroughly. Add a 2-inch layer of mulch; avoid piling it against the crown.

Climbing Vines

ANNUAL

Annual vines have an amazing will to grow. Some mature from a small, spring-sown seed into stems that reach 20 feet by the first fall frost. This trait makes them indispensable for any site needing shade or screening in a hurry. They're a good choice, too, if pruning and maintenance are not part of your schedule. And, if you're undecided about how a perennial vine might work in a certain space, you can try an annual before making a more permanent choice.

Annual vines usually climb by wrapping their stems or tendrils around a support, so provide them with something to hold onto: netting, stakes, lattice, a trellis, or a chain-link fence. These vines grow fast—put your support in place before you plant! Once they reach the support, your vines will grab on and head for the sky with little help from you.

Use morning glories to dress up a lamppost or fence; scarlet runner beans for garden accents. Hyacinth bean will provide a curtain of leaves and flowers for a porch or patio. Adorn a deck with annual vines such as climbing nasturtiums grown in pots with either a trellis for each pot or deck railings as support. Your annual vines will provide a wealth of beautiful flowers you don't even have to stoop to admire. ❧

PERENNIAL

What is more charming than a rustic rail fence smothered in a froth of sweet autumn clematis flowers? Or a pretty pergola covered with the purple or white flower chains of wisteria? Perennial climbers add a touch of romance to any garden.

Perennial climbers are practical, too. You can train them on permanent trellises to block unattractive views or provide privacy for outdoor entertaining. Grown on walls, they hide awkward architectural features. Use them to cover freestanding screens separating different parts of your yard, or to soften the look of a newly installed fence. Some vines, including clematis, make excellent partners for roses and shrubs, providing extra flowers in the same area without taking up additional space in the garden.

Perennial vines usually have woody stems and can grow substantially in one season—they normally need sturdy support. Some, such as Boston ivy and Virginia creeper, cling to walls without additional help. Others, including honeysuckle, clematis, and passionflowers, require something to wrap around, and may need guidance to get started in the right direction. Once they get going, however, your perennial climbers will provide years of easy-care beauty. 🌿

Selecting Healthy Climbing Vines

Starting with vigorous, pest-free plants will virtually guarantee your success with vines. They will live for many years once established, so it's worth taking a little time to make sure you get the best-quality climbers for your money.

Shop for vines at a reputable nursery or garden center. It is important that the plants be clearly labeled—especially if you are looking for a particular flower color and the plant is not yet in bloom. You can buy and plant container-grown vines any time during the growing season, but keep in mind that they'll settle in most quickly in fall or early spring.

Young vines are generally a better buy than older, larger plants. Since they grow so quickly, young vine plants will catch up to older ones in a relatively short time—usually within a season or two. Young vines will also be less expensive. And because the plants themselves are smaller, they are easier to handle and there is less chance of damaging their top growth during planting.

Before buying any vine, make sure you know how big it will be at maturity. To cover a small trellis or post, look for a relatively restrained vine, such as most varieties of clematis and honeysuckles. Extra-vigorous vines, such as wisteria

and trumpet vine, will need a sturdy arbor or fence to support them.

When you find a climber you absolutely must have, be prepared to provide the right kind of support for it. Keep in mind that the support you choose will have to be cleaned and maintained periodically, which can be hard to do when there are vines permanently attached. Consider the benefits of redwood and cedar; both are sturdy and rot-resistant. In any case, you'll want your vine to match its support in terms of both strengh and look (see Here's How). Inquire at your local nursery if you need advice or additional information.

Healthy climbers will have lush, unblemished foliage and sturdy stems. It's a plus if there is a stake or small trellis in the pot to support the developing shoots and prevent them from breaking during transit. Check the stems, shoot tips, and leaves (both sides) carefully for insects and signs of pest and disease problems, such as crinkled or discolored growth. Don't buy any vine with visible insects or disease damage, even at a bargain price. Your new plant—even with tender loving care—might be permanently weak or stunted, and your healthy garden will be at risk. ✿

Before you shop, decide on your planting location. Research vines that thrive in the conditions provided and take a list with you to the nursery.

Inspect the vine leaves for holes, discoloration, speckling or webbing, and other signs of pest and disease problems.

Choose vines that appear to be vigorous and healthy. The top growth should be in proportion to the container, neither skimpy nor too lush.

Select vines that have more than one stem per pot. Don't choose vines that are stressed at the base from bending.

Make sure the vine's stems are firm and evenly colored, especially at the base. Discolored stems may be a sign of disease.

Slide the vine out of its pot to inspect the root-ball. Do not buy plants with heavily matted or circling roots.

HERE'S HOW

MATCHING VINES TO YOUR STRUCTURES

It is vital to match the habit of any vine with the support structure you have available. Bear in mind that mature vines can get heavy, so be sure your structure is strong enough to hold the vine at its mature size.

Clinging vines, such as Boston ivy and Virginia creeper, fasten themselves to a support by producing rootlets or disks along the stems. These self-clingers are easy to grow on solid structures such as stone or other kinds of walls but may damage mortar or siding. Virginia creeper does well on fences, trees, trellises.

Twining climbers, including honeysuckle, morning glory, and wisteria, pull themselves up by wrapping their stems around a support; wires or posts, for example.

Passionflower and other tendril climbers produce small, coiling stems at the leaf tips. They need a thin support to wrap around, such as wire, a chain-link fence, or plastic netting.

Planting Climbing Vines

Container-grown climbers are tough and adaptable, so you can add them to your garden any time during the growing season. Spring and fall are ideal, however, since the plants will develop a more spreading root system during cool, moist weather.

Before planting, make sure the appropriate support is painted or stained and in place for your new vine. If you attempt to install a support structure later, you risk damaging the plant's root system. Once they are planted and established, new vines will grow quickly.

Thoroughly watering the rootball before planting will help your vines handle transplanting with minimal stress. After you transplant, keep vines well watered for a few weeks, until they produce new growth. Spread a 2-inch layer of an organic mulch to help the soil stay moist and cool. Keep the mulch at least 2 inches from the stems in order to prevent rot.

As the vine stems grow, direct them to their support. Ivy and other clinging vines may take a season or two to get established and start climbing. Gently tie the stems of other climbers to the support. Guide them by inserting one or more stakes next to the rootball, angled toward the support. Use soft string or strips of cloth to loosely fasten the stems to the stakes. As the stems elongate, tie them every 6 to 12 inches, until they start grasping the support on their own. 🌸

HAVE ON HAND:

► Trowel or shovel

► Water

► Mulch

► Fish emulsion or
    seaweed extract

Dig a hole 6 inches wider than pot and the same depth. Dig center of hole 12 to 18 inches from support.

Water container soil thoroughly. Slide the plant out of its pot; loosen the outer roots with your fingers.

Set the plant in the hole, with its stems angled toward the support. Replace soil around the rootball.

Water, mulch, and feed with fish emulsion. Gently guide stems in the direction of the new support.

Transplanting Climbing Vines

Vines are gratifyingly easy to move. These tough, vigorous plants may take a season or two to rebloom after transplanting, but they'll readily produce new growth once they have settled into their new site.

Climbers ideally should be transplanted in late winter or early spring, after the ground has thawed. Before digging up and moving any vine, have the new trellis, post, or other support in place. This way the root system won't be disturbed again when the support is installed.

When digging a planting hole for your vine, make the center of the hole 18 inches from the support base. By not planting directly at the support's bottom, you'll have room to work around the structure (for painting or other maintenance) without damaging stems.

In general, the planting hole should be deep enough so that stems emerge from the ground at the same level they did before. Clematis is an exception. You can set the rootball 1 to 2 inches deeper. Then, if aboveground stems are killed back by a disease called clematis wilt, the plant may be able to produce new shoots from underground. Keep mulch away from stems to prevent rot.

When new growth begins to emerge, select four to six strong shoots to train toward the support and prune out the rest. Be aware that any vines that bloom only on old wood will not flower until the following year. ❧

HAVE ON HAND:

▶ Spade or shovel
▶ Pruning shears
▶ Spading fork
▶ Tarp
▶ Water
▶ Mulch
▶ Ties for support
Optional
▶ Stakes

Install new support. Dig hole with center 18 inches from support base, 18 inches wide by 12 inches deep.

Cut stems to 1 foot or remove from old support. Dig around vine to loosen roots. Lift with spading fork.

Set rootball on tarp to move. Place plant in new hole, stems toward support, set at previous soil level.

Replace soil; water and mulch. Attach stems to support, or insert stakes to guide new shoots.

Shrubs

DECIDUOUS

Few things will accomplish as much in your garden as carefully chosen shrubs. Flowering deciduous shrubs, for example, can do many jobs: separate different parts of your yard, provide shelter and privacy, and liven up dull buildings and fences, just to name a few. A tough-to-mow slope will turn into an asset with a mass planting of low-growers such as rockspray cotoneaster. In addition to their practical benefits, flowering shrubs also offer beauty: colorful blooms as well as height and form for you to enjoy. You may want to choose one that is especially beautiful—perhaps a spirea or viburnum—as a specimen plant for accent.

The options for using flowering shrubs are limitless. Try grouping several of different sizes for the effect of a traditional flower bed with minimal work. Or plant a combination of shrubs and perennials to provide varied interest all year. Some flowering shrubs, such as winterberry hollies and viburnum, offer a display of colorful fruit well into winter. Others, including hydrangeas, have flowers or seed heads that persist for months. And, you won't be alone in your appreciation of flowering and fruiting shrubs; they also provide food and shelter for birds and other wildlife.

EVERGREEN

Evergreen shrubs are often over-looked in the garden, but that is the way it is supposed to be. Their quiet greens blend into the background, making them excellent for dividing areas without drawing attention to the boundaries themselves. They make wonderful backdrops for flower gardens, their dark foliage providing a pleasing contrast to bright blooms.

Because they keep their foliage all year, tall evergreens make a good screen to shield out unattractive views. They also filter noise and wind, important if your garden is near a street or exposed to strong winds. You can shape them or enjoy their natural beauty. Low-growing types, such as creeping juniper, are well suited for use as ground covers. Use them also along paths, to keep visitors on the walkways and subtly head them in the right direction.

Some evergreen shrubs offer more than green leaves. Camellias, rhododendrons, and mountain laurel also produce colorful flowers, while many hollies have brightly colored berries. Consider planting these in masses, where they can really show off. Some needle-leaved evergreens, including junipers, are available with golden or silvery blue leaves as well as the more common green. ❧

Selecting Healthy Shrubs

Research shrubs in early spring or fall. Identify species that will adequately fill your space and thrive in the intended location.

Shrubs will most likely be a permanent addition to your garden, so take some time to consider your requirements, and make sure you start with the best plants possible. A smart shopping strategy will help you select the right shrubs for your needs and conditions.

First, decide where on your property they will be planted. This is a good time to consult your garden map (see Making a Garden Map, page 10). Next, make sure you know what you are looking for. Check catalogs and gardening books or talk to salespeople at local nurseries and garden centers to find out which shrubs are well adapted to your site conditions and the mature height and spread of each shrub. While they may look small and manageable in a pot, shrubs can quickly overgrow their spot if not given enough room. Start by selecting a shrub that will fit in the space you have available in order to save yourself a lot of pruning and maintenance later on.

Since spring and fall are ideal shrub planting times, they're also good shopping times. You will generally find the widest selection in the spring. In addition to container-grown shrubs, some nurseries and garden centers offer balled-and-burlapped (B-and-B) plants in fall or early spring. These shrubs have been grown in a field, then dug up with soil around the roots; the rootball is then wrapped in burlap or plastic material. If you choose a balled-and-burlapped shrub, make sure the wrapping is evenly distributed around the rootball and secure. Exposed roots can dry out quickly and may not transplant well.

For any type of shrub, shop at a supplier with clean, well-organized displays and clearly labeled plants. Good labels will tell you about the shrub's flower color or other special features, as well as its size and preferred growing conditions, so you can make sure you are getting exactly what you want.

Healthy shrubs will have unblemished, evenly colored foliage. Yellowed or discolored leaves may indicate a nutrient deficiency or disease problem. When you check for signs of pest problems, make sure you look at the undersides of the leaves, too; pests often like to hide there. Avoid plants with fragile stems, an indication that the plant may not have been properly cared for. Also, avoid plants that have excessively twiggy growth. Both plants with fragile growth and those with very twiggy growth will be slow to establish. 🌺

Check the leaves for holes, speckling, insect webbing, discoloration, and other signs of disease and pest problems.

Choose shrubs with well-branched and balanced top growth that is in proportion to the size of the plant's rootball.

Select plants with plump buds and firm, vigorous stems. Avoid those with broken, shriveled, or damaged stems.

If possible, slide the shrub out of its pot so you can inspect the rootball, or ask to see it. Reject those plants with thickly matted or circling roots.

On balled-and-burlapped shrubs, make sure that the wrapping is intact, and the rootball is firm and moist.

HERE'S HOW

AVOIDING INVASIVE SHRUBS

While most shrubs are welcomed into the garden, a few may be more of a problem than a pleasure. Some barberies, for instance, reseed readily, producing many young plants throughout your garden. Other self-sowing shrubs include the multiflora rose and the butterfly bush.

Spreading shrubs can be a problem also, especially if you have a small garden. Sumacs, for example, send out underground runners (suckers), so new plants may pop up several feet from the base of the parent plant.

To avoid introducing potential problems into your garden, make sure you know what you are buying. If you aren't familiar with how a particular shrub grows, do a little research before you buy it. Visit a local botanical garden or arboretum to see firsthand how an established specimen will behave in a garden setting. If possible, talk to the staff members who maintain the plants to find out if they have any problems to report. You may still decide that you like the shrub well enough to deal with its seedlings or suckers, but at least you'll know what to expect.

Planting Shrubs

Shrubs are usually planted to grow in one spot for many years, so proper planting is an important step in helping them live a long, healthy life. Early spring is the ideal planting time, for less over-winter loss, although, with care, container-grown shrubs may be planted any time the ground isn't frozen.

If you have several shrubs to plant in one area, consider preparing a large planting bed rather than digging many individual holes (see Cultivating Your Soil, page 22). For a single shrub, a broad but fairly shallow hole (just deep enough to hold the rootball) is suffi-

cient. To check the depth of the hole, measure the distance from the ground to the top of the rootball. Then lay a stake across the planting hole. Measure from the stake to the bottom of the hole. When the measurements match, the hole is the right depth.

Thoroughly water the rootball before planting to help your shrubs survive transplanting with minimal stress. Add water until it runs out of the bottom of the rootball.

Set the plant so that it is straight in the hole. For balled-and-burlapped plants, remove the binding ropes and any nails or plastic. Then cut away as much of the wrapping as you can without breaking up the rootball. Remove wire or plastic labels attached to the plant, to prevent them from cutting into the growing stems.

Water regularly and deeply, especially during dry spells. Mulch with shredded bark or chopped leaves to keep the soil moist and cool. ❧

HAVE ON HAND:

▶ Water

▶ Shovel

▶ Mulch

Water rootball thoroughly. Dig a planting hole the same depth and twice as wide as the rootball.

If the shrub is in a container, remove the pot and loosen the outside of the rootball with your fingers.

Set shrub in the center of the hole. Remove any wrapping around the rootball. Backfill with soil.

Firm soil around stems with your foot; water. Add 2 inches of mulch; keep it 4 inches away from stems.

Transplanting Shrubs

Perhaps your shrubs have overgrown their present home, or you're planning a garden redesign. Either way, you won't have to give them up. Small shrubs are easy to transplant and will settle quickly into a new site. Established shrubs are more work to dig up and can be heavy to move; have a helper ready to carry your shrub to its new planting site.

Early to mid-fall is an ideal time to move shrubs. The air is cool but soil is still warm, providing good conditions for new root growth while discouraging energy-sapping top growth. Transplant in early spring as a second choice.

To make your job easier, tie the tops of long-stemmed shrubs with twine before digging them up. Use pruning shears or loppers to cut large roots that you can't sever cleanly with your spade.

After transplanting, untie top growth, and prune damaged stems. To prevent winter drying, protect shrubs moved in fall (especially evergreens) with a burlap or plastic mesh screen, or spray leaves with an antidesiccant to prevent moisture loss.

Regular watering during the first growing season after transplanting is critical to help your shrub settle into its new site. Water to keep soil moist if rainfall is sparse.

Fertilize transplanted shrubs in the spring. Pull back the mulch layer, scatter a balanced organic fertilizer or a 1-inch layer of compost, and replace the mulch. 🌿

HAVE ON HAND:

▶ Spade

▶ Spading fork

▶ Tarp

▶ Twine

▶ Water

▶ Mulch

Use spade to cut circle around outer spread of branches. Following circle, dig trench about 1 foot deep.

Loosen soil around rootball with spading fork. Cut roots at bottom with spade. Keep small roots intact.

Slide tarp under rootball. Gather and tie tarp around the base of stems. Move shrub to new site.

Set shrub in hole, remove tarp. Backfill with soil to previous level; water; apply 2 inches of mulch.

Roses

HYBRID TEA AND OTHERS

Roses have long been considered the ultimate symbol of romance and beauty. Among them, the hybrid tea, which comes in a dazzling array of colors and blooms all season long on elegant stems, continues to be the favorite. It's easy to understand when you see the soft shading of 'Peace' or experience the classic form, dark-red color, and strong scent of 'Chrysler Imperial'.

Of course, hybrid teas aren't the only roses you can grow in your garden. Polyanthas such as 'The Fairy'—compact plants with clusters of flowers throughout the season—are lovely in small landscapes. Floribundas—created from hybrid teas and polyanthas—are most effective planted in groups of the same kind for a mass of color. Grandifloras, typically used as cutting roses, are the tall queens of the garden, with enormous, abundant blooms on long stems. Most old garden roses are extremely hardy, as are modern shrub roses. Miniature roses resemble their larger relatives but often are hardier than hybrid teas and are especially striking placed in front of other plants.

Whichever roses you choose to own, give them full sun, fertile soil, space, and good drainage to ensure success. ❧

SHRUB ROSES

Shrub roses not only have beautiful blooms but fuller, sturdier forms than other roses. They tend to be more tolerant than hybrid teas of their growing conditions, and many, such as 'Elmshorn' with its clusters of pink blooms, do well mixed with perennials and vines to create a romantic, cottage-garden look. They can be used for colorful, informal hedges or planted in front of evergreens as highlights. A row of shrub roses often makes an attractive and quite effective barrier planting.

When choosing a shrub rose, you'll want to consider that most species and antique shrub roses (gallicas, damasks, albas, centifolias) produce one spectacular show of blossoms each season, while most modern shrub roses (hybrid rugosas, English roses, hybrid musks, polyanthas) are repeat bloomers.

Shrub roses will grow well if given full sun and fertile, well-drained soil. In fact, many of them are easier to grow than other kinds of roses, since shrub roses are often more resistant to black spot, rust, and other common rose diseases. Shrub roses also tend to need less pruning to produce a good display of flowers—a plus if pruning isn't one of your favorite gardening activities.

Selecting Healthy Roses

Research roses to consider in books, magazines, catalogs, nurseries, botanical gardens, and by asking gardening friends and neighbors.

A beautiful rose garden begins with healthy plants. Carefully selecting your roses when you shop will help reduce disease problems after planting, reduce maintenance chores, and give you more time to enjoy the fabulous flowers.

Spring is generally a good time to shop for roses at nurseries and garden centers. Bare-root roses (those sold in bags or boxes, with no soil around the roots) are sold while they are still dormant, so look for them in the early spring. Container roses are usually available throughout the growing season, although you'll find the best selection in the spring. If you buy your roses from a mail-order company, you can shop any time. The company will send your roses at the appropriate planting time for your particular area.

Whether you buy locally or through a catalog, make sure you choose a reputable supplier. Many older cultivars are available only through mail order from specialist nurseries, so if you plan to buy this way, check with gardening friends and neighbors about their experiences with different companies. Or start by ordering one or two plants, then judge their quality for yourself before placing a larger order. Regardless of where you shop, look for roses that are described as disease-resistant, either on the label or in the catalog description. By choosing roses that are naturally less prone to black spot (a fungal leaf spot), powdery mildew, and other common rose diseases, you will greatly reduce the chance of problems after planting.

Bare-root roses should be dormant when you buy them and should be planted before leaves emerge from the buds. Reject plants that have already started producing new growth. Check their stems carefully, too; they should be plump and vigorous. Wrinkled stems are a sign that the plant has dried out in the past, and it probably will not adapt well after planting.

Healthy container-grown roses have unblemished foliage that is usually a rich medium-to-dark-green color, sometimes with a reddish tinge (especially on new growth). Avoid buying plants with yellowing, dusty gray patches, or black spots; these are common signs of disease problems. When you check for signs of pest problems, make sure you inspect the undersides of the leaves; pests often hide there. Do not buy roses with any visible pests or signs of pest or disease damage, even if they are on sale. A sick plant is no bargain at any price, and will put your other garden plants at risk. ❦

If possible, slide container roses out of their pots and inspect the roots. They should be visible but not circling or heavily matted.

Look for container-grown roses that have well-balanced top growth, with at least three or four sturdy stems per plant.

Choose plants with smooth, firm green or red canes. Avoid plants with discolored, shriveled, or spindly stems.

If plant is in bloom, avoid flowers that are shriveled, or those with spotted petals, which may indicate disease.

Pick potted roses with vigorous green or reddish foliage, with no spotting, insect webbing, damage, or discoloration.

HERE'S HOW

PROPERLY SPACING ROSES

If you are planting more than one rose, make sure you consider the mature size of each plant so that you allow enough room between them at planting time. Miniature roses, such as 'Cupcake', need only 1 to 2 feet between plants, while 4 to 6 feet is generally adequate spacing for shrub roses, such as 'Bonica'. For other roses, space plants 2 to 3 feet apart in cool climates and 3 to 4 feet apart if you live in a warmer climate.

These spacings will allow your roses to grow vigorously without crowding each other, reducing your pruning chores. Adequate spacing also will encourage good air circulation around leaves and stems, so wet foliage will dry quickly. This discourages the spread of powdery mildew, black spot, and other rose diseases.

Planting Potted Roses

Potted roses adapt quickly to a new site with minimal care, whether you are introducing them into an existing garden or creating a new bed. In fact, you can plant potted roses any time the ground isn't frozen.

For a new garden, choose a well-drained, sunny site. Loosen the top 1 foot of soil with a spading fork, then work in a 2- to 3-inch layer of compost or some well-rotted manure. An existing bed will also benefit from the addition of the same soil amendments.

HAVE ON HAND:

► Gloves

► Bucket of water

► Spade or shovel

► Spading fork

► Pruning shears

► Mulch

If roses were grown in your planting bed in the past, they may have left diseases in the soil. You might want to opt for a different planting site.

Before soaking your new rose, remove all labels, wires, and plastic loops that can damage stems. Save labels for spacing suggestions and other plant requirements and information. After soaking, you may have to squeeze the pot sides in several places before the rose will slide out. You can also carefully slit the sides of the pot and peel it away from the rootball.

If your rose is grafted, you'll note a slightly swollen area called a graft union near the base of the stem. In Zone 5 or colder regions, mulch your rose heavily in winter, covering the graft union.

Fertilize 4 to 6 weeks after planting with a balanced, organic fertilizer. Water regularly and thoroughly at plant base to encourage root growth and to keep leaves dry and disease resistant. 🌿

Soak rootball in water for 1 hour before planting. Dig hole as deep as pot and twice as wide.

Loosen soil at bottom of hole. Slide rose out of pot. Free matted or tangled roots. Prune damaged roots.

Set plant in center of hole with the graft union just above soil level. Fill hole with soil and firm lightly.

Water rose thoroughly to settle soil around roots. Apply 2 inches of mulch, leaving graft union exposed.

Transplanting Roses

Roses can be successfully moved from one part of your garden to another when they are dormant; in fall or early spring. Gardeners in cold winter climates will have greater success in spring when plants are naturally gearing up for a new growing season.

Before digging up the rose you want to move, prepare your new planting site so exposed roots won't dry out before replanting.

When choosing a new place for your rose, avoid spots where other roses have grown within at least 2 years. Roses moved to sites where others have recently grown often develop a mysterious soil-borne malady known as "rose sickness." You can successfully move a single plant into an existing bed by digging a planting hole 18 inches deep and 2 feet wide, and refilling it with soil from another part of the garden. But, if you will be transplanting several roses, you may want to consider an entirely new planting area.

To make transplanting hybrid tea and floribunda roses easier, prune one-third of the canes, or enough to keep the stems and roots in proportion to each other. If you know the rose you are moving is particularly slow growing, prune more lightly. On shrub or climbing roses, carefully tie canes with twine so they won't be in your way or snap off while you are working. If you plant on uneven ground, make a lip of soil around the plant to retain water.

HAVE ON HAND:

- ▶ Sturdy gloves, protective clothing
- ▶ Spade
- ▶ Spading fork
- ▶ Tarp
- ▶ Pruning shears
- ▶ Water
- ▶ Mulch

Wear protective clothing. Use spading fork to dig planting hole 1 foot wider than rootball, 18 inches deep.

Dig a narrow 18-inch-deep trench around plant, at least 1 foot out from outermost stems on all sides.

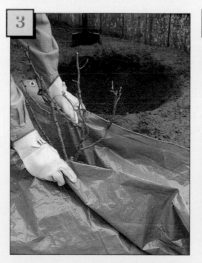

Lever rootball out of ground with spading fork. Set on tarp. Trim damaged roots; wrap with tarp to move.

Center rose in new hole at same level as before. Backfill, making soil lip if needed. Water and mulch.

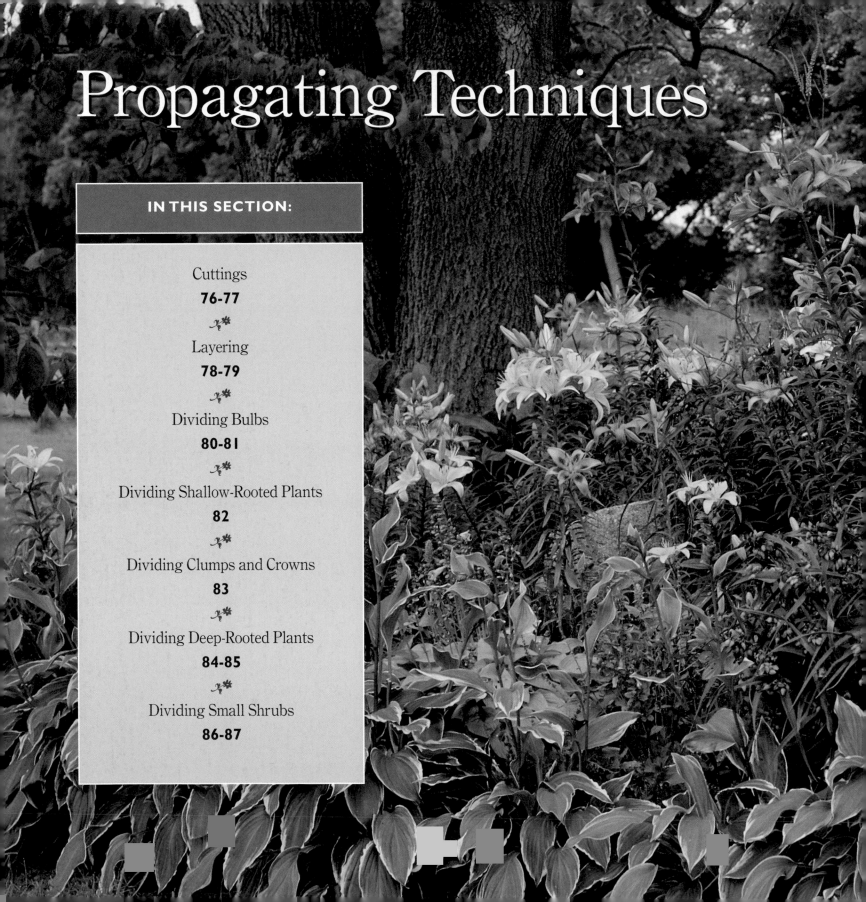

Propagating Techniques

It's inevitable—once you start your first garden, you'll want to plant another, and another. But filling your yard with gorgeous flowers and fabulous foliage can get expensive if you're buying all those new plants. The secret to having all the plants you want without draining your bank account is to learn the tricks of plant propagation.

At the beginning of the previous chapter, you learned how to grow garden plants from seed. That's a great way to start large numbers of plants quickly, but you may have to wait months or years for them to mature and bloom. In addition, the resulting seedlings may vary in height and color, which means you don't always know what you're getting. If you want large plants more quickly, or if you want to be certain you'll get an exact replica of your favorite plant, try "vegetative" propagation. This refers to taking an already-growing part of a plant—usually a piece of shoot or root—and providing the right conditions for it to develop into a whole new plant. You can also divide a large plant into two or more smaller ones, or encourage a shoot to make roots while it is still attached to the original plant.

In this chapter, you'll discover the basics of several easy types of vegetative propagation, including stem and root cuttings, layering, and division. Learn one or more of these easy techniques and your only challenge may be figuring out what to do with all the extra young plants! ❧

Cuttings

STEM CUTTINGS

Stem cuttings—small sections of vigorous, healthy shoots—will give you exact replicas of your plants in half the time it takes to grow them from seed. For best success, find pest-free shoots without buds or open flowers, and provide humidity so they won't wilt.

A 4-inch pot can hold three to five cuttings spaced so leaves don't touch (to discourage disease). Insert a small stake or pencil into the pot before covering it with a plastic bag, to keep the bag from resting on the cuttings. You won't need to water again until the cuttings have rooted and you've removed the bag.

If you can't plant the rooted cuttings right away, wrap them in a moist paper towel and place in a plastic bag. 🌺

HAVE ON HAND:

▶ Pruning shears or garden scissors
▶ 4-inch pot with drainage holes
▶ Moist potting soil
▶ Water
▶ Small stake or pencil
▶ Clear plastic bag
▶ Rubber band

1

In any season, snip a 3- to 5-inch section from end of healthy shoot, below a leaf and stem juncture (node). Remove leaves from bottom half.

2

Set bottom half of cutting in potting mix; water. Insert stake or pencil. Cover with plastic bag secured with rubber band. Set in indirect sun.

HERE'S HOW
CARING FOR CUTTINGS

Cuttings will root best in warm conditions (60° to 70°F) with bright but indirect light. Never set plastic-covered cuttings in direct sun—the air in the bag will heat up quickly and "cook" your cuttings. When new growth appears, usually in 3 to 4 weeks, remove the bag. If the cuttings resist a gentle tug, they are rooting and the bag can be left off. If not, replace the bag and check again in a week.

Two or three days after removing the bag permanently, move the cuttings to a sunny spot. Water as needed to keep the potting soil evenly moist. Wait another week or two to transplant rooted cuttings to individual pots. Your new plants are ready for the garden or for a bigger container when they are securely rooted in their pots and are growing vigorously.

ROOT CUTTINGS

Some perennials, such as bleeding heart and Oriental poppy, will produce shoots from sections of root, called root cuttings. Root cuttings generally produce plants identical to the parent. Some variegated plants, however, will have solid green foliage if you grow them from root pieces.

Mark exact location with a stake while plant is in flower but dig in late fall. Choose fleshy roots as thick as a pencil. The root piece closest to the crown will develop shoots, the other end will develop roots. A 4-inch pot will hold three to six root cuttings.

After potting, set cuttings in a cool, protected place. Water only if the soil dries; wet soil can encourage rot. Transplant when top growth appears. ❧

HAVE ON HAND:

▶ Shovel
▶ Water
▶ Sharp, clean knife
▶ 4-inch pot
▶ Moist potting soil

In late fall or winter, use a shovel to dig up the parent plant. Wash off clinging soil so roots can be seen clearly. Choose pencil-thick roots to cut.

Trim chosen roots from plant; keep track of which ends are closest to crown; keep roots moist. Trim parent plant so that roots and top are equal.

Cut these roots into 2-inch sections, making a straight cut at the crown end and a slant cut at the root end for easy identification.

Insert the cuttings into a pot of moist potting soil, with straight-cut ends at the top. Set in a cool place. Replace parent plant in your garden.

Layering

In early spring, select a young, flexible stem near the base of the plant you've chosen to layer. Gently bend the stem to the ground.

Some plant stems can be encouraged to produce roots while they are still attached to the parent plant. This technique, known as layering, involves bending a plant stem to the ground so roots will form where the stem touches the soil. Layering takes longer than stem cuttings (several months instead of several weeks), but it's a way to propagate shrubs and vines, especially woody plants, that don't root easily from cuttings. Try it with clematis, flowering quince, mountain laurel, azalea and rhododendron, and lilac.

In order to succeed at layering, you'll need a young shoot that is growing close to the ground. (Young shoots take root more readily than older, woody stems, and they are easier to bend.) If your shrub doesn't have a suitable young stem, you may be able to encourage one to develop by cutting a taller stem to within 4 to 6 inches of the ground; do this in the fall. Most gardeners layer only one or two stems at a time on each plant, but if you have enough room and enough suitable shoots, you can layer as many stems per plant as you wish.

Water thoroughly around the shrub or vine the day before layering to make the soil easier to dig. Working a few handfuls of compost into the soil of the layering hole can help promote vigorous rooting. You can also encourage faster root development by dusting the notched part of the stem with rooting hormone, a powder sold in most garden centers.

Water regularly to keep the layered area moist. Some stems will root by the end of the first growing season. If they don't feel securely rooted, check them in the fall and again the following spring. When a layer is well rooted, cut it from the parent plant where the stem enters the ground. Leave the severed layer in place for several months, until the following spring or fall; then transplant it to another part of the garden.

HAVE ON HAND:

► Trowel or shovel

► Knife

► Water

► Stake

► String

► Brick or flat rock

Bend stem so the notch is in the hole. Replace soil, leaving stem tip exposed. Water thoroughly. If needed, tie stem tip to a stake to hold upright.

Mark a point on the ground about 1 foot from the tip of the stem. Dig a hole in the soil below point, 4 inches deep and about 6 inches wide.

Cut a shallow notch on the underside of the stem, about 9 inches from the tip. Remove leaves 3 inches on either side of the notch.

Lay a brick or a flat rock over the buried part of the stem to hold the stem down and to help keep the soil moist.

In the fall, remove the brick or rock. Tug lightly at stem base to determine whether it has rooted; a well-rooted stem will feel firmly anchored.

HERE'S HOW

MOUND LAYERING

If you want to get many new plants from a single clump, use a technique called mound layering. It works well with perennials that tend to get woody stems and die out in the center, such as lavender, sage, southernwood, thyme, and wormwood. Simply mound sandy soil over the base of the stems in early spring. A 4- to 5-inch mound is sufficient; make sure at least 1 to 2 inches of each shoot tip is still exposed.

In late summer or fall, gently pull back the mounded soil to check for roots along the stems. If roots aren't visible, replace the soil and check again in spring. When you see roots, cut the rooted shoots from the parent plant. Plant them in pots or in an out-of-the-way nursery bed until they are ready to be transplanted into the garden.

Dividing Bulbs

Division is a quick and easy way to increase your bulb collection. This simple technique allows you to expand plantings of your favorite bulbs without the expense of buying new ones. It's also a great way to add new life to crowded, overgrown clumps of bulbs that are flowering poorly. Pot-grown bulbs normally need dividing every two to three years; those in the ground may only need dividing every three to five years.

The best time to divide hardy bulbs, such as daffodils, crocus, and tulips, is just as they go dormant after flowering. You will want to wait until their foliage is about half yellowed. By that time, the bulbs will have stored plenty of food, but they will still be easy to find. Replant bulbs immediately after you divide them, or store them for later planting (see Lifting and Storing Bulbs, page 39).

Plant stored bulbs as you would newly purchased ones in late summer to early fall. Large bulbs will bloom as usual the next year. Small offsets may take two to three years to flower, but will produce a beautiful display once established. If you wish, you can plant these bulblets in a corner of your vegetable garden or in another out-of-the-way spot; then move them to the flower garden once they reach blooming size.

Tender bulbs generally adapt best to division in early spring, before or just as their new growth is starting. On gladiolus, simply pick off the small cormels before you set the parent corms in the garden. Plant the cormels in a "holding bed" for two to three years (lifting and storing them each winter), until they reach flowering size. Divide dahlias, tuberous begonias, and caladiums by cutting them apart with a sharp, clean knife. In addition, dusting the cut surfaces with powdered sulfur and letting them dry for a day or two before potting them up will help prevent disease. ❧

HAVE ON HAND:

▶ Spading fork or hand fork

▶ Sharp knife

▶ Trowel or bulb planter

▶ Water

▶ Mulch

▶ Pots and potting soil

HARDY. *In summer after foliage yellows, lift bulbs with spading or hand fork, depending on depth. Shake off excess soil to expose bulbs.*

TENDER. *Remove tubers from storage in late winter. Look for small pink buds on the crown, where the roots join the stem.*

Gently break the clump apart with your fingers to separate individual bulbs. Discard any bulbs that are diseased or damaged.

Pull off or cut bulb leaves. Replant bulbs into prepared soil at appropriate depth. Water thoroughly, then top with a 1-inch layer of mulch.

HERE'S HOW

PROPAGATING LILIES

Lilies are particularly easy to propagate because they produce tiny new bulbs called bulblets and bulbils. Bulblets form along the buried part of the stem; bulbils form where the leaves join the flowering stem above ground. Gather bulbils by picking them from the stems in late summer. Collect bulblets by digging up lily bulbs when the stalk turns yellow; pick off the bulblets and replant the main bulb. Plant bulbils and bulblets in pots and set in a sheltered place outdoors over winter. Plant them in the garden or holding bed the following year; they may take another two to three years to reach flowering size.

Using a sharp knife, carefully cut each clump in half or into thirds, making sure each division has at least one healthy growth bud.

Plant divisions in potting soil in 6-inch pots. Set in a warm, bright place indoors; water regularly. Plant in garden in mid to late spring.

Dividing Shallow-Rooted Plants

Shallow-rooted perennials are simple and gratifying to divide, making it easy to fill your garden with your favorite foliage and flowers from only a few starter plants. Use your shallow-rooted spreaders as fillers in new beds and borders, until larger plants become well established. Then, divide the spreaders and plant them as ground cover in other areas. You'll soon have enough for yourself and extras to share.

The best time to divide shallow-rooted plants is when they are in leafy growth. As a general rule, divide spring and early summer-flowering plants such as ajuga and spotted lamium in late summer or fall. Fall bloomers, such as plumbago, adapt better to spring division. It's best to divide during a spell of cool, cloudy weather to prevent excess wilting of already stressed plants. If the ground is dry, water thoroughly the day before dividing. This is also a good time to prepare your new planting site.

Keep in mind that large sections of plants will recover more quickly than small ones. Damaged or dead sections will always be welcome in your compost pile.

After planting, regular, thorough watering is critical to help shallow-rooted plants get reestablished. If the weather is sunny and warm, protect replanted divisions for a week or so with overturned, slitted boxes or black, polyethylene-mesh shade cloth from a garden center or hardware store.

HAVE ON HAND:

▶ Spading fork or shovel

▶ Pruning shears

▶ Water

▶ Seaweed extract or fish emulsion

▶ Mulch

Lift shallow-rooted plants from the ground with spading fork or shovel. Shake excess soil from roots.

Divide plants into sections, using your hands. Make sure each section has ample healthy roots.

Cut back top growth on each section by ½ to ⅔. Replant the divisions immediately into prepared soil.

Water thoroughly; feed with seaweed extract or fish emulsion. Keep mulch away from stems.

Dividing Clumps and Crowns

Division is a fast and easy way to multiply many clump- and crown-forming plants such as iris or daisies. An established clump can yield from two to six or more new plants, all identical to the original. This is a great way to turn a single specimen into a bold, showy drift of plants. Division helps keep clumps vigorous, since you can discard the dead inner parts that develop as new outer growth crowds out the center. Most perennials grow best if divided every three to five years.

As you work in or walk through your garden, you will recognize the plants that look ready for division. They will be the plants that are flowering poorly or not at all, or look too big for the spot they are in. Jot down their names in your gardening notebook so you'll remember which plants to divide when the time is right (fall for early bloomers, spring for others).

To prevent wilt, divide plants during cool, cloudy weather. If it's hot and dry, water thoroughly the day before you plan to divide. Save only the most vigorous-looking sections for replanting; dead or unproductive parts can join the compost pile. A dose of seaweed extract or fish emulsion will give an immediate boost to developing roots. Laying down 2 inches of organic mulch will also promote root growth by keeping roots from drying out. But avoid moist mulch piled against stems, which can lead to rot. 🌿

HAVE ON HAND:

- ▶ Spade, shovel, or trowel
- ▶ Knife (for tough clumps)
- ▶ Hand fork (for loose clumps)
- ▶ Water
- ▶ Seaweed extract or fish emulsion
- ▶ Mulch

Dig a circle around plant, 2 to 3 inches from the outermost stems. Lift the rootball; shake off loose soil.

Cut back top growth by ½ to ⅔. Pull or cut clump apart so each section has roots and top growth.

Replant only the healthiest-looking sections in prepared soil. Firm the soil around crowns.

Water deeply. Feed with seaweed extract or fish emulsion for root growth. Mulch away from crowns.

Dividing Deep-Rooted Plants

While most perennials thrive when divided every three to five years, there are a few that grow best when left undisturbed. These include columbines, purple coneflower, lupines, monkshood, Oriental poppies, and peonies. Whenever possible, it's better to start new plants of these perennials from seed. But if a long-established clump is beginning to flower poorly, or if you want to share part of a special plant with a friend, you may need to resort to division. You have a good chance of success if you take extra care.

For best results, choose a spell of cool, cloudy weather in spring or fall so that already stressed plants don't suffer from wilting. Prepare your new planting site first, so that divisions can be replanted immediately. If the weather has been dry, water your plants deeply the day before you plan to divide them.

Check around the base for rooted sideshoots before digging up the whole clump. If you find some, carefully separate them from the parent with a trowel or spade, then move them to the new location. Where no offsets are visible, you'll need to dig up the whole plant and separate at the crowns, the portion of the plant where root meets stem.

Remember that larger sections of plant will tend to reestablish more quickly. Smaller, or weak-looking parts, along with some inevitable broken roots and stems, can be set aside for compost.

Regular watering after replanting is vital in order to help divided plants produce new roots. A dose of seaweed extract or fish emulsion (follow application instructions on the package) will encourage quick root growth. Adding a layer of organic mulch will help keep the soil evenly moist. If the weather is warm and sunny, shade your new divisions for a week or so after planting with tented newspaper weighted around the edges or overturned, slitted boxes or black, polyethylene-mesh shade cloth. ✿

HAVE ON HAND:

▶ Spade

▶ Spading fork

▶ Water

▶ Knife

▶ Seaweed extract or fish emulsion

▶ Mulch

Cut a deep circle around plant with a spade, 3 to 4 inches out from the outermost stems so that damage to roots is minimal.

Carefully separate tightly packed crowns with a sharp knife. Make sure each piece has both roots and either buds or top growth.

Lift the clump with care by inserting a spading fork deeply in order to get as much of the root system as possible without damage.

Wash off soil so that you can see the roots you're working with. If possible, separate the roots with your fingers.

Replant sections immediately into prepared soil to the crown level. Firm soil around the crown by tamping with foot, and water thoroughly.

Feed with seaweed extract or fish emulsion to encourage root growth. Apply a 2-inch layer of mulch. To prevent rot, do not cover the crown.

HERE'S HOW

WHEN TO DIVIDE

The best time to divide most spring- and early summer-flowering plants is in late summer.

Midsummer is better for Oriental poppies and bearded iris.

Spring is an optimum time for other summer- and fall-flowering plants.

If you can't divide a particular plant during the ideal season, you can still get good results at other times. Cut leafy growth back by ½ to ⅔ before replanting to reduce water loss. Then proceed with division as described.

Dividing Small Shrubs

SUCKERING SHRUBS

Small shrubs are invaluable for adding height and seasonal color to the garden. Those with shallow roots are particularly useful as screens and hedges, since they tend to send out "suckers" or new shoots from their roots, which spread to produce a dense barrier. You can help them fill in more quickly by digging up rooted suckers in spring or fall and transplanting them to empty spots. You can also move these divisions into your flowering beds and borders for additional color.

This technique works well with many common shrubs, including barberries, deutzias, shrubby dogwoods, Japanese kerria, nongrafted lilacs, mock oranges, and spireas. Be aware that suckers from the bases of grafted plants, such as many lilac cultivars and hybrid roses, will not resemble the top growth of the parent plant; they will instead look like the plant that was used for the root system.

With regular watering and mulching, divisions with sturdy root systems will reestablish themselves fairly quickly after replanting. If a division has only a few fibrous roots, however, it will need your special attention. Instead of transplanting directly into its permanent location in the garden, plant it first in a container of potting soil, set it in a shady spot for a few weeks, and water it regularly to keep the soil moist and encouraging to the formation of new roots. After one or two seasons, when the division is established and growing vigorously, transplant it to the desired location. ❧

HAVE ON HAND:

▶ Spading fork

▶ Pruning shears

▶ Water

▶ Mulch

When plant is dormant, loosen soil around sucker with spading fork. Ensure it has fibrous roots at base.

Cut underground link between sucker and parent; lift from soil. Replace soil around parent plant.

Trim new division's main root to where fibrous roots branch out. Replant into prepared soil.

Firm soil around the crown. Water thoroughly. Apply a 2-inch layer of mulch; do not cover the crown.

CLUMPING SHRUBS

Divide your clumping shrubs to create mass ornamental plantings that will produce a striking effect. They are a bit more work to divide, since you'll need to dig up the entire plant, but your result will be several useful divisions of the same size. Division is also a smart way to extend your plant-buying budget. You can, for instance, buy and plant one shrub in your garden and multiply your collection by division in a few short years.

Division works best when plants are dormant, in early spring or in fall. If the weather has been dry, soak the ground around the shrub the day before you plan to divide.

Make sure the shrub you want to propagate has multiple stems and plentiful roots at ground level before you dig it up. Ideally, there should be at least 1 inch between the stems. Tightly packed woody stems are difficult to divide without injuring the plant.

After replanting, prune out any damaged stems, and water deeply. Maintain a thorough and regular watering schedule to help the plant re-establish its deep root system. A 2-inch layer of organic mulch will help to keep the soil evenly moist; but keep mulch away from stems to prevent their rotting. A dose of seaweed extract after planting will help promote quick rooting since its liquid form is easily absorbed by hungry roots. ❀

HAVE ON HAND:

▶ Spade or shovel

▶ Spading fork

▶ Ax (for tough clumps)

▶ Pruning shears or loppers

▶ Water

▶ Mulch

Dig a trench about 1 foot out from the outermost stems. Loosen soil around roots with a spading fork.

Lift the rootball from the hole, and shake off loose soil so you can clearly see where stem meets root.

Separate into sections, each with root and top growth. Pull apart with hands, or cut with spade or ax.

Replant sections into prepared soil. Water thoroughly and mulch; keep mulch away from stems.

Maintaining Your Garden

As your garden grows and thrives, there are a variety of techniques you can use to keep it looking its best. You don't have to be tied down to garden maintenance every summer weekend if you do a little bit each time you're outside. Keep a bucket and pruning shears handy, so you can take them each time you walk around the garden. Make a habit of pinching off dead flowers and pulling out seedling weeds as you see them, and you won't have to set aside whole hours for deadheading or weeding later on. You can also set up stakes and other plant supports early in the season to save emergency staking later on.

When rainfall is lacking, recharge your soil's water reserves with the most efficient and effective irrigation technique for each planting area. You'll also need to apply fertilizers to replace the nutrients used up by your plants as they grow. To minimize watering chores and add some nutrients at the same time, cover the ground between plants with chopped leaves, shredded bark, or other organic mulch.

Don't give up on your garden when the chrysanthemums and other late bloomers signal the approach of cold weather. Fall is the ideal season for many garden projects, including digging new beds, planting, and transplanting. It's also the time to clean up tired, frost-nipped plantings, so they'll be in top shape for spring's return. If you live in a cold climate, you'll also want to take steps to protect your plantings from cold temperatures, drying winds, and hungry animal pests.

This section covers all the basics of caring for your garden throughout the year, so you'll have the pleasure of seeing your ideas—and your plants—grow into a garden you'll enjoy and enjoy showing to others. ❧

Watering

Proper watering is a large part of keeping your garden healthy and beautiful. When you choose the right equipment for the job and use it efficiently, you'll be able to irrigate with a minimum of time and water.

While many garden centers carry a dizzying array of watering equipment, your garden may require only a few basic items. A hose, nozzle, watering can, sprinkler, and soaker hose are among the most useful tools.

The rule of thumb is that a garden requires approximately 1 inch of water per week, either from rain or watering. In reality this can vary widely, depending on the plants you are growing, the amount of

sun and wind, and your soil type. For instance, watering is less critical during cool, cloudy weather than in hot, sunny, or windy conditions. And sandy soil will need more frequent watering than soil high in clay. The best way to gauge the need for water is to check below the soil surface to see if the root zone is moist. (Perennials and shrubs generally form most of their roots in the top 6 to 18 inches of soil, while annuals tend to have more shallow roots.)

Water deeply rather than often. Frequent light sprinkling encourages roots to form close to the surface, where they will suffer quickly from drought. Moistening to a depth of 1 foot or so will encourage deep root systems that better withstand surface drying.

Water the soil and not the tops of plants. The easiest and most effective way to water an established planting is with soaker hoses. These hoses release water through holes all along their length. Water goes directly into the soil without wetting plant leaves, which can help avoid disease. Lay soaker hoses in the spring, before plants fill in. Cover them with mulch, leaving the connector end exposed. Attach to your water supply and let them run for two hours before checking soil. Turn water off when the root zone is moist. ❧

HAVE ON HAND:

▶ Trowel

▶ Watering can

▶ Hose

▶ Sprinkler

▶ Soaker hose

CHECKING MOISTURE. *Pull back mulch around plant to expose the soil, then dig a small, 6- to 10-inch-deep hole with a trowel.*

HAND WATERING. *Use a watering can to irrigate container gardens and individual plants as needed; avoid wetting leaves.*

Look at and feel the soil on the sides of the hole. If the top 4 to 6 inches of soil are dry, it's time to water.

If top 4 to 6 inches of soil are moist, refill hole, test every 2 to 3 days until topsoil dries. Note time it takes soil to dry as rough gauge for future.

SPRINKLERS. Seedbeds need frequent watering to keep them moist; water with overhead sprinklers until seedlings appear.

SOAKER HOSE. To water beds and borders efficiently and without wetting leaves, snake soaker hose through planting in spring.

HERE'S HOW
SUPPLEMENTAL WATERING

During periods of drought, some plants will need extra irrigation to stay vigorous. You can give moisture-loving plants special treatment by sinking a small, unglazed clay pot into the soil next to the base of the stems. Place a cork in the hole at the bottom of the pot, and set the rim of the pot even with the soil surface. Fill the pot with water. The water will gradually seep out of the pot into the soil. Add more water as needed to keep the pot filled.

To supply extra water to new plantings, you can use a plastic milk jug instead. Poke one or two small holes in the base of the jug, set it next to the plant, and fill it with water. Refill as needed to replace the water as it seeps into the soil. Remove the jug once plants get established and start producing new growth.

Fertilizing

To stay healthy and vigorous, your garden plants need both a steady and balanced supply of nutrients. Fortunately, it's easy to apply supplemental fertilizers to keep soil fertility at the right level for good plant growth.

Before adding fertilizers to your garden, take a soil test (see Testing Your Soil, page 20). You can then tailor your program to add only the nutrients that are lacking. Adding too much of a nutrient can be as much of a problem as not adding any at all.

In most cases, however, you'll be applying a "complete" or "balanced" fertilizer to your garden. It will contain

HAVE ON HAND:

▶ Balanced, dry organic fertilizer

▶ Shovel, spade, or tiller

▶ Hand fork

▶ Liquid organic fertilizer

▶ Watering can

▶ Sprayer

nitrogen, phosphorus, and potassium— the three major nutrients that plants need for healthy growth. Nitrogen promotes lush, leafy growth. Phosphorus promotes flowering and fruiting, and potassium encourages a strong root system. The label of any fertilizer will have a series of three numbers—5-10-5, for example—indicating the available percentage of nitrogen, phosphorus, and potassium, respectively. To encourage flowering, the middle number should be higher than the other two.

The best time to apply organic fertilizers is when you prepare your soil for planting. Nutrients will be spread evenly through the root zone, where plants need them. You can add fertilizers after planting, but it will take longer for nutrients to reach plant roots. Dry organic fertilizers (manures, rock phosphate, granite dust) release nutrients slowly but steadily, so one application usually lasts several months. However, if your annuals, container plants, new plantings—or other flowers and shrubs— start blooming poorly or growing slowly during the summer, treat them to a dose of a liquid fertilizer such as fish emulsion or seaweed extract. Already in liquid form, it will immediately be available to developing roots. ❀

APPLYING DRY FERTILIZERS. *Scatter a balanced organic fertilizer over the soil before planting; dig or till into top 6 inches of soil.*

APPLYING LIQUID FERTILIZERS. *Immediately after planting, water with diluted fish emulsion or seaweed extract.*

Feed perennials and bulbs in the fall or spring. Spread fertilizer or compost over the soil; scratch it in lightly with a hand fork.

Fertilize shrubs in the fall or spring. Pull back mulch, scatter fertilizer or compost over the soil, then replace mulch.

Give annuals and container plants a mid-season boost by watering them with liquid fertilizer during the summer.

Spray perennial and shrub leaves with liquid fertilizer in early to midsummer; apply in morning or on a cloudy day to prevent possible leaf burn.

HERE'S HOW

MAKING COMPOST TEA

Compost makes a good dry fertilizer, either worked into the soil before planting or scattered around growing plants. Your plants can also enjoy the goodness of compost in liquid form if you treat them to a cup of compost tea. It's easy to make:

Use an old pillowcase or a piece of burlap 2 feet square to hold a shovelful of finished compost. Tie the top of the bag with string, then drop the bag into a 5-gallon bucket of water.

Let steep for 7 to 10 days; then lift out the bag. Apply the wet compost to your garden or return it to the compost pile. Add water to dilute the remaining liquid to the color of weak tea. Use as you would fish emulsion or seaweed extract, to water new plantings or to feed annuals, perennials, and shrubs.

Making Compost Fertilizer

You can easily turn food scraps, grass clippings, leaves, and other plant debris into valuable fertilizer and soil conditioner by making a compost pile. Microorganisms create compost by slowly breaking down organic matter into humus, the nutrient-rich, moisture-holding component of soil. You can speed up the natural process by giving microorganisms the conditions they need to do their job.

All organic matter eventually decomposes, but the process may take a year or

longer. A balanced and well-tended compost pile, on the other hand, can be ready to use in just a few weeks. As the microorganisms work, the pile heats up, reaching an internal temperature of between 140° and 160°F. Many weeds, seeds, and plant diseases are killed when this process, known as hot composting, occurs. To achieve the optimum temperature, organic matter needs air, moisture, and roughly equal amounts of nitrogen- and carbon-rich material.

Nitrogen-rich materials, such as grass clippings, barnyard manures, and kitchen waste, are generally moist and fresh. Carbon sources, which tend to be dry and brown, include fallen leaves, shredded bark and wood chips, straw and hay. Put tough branches through a chipper/shredder and chop up large kitchen scraps before adding them to your compost pile. Do not compost bones and meat scraps, as they may attract animals. Pet waste can carry harmful bacteria and should not be used, nor should diseased plant material.

Composting works best when materials remain warm and moist but not soggy, so set your pile in a well-drained spot. Choose a well-ventilated container, such as one made of chicken wire, to keep compost in and animals out. 🌿

HAVE ON HAND:

- ▶ Moist organic material
- ▶ Dry organic material
- ▶ 36-inch chicken wire, 14 feet
- ▶ Three or four 48-inch stakes
- ▶ Mallet
- ▶ Garden soil
- ▶ Water
- ▶ Garden fork
- ▶ Tarp or plastic sheet
- ▶ Metal rod

Collect moist materials, such as grass clippings, barnyard manure, and food scraps, as well as dry materials, such as leaves, straw, and wood chips.

Cover the pile loosely with a tarp to keep off rain. Pile should begin to heat up within 7 days. Insert a metal rod into center to check for heat.

Make a 4-foot-diameter, chicken wire cage by intertwining ends. Set on a well-drained spot. Drive 48-inch stakes just inside cage for stability.

Stack alternating 4-inch layers of moist and dry materials in cage. Sprinkle 2 or 3 handfuls of soil between layers. Dampen each layer. Mix.

Remove the wire cage and stakes after the temperature of the pile drops, in about 2 weeks. Reassemble the cage next to the pile.

Fork the contents of pile back into cage. Moisten if material feels dry. Repeat Steps 4, 5, and 6 twice, or until materials appear crumbly.

HERE'S HOW

THE CASE FOR ORGANICS

Organic fertilizers are made from plant or animal materials that release their nutrients slowly as they are decomposed by microorganisms in the soil. The organic matter released in the process improves the capacity of the soil to hold air and water. Synthetic fertilizers, on the other hand, are made from chemical compounds that supply plant nutrients but contribute little to the health of the soil.

Organic matter improves drainage in clayey soil and water retention in sandy soil. Compost provides a balanced source of food at a rate that plants can absorb without harm. Synthetic fertilizers, on the other hand, especially those high in nitrogen, can burn plant tissue if applied incorrectly. They may also leach through sandy soils quickly, wasting nutrients, causing ground water pollution, and leaving plants hungry.

Deadheading

Deadheading—removing flowers after they have finished blooming—benefits your plants in more ways than one. The most obvious is that your garden will look neater without dead flowers drooping off bloom stems and spoiling your display.

Beyond that, deadheading can extend your flowering season, help keep your plants vigorous, and encourage an even better display of flowers the next year. Annuals will respond to deadheading by producing more flowers. You'll extend their bloom season by as much as several weeks. By removing spent flowers, your plants won't use up energy producing seeds. Instead, many shrubs, bulbs, and perennials will primarily direct their energy into leaf and root growth. The increased plant vigor will promote a better flower display the following year.

Preventing seed formation reduces weeding chores around plants that reseed readily, such as feverfew, foxgloves, and mulleins. Leave a few seed pods if you enjoy the self-sown seedlings or want to collect seed to sow next year. But keep in mind that deadheading will prevent fruit formation, a drawback on plants that produce attractive fruits, such as roses. Prolong the bloom season while still getting the showy fall fruit by stopping deadheading in the late summer.

Deadhead at least once a week. Collect your spent flowers in a bucket and place them in your compost pile. ✿

HAVE ON HAND:

► Pruning shears or garden scissors

► Bucket to collect trimmings

On clustered flowers, cut or pinch off individual blooms as they fade, or cut the whole stem at the base.

Trim off single-stemmed blooms just above uppermost leaves, or cut to the ground if stems are leafless.

Prune spent roses just above the uppermost five-leaflet leaf, or to a strong three-leaflet leaf.

On rhododendrons, pinch the base of the finished flower cluster and carefully snap it from the stem.

Staking

Annuals and perennials with long or slender stems often need help to stay straight and tall. Staking prevents tall plants from smothering smaller companions and keeps their flowers upright and visible.

The secret to successful staking is to support them before they need it. Once stems start to sprawl, it is very difficult to make them look natural again. Place supports in early to mid-spring so that your plants grow up through or around them, covering the stakes or wires.

Individual stakes are best for plants with a few tall stems, such as hollyhocks, delphiniums, and lilies. Choose a stake as tall as the plant's ultimate height. When you insert it firmly into the ground, it will be somewhat shorter than the stem and thus less visible. Tie plant to stake carefully, making a figure eight with green garden cord.

Large, bushy perennials, such as peonies, asters, and bleeding hearts, look better when supported by hoop-type stakes. You can buy them or make a similar structure with stakes and string.

Keep short, thin-stemmed plants from sprawling by "pea staking." Cut 9- to 18-inch lengths of twiggy branches (use your late-winter shrub prunings) and insert them firmly into the ground behind or within the developing clump. Snip off visible twig-stake tips if plants don't cover them when they mature.

At the end of the season, remove all of the stakes and wash, dry, and store until next season. ❦

HAVE ON HAND:

► Stakes

► Soft string or yarn

► Scissors

SINGLE STEM. *In mid-spring, insert stake ⅓ of its length into soil, 3 to 6 inches from stem base.*

Tie a 6-inch string to stake, then loop it around the stem and tie it loosely. Repeat every 4 to 6 inches.

BUSHY STEMS. *Set four to six stakes evenly spaced around clump firmly into the soil.*

Tie string to one stake. Wrap free end around other stakes near top of all stems to form circle; tie again.

Pruning Flowering Shrubs

SPRING-FLOWERING

Few sights are more welcome to a winter-weary gardener than the brightly colored blooms of spring-flowering shrubs. Treating these early bloomers to a light yearly pruning will keep them looking their best.

Pruning dead or diseased wood back to healthy growth or to the ground improves appearance and allows your shrub to keep its natural form and remain healthy. Be aware, however, that some dead and diseased growth won't be obvious until your shrub has leafed out, so plan for a second pruning a bit later in the season. Of course, you can remove misplaced or weak stems any time. Thinning out crowded, twiggy growth in the center of your shrub will encourage production of vigorous new flowering shoots.

Shrubs that bloom in spring and early summer flower on stems that were produced during the previous growing season or on short sideshoots from those stems. These shrubs need pruning after they flower. Many common garden shrubs fall into this category, including azaleas, flowering quince, deutzias, forsythias, big-leaved hydrangea, Japanese kerria, mock oranges, firethorns, lilacs, viburnums, and old-fashioned weigela.

Avoid the temptation to shear stems uniformly with hedge clippers. Most flowering shrubs respond better to hand-pruning, and retain their natural beauty as well. 🌺

HAVE ON HAND:

▶ Pruning shears (stems up to ¾-inch diameter)

▶ Loppers (stems up to 1 ¾-inch diameter)

▶ Pruning saw (stems over 1 ¾-inch diameter)

After flowering, prune dead, damaged, or diseased stems back to a bud, another stem, or the ground.

Remove up to ⅓ of the oldest stems at the shrub base to stimulate new growth.

Thin crowded growth to base, and spent flower clusters to next strong buds, at a 45° angle away from bud.

Cut back overly long shoots to match other stems, and to give the shrub a well-balanced shape.

LATE-BLOOMING

Summer- and fall-flowering shrubs are valuable additions to any garden, providing height and color to complement low growing perennials and annuals. Examples of these late bloomers include abelias, orange-eye butterfly bush, shrubby crape myrtles, heavenly bamboo, hibiscus, and most hydrangeas.

Unlike spring-flowering shrubs, late-blooming shrubs usually flower on the current season's growth. A yearly pruning in late winter or early spring will promote vigorous new growth, ensuring a super flower display later in the season. Always remove dead or diseased wood first in order to see what you're left with to prune. On newly planted shrubs, trim the main stems back by about a third to produce a strong framework. On established plants, cut out up to half of the oldest stems each year. Cut the remaining stems of orange-eye butterfly bush and shrub-form crape myrtles back to 1 to 2 feet.

Some shrubs are grown more for their colorful stems than for their leaves or flowers. Many shrubby dogwoods, for instance, produce bright red or yellow stems that add a spark of color to winter gardens. On young plants, cut out a third of the oldest stems at the base in spring to promote colorful new growth. Established, vigorous plants grown for their colorful winter stems can withstand hard pruning; to 2 to 3 inches from the base each spring. ❧

HAVE ON HAND:

▶ Pruning shears (stems up to ¾-inch diameter)

▶ Loppers (stems up to 1¾-inch diameter)

▶ Pruning saw (stems over 1¾-inch diameter)

Prune dead, diseased, damaged stems to the ground, other stem, or above healthy bud to spur growth.

With loppers or saw, cut out up to ½ of oldest stems at the base to make room for new growth.

Thin crowded, twiggy, or poorly placed growth. If two branches rub against each other, remove one.

Prune over-long stems to create a balanced framework. On very vigorous shrubs, cut stems to 8 inches.

Pruning Evergreen Shrubs

Evergreen shrubs form the backbone of the garden, with their handsome forms and soothing green foliage. Many don't need much pruning, but a few well-placed snips at the right time will keep them in peak condition.

Needle-leaved evergreens include such traditional favorites as arborvitae, junipers, and yews. Most can't tolerate heavy pruning, so it's important to trim young plants lightly during their active growing season, when cuts heal faster, to develop the desired shape. Yews are one exception. Reclaim overgrown plants by cutting them back to a 1- to 2-foot framework of branches in spring.

When pruning too-long shoots on established needle-leaved evergreens, reach back into leafy growth to hide your pruning cuts. Don't shear them unless you are willing to do it frequently during the growing season to maintain their formal appearance.

Pruned in late spring, broad-leaved evergreens, including aucuba, boxwoods, camellias, euonymus, and mountain laurel, will reward you all year long. Boxwoods, like yew, will tolerate severe pruning. Rejuvenate your overgrown boxwood by cutting back to a 1- to 2-foot framework of stems in the spring. Consider waiting until November or December to prune shrubs such as hollies, aucuba, mahonia, and euonymus, then use the pruned branches for holiday decor. ✿

HAVE ON HAND:

▶ Pruning shears (stems up to ¾-inch diameter)

▶ Loppers (stems up to 1¾-inch diameter)

▶ Pruning saw (stems over 1¾-inch diameter)

NEEDLE-LEAVED. *Pinch tips on arborvitae and yews after new growth has hardened off to limit size.*

In early to midsummer, remove any dead tips. Cut longest shoots back to maintain shrub's shape.

BROAD-LEAVED. *In late spring, prune dead, damaged growth. If stems cross, remove one.*

Trim overly long and poorly placed shoots to shape the plant, cutting back to a bud or another stem.

Pruning Vines

If you're nervous about pruning, vines are the right plants to practice on. These tough, vigorous plants can take a hard pruning and come back for more.

Clinging vines, such as Boston ivy and Virginia creeper, often need little more than a bit of thinning to open up crowded growth and remove dead or diseased stems. Since clinging stems won't reattach if they come off their support, it's best to trim loose stem tips back to where they cling.

Other vines need different approaches, depending on flowering time. Vines that flower on new growth, such as hops, passionflowers, and porcelain vine, need heavy pruning in late winter or early spring. Vines that bloom on the previous year's stems, such as honeysuckles, are pruned within a month after flowering ends, so next year's buds have time to form. Trim long shoots back to another stem or to the ground to control size and shape.

Clematis vary in their requirements. Those that bloom once in spring or early summer need pruning just after flowering, to allow next year's flower buds to form on new growth. Prune summer- and fall-bloomers in early spring for strong new stems and blooms. On reblooming clematis, trim shoot tips back to the topmost pair of strong buds in early spring. Or, for one showy display later in the season, cut all of the stems back to the lowest buds. ❧

HAVE ON HAND:

▶ Pruning shears (stems up to ¾-inch diameter)

▶ Loppers (stems up to 1¾-inch diameter)

▶ Pruning saw (stems over 1¾-inch diameter)

WISTERIA. *In early spring, remove any dead stems. Cut back remaining sideshoots to 2 or 3 buds.*

After bloom, cut off spent flowers. Trim overly long shoots to keep them in balance with rest of plant.

CLEMATIS. *In early spring, cut back summer- and fall-bloomers to lowest pair of strong buds on stem.*

Prune spring-blooming clematis after flowering. Trim new sideshoots back to 2 or 3 pairs of buds.

Pruning Roses

HYBRID TEA

Rose pruning doesn't have to be difficult or complicated. All you need are the right tools and a little knowledge about your particular plants. Pruning your roses will stimulate new growth and result in healthy, vigorous, and attractive plants.

Prune roses when they are dormant (after their leaves drop in fall and before new growth starts in spring), but not when they are frozen. In mild-winter zones you can accomplish most of the necessary pruning in fall and snip out any frost-damaged shoot tips in spring. In cold-winter regions, cut back hybrid tea roses by about half in fall and leave the detailed pruning until late winter or early spring. In this way, buds near the cuts won't be damaged by below-freezing temperatures. Chances are you will only have to prune lightly again in the spring. At worst, you may lose a few stems.

Hybrid tea roses bloom on new wood, so they need moderate to heavy dormant pruning in order to produce a strong framework of main flowering shoots. Keep an eye on your roses during the growing season, pruning out weak, nonflowering stems as necessary. When you cut blooms for the house, cut to a five-leaflet leaf to encourage a second flush. Newly planted roses require food-producing leaves, so when you take flowers take as little of the foliage as possible. ❧

HAVE ON HAND:

- ▶ Pruning shears (stems up to ¾-inch diameter)
- ▶ Loppers (stems up to 1 ¾-inch diameter)
- ▶ Pruning saw (stems over 1 ¾-inch diameter)
- ▶ Sturdy, thornproof gloves
- ▶ Wood glue

During dormancy, prune out dead, dying, or diseased shoots. If two stems cross, prune out one.

Thin crowded growth. Make 45° angle cuts, ¼ inch above and away from outward-facing bud.

Prune main stems to 18 inches for small, abundant flowers, or to 1 foot for large, long-stemmed flowers.

Seal all cuts with wood glue to prevent destructive cane borers from entering stems.

SHRUB ROSES AND OTHERS

Different kinds of roses require different pruning approaches. Shrub roses generally need little pruning, but each year you will want to remove diseased or dead wood and cut out a few of the oldest stems at the base. Also, you will want to shorten the longest canes to shape the plant and create a balanced framework of flowering stems. It's important to remove "suckers," shoots from the root of your grafted rose. If allowed to grow, suckers will eventually kill the flower-producing grafted stock. Snap—don't cut—them off at the base, as cutting can leave buds that will resprout.

Climbing roses generally don't need pruning for the first two years after planting. After that, prune them in the spring. Trim sideshoots to 3 to 6 inches, leaving three or four buds on each. On established plants, cut out one or two of the oldest stems each year.

Floribundas (the term for cluster-flowered roses) form bushy plants that flower best with light pruning, as shown.

To encourage upright growth on a spreading rose, prune to a bud that faces upward, not outward.

Thinning out dense, twiggy growth on any rose will allow for good air circulation around stems and leaves. This enables foliage to dry quickly after rainfall or watering, thereby reducing the risk of the spread of waterborne disease. 🌹

HAVE ON HAND:

- ▶ Pruning shears (stems up to ¾-inch diameter)
- ▶ Loppers (stems up to 1 ¾-inch diameter)
- ▶ Pruning saw (stems over 1 ¾-inch diameter)
- ▶ Sturdy, thornproof gloves
- ▶ Wood glue

SHRUB. *During dormancy, remove dead, diseased, or awkward stems. Prune at base, above graft union.*

Thin crowded, twiggy growth. Make 45° angle cuts, ¼ inch above and away from outward-facing bud.

CLIMBING. *Select 6 to 8 best canes; prune out others. Cut main shoots to 2 feet above the ground.*

Reduce sideshoots by ⅓ to ⅔. Seal all cuts with wood glue to prevent cane borers from entering plant.

Pruning Hedges

Hedges define boundaries, create privacy, hide unwanted views, and provide backdrops for lawns and gardens. They may be evergreen or deciduous, formal or informal, flowering or not. How and why you prune your hedge depends on all these factors.

Formal hedges are sheared as if they were a single plant, while shrubs in informal hedges are pruned as individuals. Cutting or shearing the tips of branches causes buds along the stem to begin growing, which results in denser branching. Formal deciduous hedges, such as border privet, and fine-textured evergreens, such as yews and arborvitae, should be sheared frequently throughout the growing season to keep them compact and lush. You'll want to stop pruning around midsummer to allow new growth to mature for the winter and to prevent possible cold weather damage.

Prune informal hedges by thinning out individual branches to control their size and promote new growth. Maintain their natural shape and encourage neighboring shrubs to grow together by not pruning the branches in between.

The correct time of year to prune your informal hedge depends on if, and when, the shrubs bloom. In general, prune shrubs that bloom in the spring right after flowering but prune summer-blooming shrubs in late winter.

Always prune formal hedges so that they are wider at the bottom than at the top, to allow sunlight to reach all leafy parts of the plant. Hedges with shaded lower limbs will become leggy and top-heavy. You can renovate many leggy deciduous hedges by cutting the shrubs to within 6 to 12 inches of the ground in late winter. Pruning this hard will leave your hedges looking bare for a growing season or two, but your patience eventually will be rewarded with fresh, new growth. Prune and train your renovated hedge using the same methods you would use for newly planted one. ❧

HAVE ON HAND:

▶ Hedge shears

▶ Wooden stakes

▶ Mallet

▶ String

NEW. *In spring, to establish a formal hedge, prune bare-root stock by $1/2$ or to within 6 inches of ground at planting to encourage branching.*

ESTABLISHED. *To shape, set four stakes at each end to mark desired bottom width and top width. Make bottom wider than top.*

The first summer, shear off about ½ of new growth whenever it reaches 2 to 3 inches. Repeat as necessary, stopping by midsummer.

Late in the winter, before plants resume their growth, shear off ½ of previous year's late-summer growth to encourage branching.

Attach strings near bottom of outer stakes at one end of hedge to those at other end. Attach strings likewise to inner stakes at desired hedge height.

Shear tips of branches from bottom to top using strings as a guide to achieve desired height and width. Stop pruning by midsummer.

HERE'S HOW

CREATING TOPIARY

Create landscape accents that resemble animals or geometric shapes with fancifully sheared topiary shrubs. Select an evergreen shrub that is densely branched and fine-textured, such as boxwood or yew. Choose a plant with a structure similar to your chosen design, such as a short, round shrub for a ball-shaped topiary.

Thin out crossed branches, dead wood, and weak growth for the first year or two. Encourage branches to grow in the desired direction and remove shoots that do not fit into the overall pattern.

Begin shearing the shrub into its final shape when it is a few years old. Shear in early spring and summer, but stop by midsummer.

Be patient. Topiaries may take many years to complete, depending on the plant and design you choose.

Mulching

A mulch is any material that is used to cover the soil around and between plants. Using mulch effectively can help make your garden a long-term success. Although mulches can be inorganic (nonliving) materials, such as black plastic or gravel, organic mulches—those derived from formerly living materials—are preferable because they provide extra benefits in the garden.

Both organic and inorganic mulches will shade soil, preventing weed seeds from sprouting and minimizing water loss due to evaporation. Mulch will also keep soil from splashing up on plants, keeping flowers clean and reducing the likelihood of disease. In winter, mulches moderate soil temperature changes, which prevent freeze-and-thaw damage (see Winter Protection, page 112). In addition, an organic mulch, such as chopped leaves, shredded bark, or other material, provides an attractive background for flowers and foliage. Organic mulches also improve your garden soil as they break down over time and release nutrients and organic matter.

When you select a mulch, consider appearance, availability, and price. Coarse mulches, such as wood chips, are well suited to shrubs and trees; fine-textured mulches, such as shredded bark, are more attractive in flower gardens and other high-visibility areas. Don't overlook the mulch materials found right in your yard: grass clippings and shredded leaves are two. To cut down on expense, buy mulch for beds near the house and use home-made mulches for less visible areas.

While mulches can do wonders for your garden, they can also cause problems if not handled properly. Mulches are ideal hiding places for slugs, snails, and other soil-dwelling pests. If you have serious damage to your plants (leaves or flowers that have large holes or have been totally eaten), rake off the mulch and allow the soil surface to dry out before replacing it. If damage continues, reduce mulch by half or stop using it. Mulch can also hold moisture against leaves and stems, which can encourage rot to develop. Keep all mulches at least 2 inches away from the base of stems. 🌺

HAVE ON HAND:

▶ Hoe
▶ Shovel or pitchfork
▶ Mulch
▶ Trowel

APPLYING ORGANIC MULCH.
Cultivate the area thoroughly to remove existing weeds before applying mulch.

MANAGING MULCH. *During the growing season, pull or dig out any weeds that surface through the mulch.*

Use a shovel or pitchfork to spread mulch evenly over the cultivated soil. A 2-inch layer of mulch is usually sufficient for most plantings.

Pull mulch away from the base of each plant with your fingers, so the mulch is at least 2 inches away from plant stems.

Check the depth of the mulch layer 2 or 3 times a year; add more mulch if needed to maintain enough thickness to foil weeds.

In early spring, rake mulch from beds to let the soil warm up and dry out; replace the mulch layer in late spring.

While materials such as shredded bark, chopped leaves, and wood chips are traditional favorites for mulching, you may also be able to find other excellent mulches, depending on the nature of your local industries. Some industry by-products can work just as well as more common mulches and are usually available at reasonable prices.

In some areas gardeners can buy bags of cocoa shell mulch from candy or chocolate factories. Cocoa shells make an attractive, lightweight, easy-to-apply mulch; they also have a pleasant chocolate aroma for the first week.

If you live near a mushroom production area, you can usually find mushroom compost (the "soil" that's left after the mushrooms are harvested). Look for mushroom compost that has been aged for a few months; fresh compost can be high in salts or other materials that can damage your plants.

Other specialty mulches include grape pomace (pulp), apple pomace, buckwheat hulls, pecan shells, and seaweed, to name a few. To find out which materials are available in your area, talk to gardening friends in your community or check the garden-related classified ads in your local newspaper.

Trellising and Training

Directing plant growth with trellising and training can keep plants in top form. The techniques described here don't take much time, but they can work wonders by turning floppy or spindly plants into attractive, well-formed ones.

Trellising is the technique of choice for plants that have long, trailing stems, such as wisteria vines. A well-constructed trellis will support your vines' top growth while providing an attractive background for leaves and flowers. When selecting a trellis, consider the vine you'll be growing on it. Twining vines (such as Lonicera honeysuckles) can grow on just about any trellis. Vines that climb with tendrils (such as crimson glory vine) or twining leaf stems (such as clematis) grow best on a trellis with thin crosspieces—½ inch wide or less. You can grow them on a thicker trellis, but the vine would then have to be tied as climbing roses are.

You can train your plant by taking steps to direct its growth and flowering. Proper pruning and staking (see Staking, page 97) are essential but there are other important techniques as well. If you pinch off the top bud, for example lower buds will be encouraged to grow. This is a great way to promote dense, bushy growth—and more flowers—on many leafy-stemmed plants such as clematis (also see Deadheading, page 96). Pinching can help delay flowering, so you will have flowers over a longer period of time than you normally would. Stop pinching in early July so that flower buds have time to form flowers for the fall. Pinching is also a promoter of sturdy stems, which can help reduce your staking chores.

Disbudding is another training method. By cutting or rubbing off sideshoots, the plant is encouraged to put its energy into the top flower bud. Each stem will then produce only one flower, but that bloom will be large and showy. Disbudding is not often used on vines but is common with bedding plants such as chrysanthemums and dahlias, and even hybrid tea roses. ❦

HAVE ON HAND:

▶ String or soft twine

▶ Scissors

▶ Grass or pruning shears

ATTACHING A VINE TO A TRELLIS. *Cut a piece of string or soft twine 6 inches long. Tie it around a crosspiece on your trellis.*

PINCHING. *Use your thumb and forefinger to pinch or snap off individual shoot tips, just above a leaf or pair of leaves.*

Gently pull the loose ends around a stem; tie again, leaving some slack around the stem. Trim extra string so it won't be visible.

Tie again every 6 to 12 inches. Check every few months to make sure ties are not cutting into stems; use a looser tie if needed.

HERE'S HOW

ATTACHING TRELLISES TO WALLS

When you install a trellis next to a wall, use small blocks of wood as spacers to hold the trellis 2 to 3 inches away from the structure. This will allow air to circulate between the vine and the wall, discouraging disease problems and minimizing damage to the wall as well.

To make future wall maintenance easier, attach the bottom of the trellis to hinges, and use hooks and eyes to hold the top of the trellis to the spacers. When you must reach the wall, simply unhook the top of the trellis. Carefully lower it away from the structure and prop it on a ladder. When you are finished with the wall, raise the trellis again and rehook.

SHEARING. *If plant has too many stems to pinch, cut top growth back by ½ of total length of stems with grass clippers or pruning shears.*

DISBUDDING. *Pinch or rub off sideshoots; leaving top flower bud. Don't remove leaves that grow directly from the stem.*

Fall Cleanup

When fall frost nips at your flowers and leafy growth slows down, it can be tempting to give up on your garden. However, it's worth taking the time to do a final cleanup before winter sets in. Putting your garden to bed properly can prevent problems next year, and gives it a tidier appearance for the winter months.

Dead leaves, flowers, and stems provide ideal overwintering sites for insects and disease organisms. You can remove these problems before they develop. If you know a plant is diseased, discard its top growth in your trash or bury it in an out-of-the-way spot. Otherwise, it's safe to add plant debris to your compost pile.

HAVE ON HAND:

- ▶ Pruning shears
- ▶ Leaf rake
- ▶ Water
- ▶ Rags
- ▶ Spading fork
- ▶ Hand fork

Cut back spent flower stems after bloom to prevent plants from dropping seed and self-sowing. While a few self-sown seedlings may be welcome, some plants can produce copious amounts. (Foxgloves, columbines, and coneflowers are a few examples.) If you like, leave just one or two flower heads to get a few seedlings without creating a problem.

While it may seem like a good idea to let fallen leaves accumulate on beds, it's best to rake them off regularly. It's also a good idea to rake mulches away from shrubs and perennials in mid-fall. Mulches and fallen leaves provide ideal shelter for mice, voles, and other animal pests, encouraging them to nest in your garden. They'll feed on your plants through the winter, chewing roots or devouring crowns and buds. By removing these sheltering materials, pests will make their homes elsewhere, minimizing the risk to your plants. It's safe to replace the mulches once the ground is frozen.

Some perennials, such as purple coneflowers, sedums, and asters, have attractive seed clusters that appeal to wintering birds. Many ornamental grasses also provide winter interest. If you enjoy the look of these plants, wait until late winter to cut them down. ❧

Pull out dead annuals, roots and all. Cut back dead growth on perennials. Start a new compost pile with these materials.

Dig dahlias, gladiolus, and other tender bulbs before frost or when leaves turn brown. Dry and store indoors for the winter.

Rake mulches and fallen leaves away from shrubs and perennial beds. Shred leaves for mulch or add to compost pile.

Dump annual container plantings into the compost pile. Rinse clinging soil out of containers; dry and store indoors for winter.

Do a final, thorough weeding to catch weeds you missed earlier, as well as to eliminate newly sprouting cool-weather weeds.

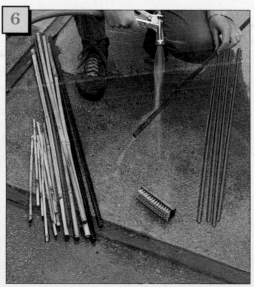

Remove stakes from the garden. Discard twiggy stakes. Wash soil off permanent stakes and let them dry before storing for the winter.

HERE'S HOW

FALL CHECKLIST

Fall is a great time to get many garden jobs done. The air is cool but the soil is still warm, providing ideal conditions for root development. When you plant, transplant, or divide plants at this time of year, they'll settle in well and be in prime condition for growing next spring. Here are a few other gardening jobs that you can do in the fall:

Take soil tests and add any needed amendments.

Dig new garden beds for planting in fall or spring.

Fertilize perennials, bulbs, and shrubs with compost.

Sow perennial seeds; plant bulbs.

Drain and store hoses.

Clean, sharpen, and store garden tools.

Fall is also the time to review the past year's triumphs and tragedies. In your gardening notebook, make a note of disease or pest problems you encountered during the year so you'll be able to take the correct control measures early next year. Also, jot down new ideas and plant combinations you want to try so you'll be ready when the spring shopping season arrives.

Winter Protection

For cold-climate gardeners, winter is a time to dream, to think back on successes of the season past and plan for next year's plantings. But while you are comfortable indoors with your catalogs and coffee, your plants are coping with winter's stresses: fluctuating temperatures, drying winds, and hungry animals. Protecting your perennials and shrubs to help them weather the winter will be time well spent.

If your perennials and bulbs are naturally adapted to your climate, they will tolerate the winter cold on their own. Top growth dies back to the ground, and roots are insulated by the soil. Problems arise

HAVE ON HAND:

▶ Water

▶ Pruning shears

▶ Mulch

▶ Evergreen boughs

▶ Antitranspirant

▶ Burlap and stakes

when warm spells are followed by cold snaps, especially in late winter. Warmth tricks plants into producing new growth, then frost kills the tender shoots. But you can use a trick as well. Cover soil with winter mulch to keep it evenly cool. (Wait until soil is frozen, to avoid providing shelter for pests.) Choose a loose, lightweight mulch: shredded leaves, pine needles, or straw. (Do not use hay, and remove all mulches in early spring.) Snow, if you're lucky enough to have it, is excellent, insulating the soil from swings in air temperature.

Shrubs need different protection. Top growth is subjected to dry winter wind, which draws moisture out of stems that frozen roots can't replace. To minimize winter damage, stop fertilizing shrubs by midsummer; this stops the tender growth that is most susceptible to drying. Water thoroughly before the ground freezes, and place burlap screens on the windward side of the plant to block wind. Foliage can be protected by antitranspirants (available at garden centers).

Protect the bark and stems on shrubs from rabbits and other small critters with wire-mesh "collars." To foil deer, however, you'll need to put an 8-foot fence around your yard or create temporary fences 6 feet tall around individual plants. 🌾

PROTECTING PERENNIALS. *If the fall has been dry, water regularly until top growth dies back; then cut back dead tops.*

PROTECTING SHRUBS. *Water deeply around shrubs before the ground freezes to ensure that the root zone is moist.*

Once the soil is frozen, add a 3- to 6-inch layer of mulch over the bed. Any falling snow will be a bonus, increasing the insulation.

Where winter snow cover is unreliable or nonexistent, lay evergreen boughs over mulched plants to provide extra protection.

When the soil has frozen, replace the mulch you raked off in the fall; add more, if needed, to keep the layer 2 to 3 inches thick.

Spray evergreen foliage with an antitranspirant according to package directions, or install a burlap screen to block wind.

HERE'S HOW

HANDLING FROST HEAVES

Frost heaving is the result of fluctuating temperatures around unmulched plants. Alternating freezing and thawing pushes plant crowns out of the soil, breaking the roots and exposing buds and tender roots to drying winds.

Mulching frozen soil in late fall or early winter and covering beds with snow, as described, will usually prevent this problem. But it's a good idea to walk through your garden during warm spells to spot any plants that may have been heaved out of the soil. If you can, push the tops back into the soil; otherwise, pile on extra soil or compost to cover exposed roots. Replant heaved clumps at their proper level once the soil thaws in spring.

Creating a Healthy Lawn

Lawns beautify the ground around a home, carpet play areas and outdoor spaces, and connect the various sections of the landscape. When installing a new lawn, thoughtful planning and thorough preparation are needed to ensure that the grass you choose will thrive for many years with minimum care. Modern grass hybrids make your job easier because they resist diseases and insects better than older varieties and grow in a wider range of conditions. Many offer deeper color, finer texture, and slower growth, which means less frequent mowing.

Next to grass selection, soil preparation plays the greatest role in the longevity and appearance of your lawn. Unlike gardens, lawns usually remain in place for a generation or longer. Take time to level the soil, improve its structure and fertility, and correct drainage before planting seed, sprigs, or plugs, or installing sod.

As you plan the layout of your lawn, remember that large, uninterrupted areas are the easiest to mow. Group plants, trees, and shrubs into connected planting beds wherever possible. Keep edges straight or gently curved. Avoid sharp angles and leave spaces wide enough for your mower to pass through comfortably. After you plant your lawn, mulch or plant ground cover on large areas around trees to prevent mower damage to their trunks and eliminate the need for trimming. ❧

Selecting Lawn Grass

Play and heavy traffic areas need to recover quickly from abuse. Choose perennial ryegrass, tall fescue, Bermuda, Bahia, and zoysia grasses.

Your lawn's appearance, durability, and ease of maintenance depend largely on the type of grass you choose for your site. When selecting grass or sod, consider your climate, how you will use your lawn, the amount of time and money you plan to spend on maintenance, and whether your site is sunny, shady, or has areas of each.

Plant breeders have developed many new grasses adapted to a wide range of lawn needs and growing conditions. Lawns with a variety of conditions, such as sunny and shady or wet and dry, do well with a mixture of several seed types. Lawns in northern climates are more likely than those in the South to need a mix of grasses. If you select just one type of grass, you may not achieve the results you want. For instance, cool-season grasses, such as Kentucky bluegrass, grow quickly in spring and autumn when weather is cool and moist but become nearly dormant during hot summer months. Warm-season grasses, such as Bermuda grass, grow vigorously in summer but do not tolerate freezing northern temperatures. A mixture of native grasses suited to your climate may be your best bet for a healthy lawn.

Your outdoor activities will also help you determine the best grass combination for your lawn. Children's play spaces and heavy traffic areas will need tough grasses, such as perennial ryegrass or tall fescue. For ornamental lawns with little traffic, you may want to choose a more finely textured grass that will provide a neater, more elegant look.

Consider the maintenance requirements of various lawn grasses before you decide which ones are for you—their needs can vary widely. Bluegrasses and St. Augustine grass may require frequent watering, for example, while fescues and Bermuda grass will tolerate long periods of drought. Some grasses need large amounts of fertilizer, while others don't. The growth rate of your grass, especially during its season (or seasons) of fastest growth, will dictate how frequently your lawn will need to be mowed.

The amount of sun your lawn receives, as well as your soil type, will help you choose the grass you need. There are now many grasses that will grow well in the shade. Some even tolerate the salty soil found in coastal areas and near snowbelt roads.

A good match between your selection of turf grass and your lawn conditions will ensure that you and nature are working together to create and maintain a beautiful and sturdy lawn. 🌸

Plant native prairie grasses, buffalo grass, and blue grama grass in sites where maintenance—and water—may be infrequent.

Use tall fescue, Bermuda, zoysia, or buffalo grass where water availability is limited. Their deep roots make them especially drought tolerant.

Fescues and St. Augustine grass are more tolerant of salt than most. Use them in coastal areas and along roads that are often snow covered.

Plant Kentucky bluegrass in ornamental lawns with light foot traffic. During summer, this cool-season grass will need to be watered frequently.

Use seed mixtures for lawns with varied conditions such as sun and shade. If one grass fails, others will keep your lawn looking attractive.

HERE'S HOW
BUYING GRASS SEED

When buying grass seed, be sure to read the label on the package to learn specifically what grasses are contained, the percentage of each, and expected germination rates.

Look for germination rates of 80 to 90 percent for cool-season grasses and at least 70 percent for warm-season and native grasses. The mix should contain less than 1 percent weed seeds. For best results, plant seed dated for use in the current year.

Some mixes are largely annual grass species. While these germinate rapidly and provide instant cover, choose a mix with at least 75 percent perennial species that will persist beyond the first growing season.

Preparing and Seeding Your Lawn

Perhaps you have a new house surrounded by bare soil, or you want to spruce up a neglected plot. Sowing grass seed over carefully prepared soil will be the most economical way for you to establish your new lawn.

Thorough soil preparation is the key to even and vigorous lawn growth for many years. The first step is to conduct a soil test (see Testing Your Soil, page 20) to determine what, if any, amendments you'll need to add. Next, remove weeds and any stumps, large rocks, or other

obstacles from the site. Correct dips or bumps in the lawn by removing or adding topsoil wherever necessary. Be sure to slope soil away from building foundations and correct any drainage problems (see Understanding Drainage, page 13).

Apply recommended lime or sulfur if needed to bring the soil pH close to neutral. Add compost, fish meal, or rotted manure to improve soil structure and fertility. Spread a fertilizer high in potassium and phosphorus over the lawn area to promote strong root growth. Rototill both the length and width of the lawn to a depth of 6 to 8 inches to incorporate the soil amendments and to loosen and aerate the soil.

Before seeding, rake the soil smooth and roll it. Water the area thoroughly to settle the soil. If soil settles unevenly, rake it and roll again. You can seed immediately or wait a few days and eradicate any weeds that may germinate in the freshly tilled soil. Sow cool-season grasses in late summer to early autumn and warm-season grasses in the spring to early summer for best results. You may want to rent some of the equipment needed to prepare and seed your lawn. Most rental agencies carry rototillers, drop spreaders, and lawn rollers. 🌺

HAVE ON HAND:

- ▶ Tape measure
- ▶ Grass seed
- ▶ Drop spreader
- ▶ Garden rake
- ▶ Lawn roller
- ▶ Water
- ▶ Mulch
- ▶ Hose
- ▶ Sprinkler

Measure site and determine square footage of area to be seeded. Purchase amount of grass seed recommended on package to cover site.

Half-fill a lawn roller with water and roll the seeded area lengthwise and crosswise to firm soil. Do not roll wet or easily compacted soil.

Using a drop spreader, spread seed at half the recommended rate in one direction. Apply second half in a crosswise pattern.

Rake seed gently into top ⅛ to ¼ inch of soil to improve soil contact. Keep seed evenly distributed to avoid bare spots and clumping.

Apply a uniform ¼-inch layer of coarse organic mulch, burlap, or floating row covers (for a small area) to hold soil moisture and deter birds.

Set up a hose and sprinkler. Water gently to a depth of 6 inches. Water daily as needed to keep soil surface moist until grass is established.

HERE'S HOW

PROTECTING SEED FROM BIRDS

The sprouted seeds of a newly germinated lawn can look like a feast to a flock of hungry birds. Protect your lawn by mixing seeds with topsoil before sowing, covering the seeds with mulch, or using scare devices.

Apply organic, weed-free mulch that can stay on the lawn: one or two bales of straw per 1,000 square feet, for example. Fabrics such as burlap, cheesecloth, and floating row covers deter birds, but must be removed before the grass grows through.

Homemade deterrents such as scarecrows or shiny aluminum pie tins hung from strings on low stakes may keep some birds away. Garden centers offer a range of devices designed to scare birds, including inflatable owls and vibrating tapes designed to be stretched between posts.

Plugging Your Lawn

Set stakes into ground at opposite ends of prepared lawn 6 inches from edge to establish straight planting lines. Attach taut string.

Plugging is a common method for starting a lawn in mild climates where turf grasses spread mainly by runners and where grasses cannot be started from seed. Plugs are actually small pieces of sod which are sometimes available at lawn and garden centers and through mail-order sources.

Plugs are an ideal choice for lawns composed of warm-season grasses, which fill in faster than cool-season grasses. But even in the best conditions, plugs can take from one season to two years to fill in, depending on the grass species, soil preparation, spacing, and the amount of care and attention they receive after planting.

When planting plugs, prepare your soil as you would for a seeded lawn (see Preparing and Seeding Your Lawn, page 118). Be especially careful to remove all weeds that could compete with the newly planted grass before it becomes established. The plugs should be planted as soon as you purchase them, so it is important to have your site ready beforehand. If you can't plant them right away, store them in a cool place out of the sun and keep them slightly moist. Allowing the roots to dry out or exposing the plants to high temperatures for even a short time will injure or even kill them.

The quantity of plugs you need depends on the type of grass you wish to grow, the size of the plugs and the area to be planted, and how quickly you want the lawn to fill in. Plan to plant plugs in the early spring so that they will root during the cooler weather and grow rapidly as the season heats up. ✿

HAVE ON HAND:

▶ Tape measure

▶ 2 stakes

▶ Mallet

▶ String

▶ Plugger or trowel

▶ Water

▶ Sod plugs

▶ Lawn roller

▶ Hose

▶ Sprinkler

▶ Topsoil

▶ Shovel

Moisten soil lightly. Set plugs into holes so that soil level of plug is level with ground. Fill in around plug to provide soil contact. Firm.

Dig holes under string with trowel or plugger, 1 inch wider and deeper than plug size, at uniform intervals between 6 and 12 inches.

Move stakes and string to next row. Dig holes in staggered pattern to give more uniform coverage. Repeat across area until all holes are dug.

HERE'S HOW

CREATING A LEVEL LAWN

Dips and ridges make mowing difficult and spoil the appearance of an established lawn. Create a level planting area before you seed, plug, or sod your new lawn.

Remove all weeds and grass from the site and then rototill the soil to a depth of 6 to 8 inches. Smooth the area with a wide landscaper's rake, filling the low spots with soil from the high spots. Bring in additional topsoil to correct large depressions. Rototill or dig high spots to remove excess soil.

Water the planting area with a sprinkler to settle the soil. Repeat raking until the entire lawn area is smooth and level.

Roll lawn with lawn roller to ensure plug and soil contact. Water with sprinkler to depth of 6 to 8 inches and daily as needed for several weeks.

Add additional topsoil between plugs if settling or erosion occurs. Begin mowing when grass is 3 to 4 inches high and roots are established.

Laying Sod

Sod provides an instant, uniform, weed-free lawn that can be installed nearly anytime during the growing season. Ideal for difficult areas, such as slopes, sod lawns can quickly solve the problems of erosion and bare spots. Unlike seeded or plugged lawns, sod lawns are often ready to be used within three to four weeks. The cost of convenience, however, is high.

Sod is expensive, so it makes sense to provide the best possible growing conditions. Even though sod comes with soil attached, the ground in which it will grow must be fertile, level, and properly prepared for your finished lawn to look its best. Prepare the soil as you would for seeding lawn grasses (see Preparing and Seeding Your Lawn, page 118). To allow for the thickness of the sod, grade carefully around sidewalks and other edges, making the prepared soil about an inch lower than the final lawn will be.

Order your sod from a sod farm, garden center, or landscape contractor well in advance of when you want to install it. Measure the square footage of your yard to determine how much sod you will need, then add another 10 percent to the total to allow for damage, ground slope, or hard-to-fit areas. If you have any special situations, such as shade or a children's play yard, tell your supplier so that the staff can help you select the best sod for your needs.

Lay your sod on prepared, evenly moist soil as soon as it arrives. Each strip will be about 2 feet wide and from 6 to 9 feet long and can weigh as much as 40 pounds. Work with a partner when carrying the strips to avoid damaging them. After planting, avoid walking on your new sod and keep it well watered for at least three weeks until the roots have grown into the underlying soil. 🌿

HAVE ON HAND:

▶ Sod strips

▶ Boards

▶ Sharp knife or lawn edger

▶ Water

▶ Sprinkler

Store sod strips in a cool, shady place while you work. Keep sod lightly moist, but not wet. Handle gently to avoid dislodging soil from roots.

Lay the next row of sod strips tightly against the first row. Cut strips if necessary to stagger the ends. Press edges together firmly.

Walk and kneel on boards laid across area to avoid soil compaction and turf damage. Take care not to tear or stretch sod strips.

Lay the first strip along a straight edge, such as a driveway. Place strips end to end across the yard, ends firmly together, avoiding gaps.

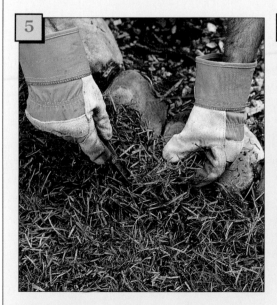

Trim around flower beds and mulched areas with a sharp knife or a lawn edger to give sod a neat and even appearance.

Water to a depth of 6 to 8 inches. Water as needed to keep edges and underlying soil moist for 2 to 3 weeks, or until roots are established.

HERE'S HOW

KEEPING SOD IN GOOD CONDITION

Sod should be installed as soon as it arrives, but if that is not possible, you can store it for a period of time if you take the proper care.

Rolled sod will keep for a day or two in a cool spot, out of direct sun. Water by spraying the sod lightly to moisten it. If you must store it for longer than 48 hours, unroll the strips on a hard, cool, even surface. Protect your sod from sun and heat, and keep it moist.

Roll the strips up again before moving them to their permanent site. Take care not to stretch or tear the sod.

Removing Weeds

Most lawns contain some plants other than desirable lawn grasses. A few undesirables, or weeds, are not necessarily a problem. Low soil fertility, unbalanced pH, soil compaction, and improper mowing, however, may give weeds the upper hand.

Correcting these deficiencies will help reduce the chance for weeds to succeed in your lawn, but you may still need to remove some either by hand or with herbicides. The method you choose will depend on the size of your lawn and the types and quantity of weeds.

HAVE ON HAND:

- ▶ Asparagus knife or narrow trowel
- ▶ Granular herbicide in shaker container
- ▶ Cardboard or tarp
- ▶ Liquid herbicide in spray container
- ▶ Water
- ▶ Sprinkler
- ▶ Drop spreader
- ▶ Granular weed and feed mix

For small weed-infested lawn areas, removal by hand makes the most sense, although herbicides may also be used. Take care to remove the entire weed, root and all. Removing only the top of the weed will allow the plant to grow back.

For large weed-infested areas, herbicides are the most practical option. Preemergent herbicides applied in the spring work by killing newly sprouted weed seeds. Preemergents will also kill grass seedlings, so read the label carefully to find out when it is safe to reseed.

Postemergent herbicides kill established weeds and can be either selective or nonselective. Selective herbicides affect only certain plants, such as broad-leaved dandelion and plantain. Apply these in late summer to control perennial weeds in your lawn. Nonselective herbicides kill all plants and are useful for eradicating weeds and grass in areas to be renovated and reseeded.

Remember that herbicides are powerful poisons that should be used sparingly. Always read and follow instructions on the herbicide label carefully. The label will tell you what kinds of plants the chemical will control, when and how to apply it, and which safety precautions are necessary. ❧

SMALL AREA. *Push an asparagus fork or narrow trowel into soil next to weed and pry up to pop entire plant and root out of soil.*

LARGE AREA. *Water area to be treated by just moistening foliage. Choose a warm, calm, sunny day when no rain is expected for 24 hours.*

SMALL OR LARGE AREA. *Apply granular preemergent herbicide directly to weed. Cover grass with cardboard or a tarp to protect.*

Spray a postemergent liquid herbicide on individual weeds. Apply when the air is still. Protect nontarget plants with cardboard.

Fill a drop spreader with a granular post-emergent herbicide (see Fertilizing Your Lawn, page 134). Adjust spreader to appropriate rate.

Push drop spreader over lawn at a steady pace. Close hopper when stopping or turning around. Stay off grass for 12 to 24 hours.

HERE'S HOW

PESTICIDE SAFETY

All pesticides, including herbicides and insecticides, are toxic and must be handled with caution. Read the label completely before purchase to be sure the pesticide is appropriate for your intended use. Before use, read the label again and follow the instructions exactly. Never apply a pesticide to a crop or pest that is not listed on the label.

Wear protective gloves, long pants, and closed-toed shoes when mixing and applying pesticides. Wear safety goggles and a dust mask or other safety equipment recommended on the label. Never apply a liquid or dusty pesticide on a breezy day. Keep children and pets out of the area.

Dispose of unused pesticides according to the label instructions; do not pour them down a drain. Store pesticides in original containers.

Removing Thatch

MANUAL DETHATCHING. *Remove a 6-inch-deep core of soil from lawn. Measure thatch depth. Dethatch if thicker than ½ inch.*

Thatch, the layer of dead plant material that lies just above the soil surface, is largely caused by the overapplication of fertilizer. It becomes a problem only when debris accumulates faster than soil microorganisms can decompose it. A half-inch of thatch is normal and even desirable in most lawns, but thicker layers can prevent water and nutrients from reaching grass roots, thereby providing an ideal environment for pests and diseases to thrive. If your lawn feels spongy or springy when you walk on it, you probably need to dethatch.

Thatch buildup tends to be more of a problem with warm-season grasses than cool-season ones and is prevalent in lawns composed of creeping grasses, such as bluegrass, bent grass, St. Augustine grass, Bermuda grass, and zoysia. These grasses spread by runners above or just below the ground, which can form a dense mat after a number of years. As the layer thickens, the lawn may show signs of decline, including dry brown spots and insect damage.

In thatch-heavy lawns, water collects in the thatch layer instead of penetrating into the soil. As a result, grass roots grow close to the surface, where they are susceptible to drought and disease. Consider purchasing a mulching mower, which cuts grass finely enough so that it becomes a natural fertilizer.

The best time to remove thatch from your lawn is just before the grass begins a period of active growth. Dethatch warm-season grasses in the spring and cool-season grasses in the spring or in late summer to early autumn. After dethatching, lightly fertilize your lawn with an organic fertilizer, correct the pH if necessary, and water thoroughly. Rake grass vigorously at least once a year, aerate your lawn periodically, water deeply when needed, and maintain healthy soil to prevent the accumulation of thatch from recurring. ✤

HAVE ON HAND:

▶ Trowel or spade

▶ Tape measure

▶ Lawn rake

▶ Thatch rake

▶ Dethatching machine

AUTOMATED DETHATCHING. *Rent a dethatcher, often called a power rake, to remove buildup over a large, heavily thatched area.*

In small areas with a thin layer of thatch (less than 1 inch), rake grass firmly with a lawn rake to pull up loose plant debris.

On small lawns with moderate buildup (over 1 inch), use special thatch rake to slice and dislodge thatch. Remove debris with lawn rake.

Adjust height of flail bars to slice through top half of thatch layer. Run machine for several feet, stop, and measure depth of slice.

Run machine over lawn in parallel rows, lifting blades when turning. Repeat perpendicular to first dethatching. Rake up debris for compost.

HERE'S HOW

PREVENTING THATCH

The best way to prevent an accumulation of thatch is to build and maintain healthy soil where microorganisms can thrive.

Microorganisms work best in neutral to slightly acid, well-aerated soil that is rich in organic matter. Leave short grass clippings on your lawn to feed the soil inhabitants and build humus. To prevent compaction, aerate the soil periodically.

You should avoid using high-nitrogen chemical fertilizers since they can slow down the decay process, and some also acidify the soil. Maintain the correct pH and fertilize with organic nutrients to keep microorganisms healthy and to promote fast decay.

Overseeding

Planting grass seed on an already established lawn is called overseeding. In mild climates where lawns become dormant and brown in the winter, lawn owners often plant a temporary layer of cool-season grass over the permanent grass for winter color. In the North, overseeding the lawn with improved grass cultivars can permanently enhance the quality of your turf.

Many older lawns contain weak and unattractive grasses. Perhaps your growing conditions or needs have changed; the young tree that you planted many years ago may now be casting deep shade, or the once-ornamental lawn has become a children's playground. Perhaps you'd like to replace a water-thirsty lawn with a more drought-tolerant grass, or your current lawn is plagued by a persistent disease. These new grasses have improved resistance to diseases, pests, and traffic. Plant breeders have also managed to make them drought- and shade-tolerant and given them darker, greener tones and finer textures.

You can overseed existing grasses with these newer cultivars to gradually improve your lawn. The best time to overseed depends on your climate and the type of grass you have. Cool-season lawns should be overseeded in the early spring or late summer, just before active growth begins. In the South, plant perennial or annual ryegrass seed over a nearly dormant lawn in mid-autumn as the temperatures begin to drop.

Grass seed must have good contact with the soil to germinate. It will not grow well in heavy thatch or severely compacted soil. Prepare your lawn by dethatching or aerating, if necessary, before overseeding. Mow the grass shorter than usual prior to overseeding. After sowing the seeds, avoid walking on the lawn and keep it well watered until the new seedlings have established.

HAVE ON HAND:

▶ Lawn mower

▶ Lawn rake

▶ Grass seed

▶ Compost or topsoil

▶ Sprinkler

▶ Water

▶ Vertical mower

▶ Drop spreader

SMALL AREAS. *Mow lawn to the minimum recommended height. Rake vigorously with lawn rake to dislodge thatch and expose soil.*

LARGE AREAS. *Rent a vertical mower with firmly mounted blades that will slice through thatch and top 1/2 inch of soil.*

Scatter seed by hand at 2 to 3 times the rate recommended for establishing new lawns. Rake lightly to work seed into the soil.

Sprinkle ½ inch of compost or topsoil over area. Water thoroughly to 6-inch depth. Maintain soil moisture until new seedlings are established.

Run machine over lawn in parallel rows, and again crosswise at right angles. Rake up debris and add it to your compost pile.

Sow seed with drop spreader at 1 or 1½ times the rate for new lawns. Repeat crosswise to first application. Rake, top-dress, and water as above.

HERE'S HOW

CORRECTING HIGH AND LOW SPOTS

High and low spots give an established lawn a rough appearance and make uniform mowing impossible. Weeds gain an advantage in areas where the grass is cut too low; water tends to accumulate in depressions. Sod can be replaced, but you may need either to overseed or reseed.

Remove sod with a sod cutter or spade. Roll up and keep cool and moist. Remove soil from high spots or add soil to low places. Lay a long piece of 2 x 4 lumber to check soil level. Allow for the depth of the sod when grading where you plan to replace it; otherwise, level the soil and reseed.

Replace the sod carefully. Overseed as necessary. Water deeply and keep the area moist until the grass grows roots into the underlying soil.

Aerating Your Lawn

Healthy soil has spaces between the soil particles where air and water can move freely. Plant roots grow through these pores, too, seeking the moisture and oxygen they need. When soil becomes compacted from heavy traffic, walking on or working in wet soil, or depletion of organic matter, the air and water-holding spaces are reduced or eliminated. Roots may suffocate or dry out.

Compaction occurs frequently in play areas, along paths, and at the edges of lawns where cars park. Soil composed of naturally small particles, such as clay and silt, is more prone to compaction than large-particled sandy soil. Soil rich in organic matter and teeming with earthworms and microorganisms is less likely to become compacted because, as the worms tunnel through the soil, they open passages for water and air to penetrate.

Symptoms of soil compaction include poor drainage, worn or bare spots, and patches of thin or uneven growth. If your lawn becomes less drought tolerant or less responsive to fertilizer and pest control, soil compaction may be to blame. Thatch also tends to accumulate more quickly on compacted soil.

Slicing or punching holes in the turf loosens the soil and allows water and air to permeate. Methods that remove a plug of soil are even more effective than those that slice or pierce the soil. If your lawn receives moderate use, aerate every two years or so to maintain soil health. Heavy traffic areas and neglected lawns benefit from aeration once or twice a year until their health is restored. The best time to aerate your lawn is when grass is beginning to grow actively. Aerate in spring or autumn in the North and in late spring in the South, when the soil is moist. ❀

HAVE ON HAND:

▶ Square-tined spading fork

▶ Foot-press aerator

▶ Spiked lawn roller

▶ Motorized core aerator

▶ Sprinkler

▶ Water

▶ Lawn rake or mower

▶ Compost or organic fertilizer

SMALL AREAS. *Push a square-tined spading fork 6 to 8 inches deep into your lawn every 6 inches throughout the compacted area, or....*

LARGE AREAS. *Rent a motorized core aerator with hollow spikes that remove 1-inch-wide plugs of soil and turf.*

Rent or purchase a foot-press aerator with hollow tubes that remove narrow plugs of soil. Push into soil at 6-inch intervals, or....

Rent a roller-mounted aerator with triangular spikes welded onto a steel jacket. Push manually or drag it behind a lawn tractor.

Moisten soil with sprinkler. Drive machine over compacted lawn in parallel rows. Lift tines from ground when turning. Do not overlap your rows.

Allow soil plugs to dry. Rake up and compost or run over with mower to distribute. Apply compost or organic fertilizer. Water thoroughly.

HERE'S HOW

AERATING WHILE MOWING

You can loosen and aerate the soil while you mow your lawn or walk through the grass doing other chores by wearing special shoes with spikes. To be effective, the spikes must reach through the thatch and into the soil. The cleats of most golf and other athletic shoes are not long enough to aerate effectively.

Many mail-order gardening supply companies offer cleated sandals with 1½-inch spikes screwed into the plastic soles. The sandals simply strap onto your regular shoes. As you walk, the spikes make small holes in the soil, allowing air and water to penetrate.

Watering Your Lawn

Lawn grasses are among the most durable of our landscape plants. They will thrive under foot traffic and mowing, shade and sun, but even the toughest grasses do not tolerate prolonged drought. The amount and frequency of lawn irrigation depends on many factors, including the weather, grass and soil types, and your own schedule and expectations.

Some grasses, such as fescues, Bermuda grass, and zoysia, are much more tolerant of drought than others—for example, creeping bent grass and St. Augustine grass. Sandy soil that drains

HAVE ON HAND:

▶ Spade

▶ Portable sprinkler

▶ Garden hose

▶ Outside water faucet

▶ 12 same-sized containers

▶ Tape measure

▶ Ruler

rapidly will need more frequent watering than clay soil or soil that is rich in organic matter. Plants use more water in hot, dry, windy weather than they do at cooler times of the year.

Your watering and lawn-maintenance habits will also affect how often and how much you will have to water in the future. Plants with deep roots can draw water from a larger area than shallow-rooted plants and require less frequent watering. You can encourage deep rooting by watering your lawn until the soil is moist to a depth of 6 to 12 inches. Allow grass to grow about one-half inch longer than usual during the dry season to help keep the soil shaded and cool. Always mow with a sharp blade. Dull blades tear the grass and cause it to lose more water than it normally would.

If possible, water your lawn before the grass wilts. (Water-stressed grass looks dull or silvery green. When you walk across dry grass, your footprints will remain.) Water either in the early morning or in the evening, when wind and temperature are lower, to avoid evaporation loss. If lawn diseases are common in your area, confine your watering to the morning so grass dries quickly. ❧

Determine soil moisture by making a spade-deep wedge in the soil. Water if the soil is dry at a depth of 6 to 12 inches.

Determine evenness of water distribution by placing 12 shallow, same-sized containers at equal intervals throughout spray pattern.

Water your lawn in the early morning to allow grass to dry before nightfall. Grass left wet overnight is more prone to disease.

Adjust position of sprinkler or water pressure so that water falls only on lawn. Avoid watering streets, sidewalks, and buildings.

After a period of time, 1 hour for example, stop watering. Measure water in each container. Level should be the same in each.

Adjust or move sprinkler to achieve uniform coverage. Recheck soil moisture as described in Step 1. Water to a depth of 6 to 12 inches.

HERE'S HOW

HOW MUCH IS ENOUGH?

Applying just the right amount of water keeps your lawn healthy, saves you time and energy, and helps conserve water. Most grasses require about 1 inch of water per week during the growing season, depending on weather conditions.

There are areas of the country that receive enough rainfall to make watering rarely necessary. When you do need to water your lawn, give it a good soaking—about 1 inch in a single weekly application.

Remember that different types of soil absorb and hold water at different rates. Lawns planted in clay soil will benefit from sprinklers with a low flow rate (less than ¼ inch per hour) to avoid puddling and runoff.

Fertilizing Your Lawn

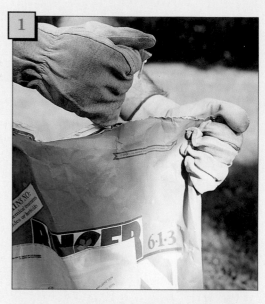

Fertilize each month during the growing season when not hot and dry, ideally in the evening before rain. Wear gloves; keep fertilizer from eyes.

Lawn grasses, like other plants, need a steady supply of essential nutrients to grow and to maintain their vigor. They demand more food than many other landscape plants because grasses grow quickly and close together, and receive frequent mowing. Building a healthy, nutrient-rich soil helps your lawn withstand drought; resist pests, diseases, and winter damage; and maintain slow, steady growth throughout the growing season. Applying a balanced fertilizer can help your lawn flourish.

Every few years, take a soil sample from your lawn and have it tested for pH and nutrients (see Testing Your Soil, page 20). The ideal pH for most lawn grass is about 6.5, which is slightly acid. Too low or too high a soil pH encourages weed growth and makes nutrients less available to the grass. Based on the results of the soil tests, apply lime or sulfur to correct the pH and apply fertilizer to provide the recommended amounts of necessary nutrients.

As for other plants, nutrients can come from either natural or synthetic fertilizers. Most garden centers carry both kinds in easy-to-use granular form. Synthetic fertilizers are sometimes less expensive, but they do not build soil health. Often, their nutrients leach out quickly. Fertilizers from natural materials, such as manure or compost, add organic matter to your soil. This holds water and air and provides food for beneficial soil organisms. Humus-rich soil is also less prone to drought and compaction.

Choose a balanced fertilizer with an N-P-K ratio of about 3-1-2—or a multiple thereof, such as one labeled 6-2-4 or 12-4-8. Fertilizers with high amounts of nitrogen stimulate leaf growth, so if you choose one of these for your lawn you may need to mow more frequently. Slow-release lawn fertilizers are applied only once, early in the growing season. To avoid plant damage, use only recommended amounts. The use of a mulching lawn mower can help reduce the need for fertilizers.

HAVE ON HAND:

▶ Garden gloves

▶ Granular fertilizer

▶ Broadcast spreader

▶ Water

Cover ends of lawn first. Then walk in rows over entire area, overlapping edges of each row. Close vent when turning, backing up, or stopping.

Check fertilizer container, using directions to set rate-of-flow lever on spreader. When in doubt, broadcast at a slower rather than faster rate.

Close hopper on the broadcast spreader, then fill with granular fertilizer. Open vent to distribute fertilizer slowly, walking at an even pace.

Water lawn thoroughly to depth of 4 to 6 inches, to get fertilizer into root zone. Do not leave fertilizer on the surface where it can burn grass.

Keep children and pets away from lawn for 24 hours. Store leftover fertilizer in securely closed bag. Lock in a cool, dark place.

HERE'S HOW

WHEN TO FERTILIZE

Fertilize lawns during or just prior to periods of active growth. Recommended fertilizing times are somewhat different for cool- and warm-season grasses.

In the North, cool-season grasses grow rapidly in the spring and early fall but less during summer months. Apply fertilizer in late summer to early fall to give grass a boost and provide food for winter storage. In the spring, fertilizing should not be done routinely. It is only necessary if your lawn indicates a need for it. Test soil after the ground has dried out somewhat and begun to warm up.

In the South, warm-season grasses should be fertilized as soon as they start growing in the spring. Fertilize again in the fall.

In both areas, be careful to avoid fertilizing in midsummer when the weather is hot and dry.

Growing Lawn Under Shade Trees

Lawn grasses grow best in moist, fertile soil in full sun. Trees in or near lawns can create problems for grass because they produce shade and compete for water and nutrients. Many deciduous trees have roots that protrude from the soil surface, making mowing a challenge. Also, deciduous trees drop leaves that smother grass in the autumn. Despite these obstacles, there are a number of simple steps you can take to grow healthy grass under most shade trees.

Help grass succeed by eliminating as much competition as possible. Thor-

HAVE ON HAND:

▶ Sprinkler

▶ Water

▶ Spade

▶ Square-tined garden fork

▶ Shady lawn grass seed mixture

▶ Lawn mower

▶ Lawn rake

▶ Pole pruning saw

oughly water the lawn around the tree several times during the growing season, allowing the water to penetrate several feet into the ground. Shallow watering encourages both grass and tree roots to grow close to the surface and can increase competition for water. If your tree roots are watered deeply, they will stay far underground and leave the soil surface for your grass.

Aerating the soil under and around trees more frequently than other parts of your lawn will help water and fertilizer soak in deeply, especially in a heavy traffic area. When you aerate, add ½ inch of organic material, such as compost or rotted manure, to enrich the soil and help it retain moisture. Driving tree fertilizer spikes into the soil around the tree as needed will get nutrients down to the tree's root zone so it won't have to depend on fertilizer that was intended for the lawn.

When mowing your lawn, cut the grass under trees or in shady spots about an inch higher than normal. This gives the grass more leaf surface with which to collect light and make food. Ultimately this grass will be stronger and better able to withstand the adverse conditions found beneath shade trees. ❧

Water grass under trees to a depth of between 1 and 3 feet during long dry periods. Remove a wedge of soil to check water penetration.

Rake up fallen leaves, fruit, and twigs that can smother grass and invite disease. Thorough raking also helps prevent thatch buildup.

Use square-tined garden fork to aerate soil under tree canopy. Overseed with shady lawn grass seed. Top-dress with ¼ inch of soil; water.

When cutting grass in shady areas, raise mower deck 1 inch higher to encourage deeper rooting and give grass blades more surface area.

Thin out up to ¼ of tree canopy by pruning branches back to the trunk or a large limb in autumn or late winter, depending on the species.

If acid-loving moss is competing with your grass, increase soil pH with lime to improve the growing conditions for grass.

HERE'S HOW

TACKLING BARE SPOTS

When you have a bare spot in your lawn where grass has refused to grow under a shade tree or for any other reason, treat the area as you would a new lawn. Prepare the soil by incorporating compost or organic material and raking it smooth. Mound the soil slightly to allow for settling and water it thoroughly. Add more soil, if necessary, to correct the grade.

Match the grass species and cultivars growing in the rest of the lawn whenever possible, but you will need to give special consideration to the nature of the shady area under trees if that is where you are making repairs. If you need help in identifying your lawn grasses, take a sod sample to a turf specialist, such as a local Cooperative Extension Service agent, lawn care contractor, or garden center expert. Plant seed, plugs, or sod, then water and mulch (see Creating a Healthy Lawn, page 114).

Alternatives to a Lawn

IN THIS SECTION:

A velvety-green lawn surrounding a home may be traditional, but it may not always be practical or desirable. Grass can be difficult to grow in arid climates and in shaded places, and it is troublesome to maintain in heavy traffic areas, play spaces, and on slopes. Mowing around trees, shrubs, flower beds, and vegetable gardens is time consuming, frustrating, and can damage plantings. But don't despair: you can reduce maintenance, save on energy and other resources, and add variety to your landscape with mulches and ground-covering plants.

Planted under trees and on the north side of buildings, shade-loving ground covers make a fine alternative to grass. Ground-hugging herbs are a natural to tuck between the paving stones of a path. On difficult slopes, replace grass with drought-tolerant shrubs and vines or create rock gardens. If your lawn looks brown and dry in the winter, try an evergreen ground cover instead.

If a particular growing area is not suitable for a plant type you like, try one of the many organic mulches available. They improve soil quality and discourage the growth of weeds around ornamental plants, shrubs, and trees. Use gravel and stones to line paths and low-lying drainage areas or to protect spaces for foot traffic around your house. A wide range of colors and textures is available to complement your house and yard. ❧

Blooming Ground Covers

Many low-growing plants are useful for covering shady spots, slopes, and rocky terrain where lawn grasses won't grow or are difficult to maintain. Blooming ground covers are any low-growing annual, perennial, vine, or shrub that spreads and offers colorful flowers. Before choosing from among the many species available, assess your needs and growing conditions.

Look at your intended planting site and note the amount of sun it receives.

HAVE ON HAND:

▶ Garden hose
▶ Spade
▶ Shovel
▶ Compost or shredded leaves
▶ Lime or sulfur
▶ Bulb planter
▶ Garden rake
▶ Trowel
▶ Pine needle or shredded leaf mulch
▶ Sprinkler

Optional
▶ Spring- and summer-flowering bulbs

Check for drainage problems and test the soil to determine whether it is acid or alkaline, fertile or poor.

Sites are considered partly shady if they get up to six hours of direct sun per day during the growing season or only receive sunlight filtered through leafy trees. Buildings and many evergreen trees cast dense shade. To brighten dark areas, choose shade-tolerant ground covers with light-colored blooms. Flowering bulbs can be tucked under ground covers for an added dash of color.

Underplant trees and shrubs with a ground cover such as periwinkle that grows well in dry shade. Slopes, too, are often dry. For exposed banks choose a drought-tolerant plant such as Roman chamomile that thrives in full sun. For low, poorly drained spots, select plants such as sweet flag that enjoy moisture.

Begin by making a list of plants that match your needs. Check your local nursery, where you can ask a knowledgeable salesperson for advice. As you look over possibilities, consider hardiness, blooms, foliage, height, how quickly the plants spread, and whether they are invasive. Ask about maintenance requirements, such as watering, pruning, winter protection, and possible diseases or pests. ❧

Lay a garden hose on the ground to mark the outline of the area to be planted. Make curves gentle; avoid sharp angles.

Spring- and summer-flowering bulbs, such as daffodils, tulips, and lilies, are an option. Plant them throughout area before ground cover.

Push spade 4 inches into the soil just inside the hose around the outline. Undercut the sod layer 2 to 3 inches deep with spade and remove.

Spread 2 to 3 inches of compost or shredded leaves plus lime or sulfur, if needed. Mix well into the top 8 to 12 inches of soil.

Smooth the soil with a rake. Plant low-flowering ground cover 2 feet apart. Space plants uniformly for best appearance.

Mulch with 1 inch of pine needles or shredded leaves, which are light in weight. Water thoroughly with sprinkler to depth of 4 to 6 inches.

HERE'S HOW

PLANTING IN STONE PATHS

You can plant very low-growing ground covers between the stones in a walkway to beautify the path and prevent growth of undesirable weeds. Some creeping herbs release a pleasant fragrance when walked on.

Eliminate any weeds or grass between the stones by hand. Replace gravel or sand between the stones with fertile topsoil or compost.

Start the ground cover from plugs or seed, depending on the plant you choose and time of the year. Sprinkle seed thinly and mix gently into the top ⅛ inch of soil. Set plugs 8 to 12 inches apart between stones. (Small plugs often work best.) Water the seeds or plugs and cover them with a thin layer of straw or pine needles until established.

Evergreen Ground Covers

Before planting ground cover on a slope, remove weeds. Purchase loosely woven jute or burlap fabric and 6-inch-long, U-shaped earth staples.

Unlike most lawn grasses, evergreen ground covers provide texture and color in the landscape throughout the year. These versatile plants may be sprawling vines, hardy perennials, or needle-bearing, broad-leaved evergreen shrubs. Many offer attractive blooms.

Low-spreading, evergreen shrubs such as creeping juniper add height to the borders of your lawn, easing transitions from grass to gardens, trees, and buildings. These 1- to 2-foot-high plants can be used to provide both visual and physical barriers around parts of your landscape. Combine them with other flowering or evergreen ground covers for a rich tapestry of color and texture.

A low-growing evergreen ground cover, such as periwinkle or pachysandra, makes a perfect surrounding for your spring-flowering bulbs. As cheerful daffodil and tulip blooms poke through a glossy, dark green ground cover, their colors are a happy surprise. Later, fading flowers and bulb foliage will be hidden beneath hardy, spreading perennials.

Vigorous evergreen ground covers, especially drought-tolerant shrubs and vines, are your best bet for blanketing steep slopes. There, strong, spreading roots can quickly grasp and hold the soil. Year-round foliage helps to soften the impact of rain and decreases the chance of soil erosion.

You can lay a loosely woven jute or burlap fabric on slopes to help hold the soil. Cuts can be made in the fabric for planting individual shrubs, such as creeping juniper, or groups of bulbs. Be sure to use a very loosely woven fabric (minimum 1-inch openings) for ground covers that spread by runners across the surface of the soil, such as ivy and periwinkle, or they will have difficulty becoming established. ❧

HAVE ON HAND:

▶ Jute or natural burlap fabric

▶ 6-inch-long earth staples

▶ Mallet

▶ Marker

▶ Knife

▶ Spade

▶ Organic mulch

▶ Water

Stagger and mark plant spacings across slope. Cut X-shaped openings in fabric at marks. Prepare planting holes.

Lay fabric across weed-free slope starting at bottom. Overlap strips by 6 to 8 inches, with the uphill strip on top of the lower one.

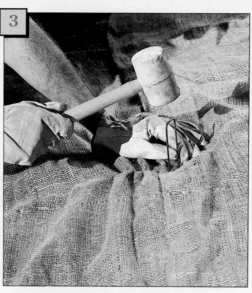

Tap earth staples through the fabric and into the soil every 3 to 5 feet at overlaps and along edges. Space closer than 3 feet for steep slopes.

Plant your evergreen ground cover. Make a little terrace for each plant and bank soil around the downhill side.

Spread 2 to 3 inches of shredded bark or straw mulch over fabric. Water gently and frequently to avoid runoff and erosion.

HERE'S HOW

CONTROLLING INVASIVES

The most useful ground covers spread rapidly to carpet the ground in which they are planted. Unfortunately, some of these vigorous plants grow beyond their allotted space.

Invasive ground covers usually spread by sending out underground stems or aboveground shoots into fertile new territory. Trim shoots back with hedge shears or clippers throughout the growing season to prevent them from taking root.

Use a sharp spade or lawn edger to cut through roots and spreading underground stems. Remove soil to maintain a 4-inch-deep and 4- to 5-inch-wide strip of bare soil around the perimeter of your ground cover bed. Plastic lawn edging may control shallow-rooted spreaders and keep grass out of the bed. Pull stray stems that grow up through the lawn or migrate from elsewhere.

Mulch

Mulch has a number of uses as a lawn replacement. It suppresses weeds, holds moisture, and moderates soil temperature. Organic mulches add humus and nutrients to the soil.

Organic mulches are usually chosen for their looks as well as benefits to the soil. They include bark, pine needles, straw, and seed hulls. Although organic mulches may need periodic renewal, they improve the structure of your soil as they decompose.

Keep organic mulches several feet away from buildings wherever termites, carpenter ants, or other damaging insects may be a problem. If you live in a fire-prone area, you will want to use gravel near your home instead of organic material.

Plastics provide effective weed control under other mulches or when used alone, but they are not biodegradable nor do they let water through. If you use them around ornamental plants, be sure to perforate the plastic. These mulches are most useful to warm the soil to the appropriate temperature before planting annual seeds.

Unlike plastics, geotextiles (papers and landscape fabrics) are water-permeable. Placed under organic mulches they help provide weed suppression, but they prevent decomposing material from enriching underlying soil with humus. They work especially well under gravel. ❧

HAVE ON HAND:

▶ Hoe
▶ Garden rake
▶ Vinyl edging
▶ Mulch
▶ Spade
▶ Geotextile mulch
▶ Scissors
▶ Earth staples
▶ Mallet
▶ Shredded bark mulch

Remove weeds with a hoe to prepare the area for mulching. Rake up plant debris; smooth soil.

Install vinyl edging, per package instructions, to contain the mulch and prevent the invasion of grass.

GEOTEXTILES. *Overlap on bare ground by 2 to 3 inches. Trim, secure with U-shaped earth staples.*

ORGANIC. *Fill prepared area with 1 to 2 inches of shredded bark. Rake lightly to smooth.*

Stone and Gravel

Natural stone or crushed gravel often can be used where grass does not grow well or is not practical. Smooth-edged stones in neutral colors give a soft appearance but are highly durable. The smaller sizes, 3⁄8 to 1⁄2 inch in diameter, make excellent ground cover in places such as footpaths and picnic areas. Gravel also is useful in heavy traffic areas. Use larger smooth stones, called cobbles, to line dry or seasonally wet low-lying areas. Flagstones, commonly used for paths and patios, become a permanent landscape feature that is almost maintenance free.

Crushed stone or gravel is available in many sizes, washed or unwashed. Its angular sides and sharp edges give it a rough but attractive appearance. Unwashed stone packs down well and forms a hard surface useful for paths but not around plants. Washed crushed stone larger than 1⁄2-inch diameter is suitable for mulch around woody plants.

Stone adds little in the way of nutrients but some, such as ground limestone, can raise soil pH. When used with an underlying layer of plastic, stone makes an effective weed barrier. In arid, drought-prone climates, gravel and stones are the safest materials to use close to buildings. They also are less attractive to destructive insects and rodents, such as termites and mice, than organic mulches.

HAVE ON HAND:

- ▶ Tape measure
- ▶ Garden hose
- ▶ Spade
- ▶ Vinyl edging
- ▶ Builder's sand
- ▶ Garden rake
- ▶ Tamper
- ▶ Flagstone, 12- to 24-inch diameter
- ▶ Gravel, sand, or topsoil

FLAGSTONE PATH. *Mark edges with garden hose. Remove sod to depth of stone with a spade.*

If desired, install vinyl edging per package instructions to keep grass from growing between stones.

Rake a 1⁄2-inch layer of coarse builder's sand evenly on the path. Tamp down with tamper.

Set flagstones on the sand in an attractive pattern. Press to level. Backfill with gravel, sand, or topsoil.

Creating a Beautiful Landscape

Well-chosen and carefully placed trees and shrubs can dramatically alter your landscape, add a lifetime of beauty, and increase the overall value of your property. They can act as walls and architectural features blocking sound and undesirable views and provide visual interest, as well as serve as a natural habitat and food source for wildlife throughout the year.

Trees and shrubs can also represent a sizable investment in terms of labor and money. Fortunately, once they are planted, maintaining their health and vigor is relatively easy. Among the most important steps are watering, pruning, and in the case of trees, staking. Each of these tasks must be performed at the proper time in the growth season for the specific type of plant, and using the correct technique. However, the small effort involved can yield great rewards including improved plant appearance, increased flower and fruit production, and vigorous new growth.

In this chapter, you will learn how best to care for the shrubs and trees in your yard. Master these easy techniques and you will be rewarded with a lush and healthy landscape for years to come.

Planting a Hedge

Check what mature length, width of hedge will be. Measure on ground. Drive stakes into center of both ends. Tie string to stakes, remeasure.

Hedges are the living walls of your landscape. They usually consist of uniform shrubs that are planted individually in a row but are grown as if they were one plant. Hedges can accent or hide views, define space, and direct movement throughout your garden.

Your choice of shrubs depends partly on the purpose of your planting. Use hedges with year-round foliage to hide views or create privacy. A hedge that defines a children's play area should be nontoxic and free of thorns. Shrubs with ornamental or edible fruit can enhance a view or attract birds. For a formal hedge, use fine-textured plants (those with small leaves or needles such as boxwood, barberries, or yew) that respond well to being sheared.

Price and future maintenance requirements will also determine your plant selection. You can purchase shrubs as bare-root, container-grown, or balled-and-burlapped. Calculate the number of bare-root shrubs you will need by figuring about 18 to 30 inches between plants. Spacing depends on the mature size of the shrubs and how quickly you want them to grow together. If you are using larger B-and-B or container-grown stock, you will want to seek advice from the nursery staff as to plant spacing.

Because hedges may require a large number of uniform plants, bare-root shrubs are usually the most economical choice. You can obtain these as dormant plants from a local nursery or through mail-order catalogs in early spring. There are some shrubs, however, that are available only as B-and-B or in containers. While these are more expensive, they can be planted anytime during the growing season. Plant your container-grown and B-and-B shrubs in individual holes, but plant bare-root shrubs in a trench. After planting, apply organic mulch to conserve moisture and deter weeds. 🌿

HAVE ON HAND:

▶ Tape measure	▶ Tarp
▶ Stakes	▶ Pruning shears
▶ Mallet	▶ Yardstick
▶ String	▶ Water
▶ Spade	▶ Garden rake
▶ Shovel	▶ Organic mulch

Space plants 18 to 30 inches apart along center of trench. Lay yardstick across trench. Place uppermost root 1 inch lower than ground level.

Measure spread and depth of bare roots. With spade, dig a trench twice as wide as spread of roots. Dig to root depth. Store soil on tarp.

Prune damaged and broken roots and any that circle the stems. Remove dead, broken, and crossed, rubbing branches. Keep roots moist.

Add soil around roots until trench is half full. Water thoroughly and let drain. Adjust shrub height. Fill trench with soil. Water again.

Lay 2 to 4 inches of organic mulch around shrubs. Pull mulch away from plant stems. Water weekly for one or two growing seasons.

HERE'S HOW

PLANTING SAFETY

Consider the location of both overhead and underground utilities when you dig planting holes. Contact Dig Safe (1-888-DIGSAFE), or individual utility companies if you are unsure where electric, telephone, gas, cable television, or water lines are buried.

Plant shrubs and trees where they can safely grow to maturity. Avoid planting tall trees under utility wires or planting wide shrubs close to sidewalks, roads, and driveways. When planting a hedge near a property boundary, position the shrubs so that their mature size will not encroach on neighboring land.

Contact the town or city clerk's office before planting close to a road or sidewalk. The town may require that trees and shrubs be planted outside the public right of way.

Protecting Newly Planted Shrubs and Trees

Shrubs and trees may take several years to become established after planting. While these young plants grow and adjust to their new home, they are especially vulnerable to damage and disease. Lawn mowers, string trimmers, and animals may damage their bark, while pedestrians and vehicles may compact the soil around their roots. Weather takes its own toll. A little extra attention after planting can make a long-term difference in your plant's health and survival.

Water and nutrients travel through shrubs and trees just under the bark.

Damage to the bark can interrupt this movement and provide an entrance for diseases and pests. If the injury circles the trunk, a condition known as girdling, the plant is likely to die. Plastic or wire guards installed around the trunks of trees will protect bark from mowers, trimmers, and gnawing animals. Keep foot traffic and machines away from shrubs with a wide band of organic mulch.

Paper guards, which protect trees during shipping, should be removed and replaced with plastic or wire guards. There are advantages and disadvantages to either. Although plastic tree guards protect against mechanical damage, they can hold moisture against the trunk, which may rot the bark. On the other hand, wire guards made of hardware cloth will let light and air reach the trunk, but they take more preparation.

In cold regions, freezing and thawing cycles can crack bark and heave roots out of the ground. Snow and ice are capable of breaking branches. Roadside salt spray and drying winter winds burn evergreen foliage. Staking trees will help control wind and frost heaving. Using tree paint, burlap, and snow barriers will also help prevent winter damage. ❧

HAVE ON HAND:

▶ Plastic tree guard

▶ Heavy scissors

▶ Hand trowel

▶ Tape measure

▶ Hardware cloth, 18- to 24-inch width

▶ Tin snips

▶ Wire fasteners

PLASTIC GUARD. *Open one end of plastic tree guard and slip it around base of tree trunk. Wind guard gently around trunk.*

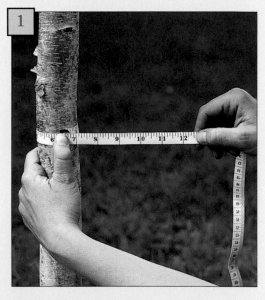

WIRE GUARD. *Measure around plant trunk, and add 6 inches. Using tin snips, cut 18- or 24-inch-wide hardware cloth to required length.*

With heavy scissors, cut plastic tree guard to several inches below lowest limb. Make smooth cut, taking care not to damage bark.

With trowel, remove soil 2 inches deep around trunk. Slide guard down trunk into trench. Replace soil. Remove guard before it becomes tight.

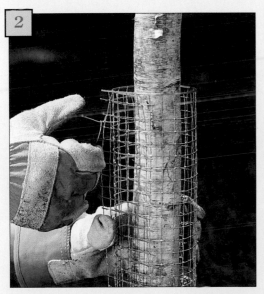

Wrap loosely around trunk, overlapping ends. Cut 2- to 3-inch lengths of wire with tin snips. Insert through overlapped ends. Twist to secure.

Bury guard 2 inches deep as described above. Check wire tree guards periodically. Remove guard before it becomes tight.

HERE'S HOW

PREVENTING ROOT DAMAGE

Damage to plant roots often goes unseen, but it can severely affect your tree's ability to grow and thrive. Common sources of root damage are poor drainage and soil compaction. In both cases, the roots suffocate from lack of air.

Healthy soil contains a balance of air, water, organic material, and soil particles. In poorly drained soils, air spaces become filled with water. Heavy pedestrian or vehicular traffic can push soil particles together, which eliminates valuable air spaces. To prevent this from happening, plant in well-drained soil, apply organic mulch, and keep traffic away from the plant's root zone.

During construction projects, fence off an area around your tree that is at least as wide as the tree's canopy. Prevent heavy equipment traffic and materials storage in the root zone. Avoid changing the soil level under an established tree or shrub.

Watering Shrubs and Trees

Newly planted shrubs and trees need regular watering for their first season or two to encourage deep rooting and rapid recovery. Older trees, especially fruit trees, may need extra water when they bear a heavy fruit crop or are suffering from insects or disease. In areas where seasonal drought is common, nonnative plants often need additional water to survive.

The roots of woody plants reach deep into the soil for firm anchorage and adequate water supply. The key to watering trees and shrubs is to get the water down into the root zone where the plant can

use it. The feeder roots of most trees are located in the top 4 feet of soil, although some go much deeper, depending on the soil type and tree species. Most roots are within the dripline, the circle formed by the tree's widest branches. Watering only the top few inches of soil encourages plants to grow shallow roots that will be more susceptible to drought.

Getting water deep into the soil takes time. Slow application methods, such as soaker hoses, work well because they prevent runoff and puddling. A soaker hose applies the water through pinprick-sized holes that either drip water or release a fine spray depending on the water pressure. Another method of keeping water in place until it can soak into the soil thoroughly is to create a raised ring of soil around the base of your shrub or tree. Both methods efficiently apply water over root zones. 🌸

HAVE ON HAND:

▶ Spade

▶ Soaker hose

▶ Outside faucet

▶ Notebook and pencil

Check moisture in a 1-foot-deep wedge of soil with spade. Water if dry at 6 to 12 inches.

Place soaker hose around tree just inside dripline. Attach garden hose to faucet and end of soaker hose.

Adjust water pressure so that the soil is able to absorb water without puddling or runoff.

Recheck soil moisture. Water until moist at 12 to 18 inches deep. Note length of time for future reference.

Helping Shrubs and Trees Retain Water

All trees and shrubs need enough moisture in their root zones to remain healthy and vigorous. Young and newly planted shrubs and trees are especially vulnerable to water stress until their roots are well established.

You can help your newly planted trees and shrubs retain water by building a berm, or low mound of soil, around the planting hole. This catch basin will hold water and direct it where the plant needs it most. It will also prevent wasteful runoff. It's important to keep the root zone moist, but not water-logged, for the first season.

HAVE ON HAND:

▶ Spade

▶ Organic mulch

▶ Rake

▶ Water

Leave the basin in place for several months unless rainfall is adequate.

Organic mulches such as shredded bark, leaves, cocoa hulls, chopped straw, and compost hold moisture in the soil around shrubs and trees. As they decompose, they also add nutrients to the soil. Cover an area one-third to one-half the diameter of the tree canopy with mulch for maximum benefit. For a grouping of shrubs, cover the entire area between and around the shrubs with mulch. Keep mulch away from trunks and stems to prevent disease, insect infestation, and rodent injury.

Mulch also suppresses weeds and grasses that compete with shrubs and trees for moisture. A 3-inch layer of mulch will eliminate most competition but consider laying a weed-barrier fabric under your mulch to smother more persistent weeds. Check the fabric to be certain water will pass through it freely. 🌷

MULCH. *Remove weeds, sod in a 4- to 8-foot circle around tree with spade. Add 2 to 3 inches of mulch.*

Pull mulch 6 inches from trunk to prevent bark from rotting. Add mulch yearly to maintain depth.

BERM. *Rake soil into 2- to 4-inch-high berm around outside of planting hole. Slope berm away from trunk.*

Fill basin with water and let it soak in. Don't disturb berm. Repeat until soil is thoroughly soaked.

Pruning Shrubs to Tree Form

You can create a miniature tree for a focal point, to fit a special place in a small garden, or to accent a patio container. Many ornamental shrubs can be pruned and trained to resemble small single- or multistemmed trees. You can start with a newly purchased shrub or consider training an existing landscape shrub that has become leggy or overgrown.

First, you'll need to decide whether you want a single- or multistemmed tree. A miniature tree with one straight trunk topped with a rounded or weeping canopy of branches is called a standard. Standards, especially roses and plants with a "weeping" habit, are often created by grafting an ornamental shrub variety onto the trunk of a different variety.

Choose either evergreen or deciduous shrubs with a strong branching tendency, especially those with interesting bark, flowers, or foliage. Avoid shrubs with small, weak stems. Shrubs with fine-textured foliage and a twiggy habit, such as boxwood and privet, can be trained into very formal, sheared trees. Those with larger leaves or a more open habit, such as red buckeye or oleander, make graceful, picturesque trees. Select a shrub whose mature size will be the same as the desired tree. Of course, dwarf varieties result in smaller trees.

Shrubs that are trained to a tree form need extra care to keep them vigorous and healthy. Staking standards keeps them straight and can prevent weather damage. Ties should be loose enough so the tree can move in strong winds without snapping. Use cloth, plastic, or rubber hose-coated wire to avoid girdling, removing bark and cutting a ring around the trunk, which can kill the tree. Give standards extra winter protection by covering them with burlap or a wooden shelter, and prune regularly to maintain their shape. Frost-tender shrubs can be grown in large containers and brought indoors before the first frost. ❧

HAVE ON HAND:

▶ Pruning shears

▶ Tree stake

▶ Cloth strip, 1 inch wide

Choose a shrub with a strong central stem for a single-trunk tree (or a group of well-spaced stems for a multistemmed tree).

Choose main branches to form canopy. Remove no more than ⅓ of undesirable growth in one year. Prune flush with trunk or main limb.

For a single-trunk tree, remove competing stems at base, leaving desired trunk intact. (Thin to 2 to 4 stems to create multistemmed trees.)

Remove crossed, damaged, and broken limbs from canopy. Make smooth cuts flush with main trunk or branch. Remove weak growth.

Direct new growth by pruning back branches to healthy stem that points in desired direction. Prune to outward- or upward-pointing buds.

Insert stake near trunk of newly planted single-stemmed shrub. Making a figure eight with 1-inch-wide cloth, tie trunk loosely to stake.

HERE'S HOW

MAINTENANCE

To prevent your miniature tree from returning to its shrub form, rub off sprouts as they develop along the trunk and remove root suckers.

Thin out crowded canopy branches and cut wayward shoots to one-half their length. Prune summer-flowering shrubs early in the spring, but wait until just after bloom to prune spring-flowering plants. Remove dead or broken limbs at anytime of year.

Mulch around the roots to keep them moist and protect them from winter damage. If your tree is growing in a lawn, protect its trunk from mower and string trimmer injury by wrapping it with hardware cloth.

Pruning Fruit Trees

Prune young fruit trees lightly during the first three years to establish an open framework of well-spaced branches and encourage early fruiting. As your fruit trees get older, prune to maintain their shape and keep fruiting branches productive. Horizontal branches with wide crotch angles produce the most fruit, while drooping or upright limbs tend to be weak and unproductive.

You can prune and train young trees to one of two basic shapes, depending on the type of fruit tree. Concentrate your early pruning efforts on establishing the tree's shape. Apples, pears, and cherries are usually trained to have a strong central leader, or trunk. The central leader

tree has four or five tiers of branches evenly spaced along and around its trunk. The overall shape resembles a Christmas tree, with wider branches at the bottom and narrower ones at the top, allowing light and air to circulate around the entire plant.

Peaches, plums, and apricots are pruned to a vase shape, gradually widening from the bottom. With this method, the central leader is cut back and side branches are pruned to encourage sunlight to reach the center of the tree and to prevent the rubbing of branches.

Some fruit trees, such as apples, pears, plums, cherries, and apricots, flower and bear fruit on short, knobby shoots called spurs. Spurs develop best on two-year-old and older branches, especially those that are horizontal. Other fruits, such as peaches, figs, pomegranates, and most nut trees, bear fruit on either current or one-year-old wood. Pruning these trees more heavily will encourage new shoots.

Prune most fruit trees when dormant, in late winter. Clean tools between each tree you prune with either isopropyl alcohol or a 1:10 bleach and water solution to prevent the spread of disease. 🌱

HAVE ON HAND:

► Tape measure

► Pruning shears

► Protractor

► Isopropyl alcohol or 1:10
  bleach and water solution

In spring, train newly planted apple trees to central leader shape by cutting leader to within 30 to 36 inches of ground. Remove side branches.

Late in first winter, choose 3 to 5 branches with 50° to 80° crotch angles, well spaced around leader, 6 inches apart, as the first permanent tier.

Late during the first summer, remove branches with crotch angles narrower than 35°. Use protractor to measure angle.

Maintain a central leader by removing competing ones. Prune limbs growing within 18 to 24 inches of ground. Do not leave stubs. Clean shears.

Remove root suckers, undesirable branches, leaving 3 to 5. Prune remaining branch tips by ¼. Cut leader back to within 30 inches of topmost branch.

The next summer, choose 3 to 5 limbs to form next tier 18 inches above top limb. Repeat Steps 2 to 6 for 4 or 5 tiers. Clean shears between trees.

HERE'S HOW

PRUNING BARE ROOTS

A newly planted bare-root tree must establish a strong root system before it can support many branches. Light root pruning can encourage root growth and development.

First, cut off damaged and broken roots just above the damaged portion. If the tree has a taproot, take care not to break it. Cut back very long roots by about one-third, but leave as many roots intact as possible. Keep roots cool and moist while you work.

Although it is best to remove all branches from bare-root fruit trees at planting time, you may leave two or three small, well-placed limbs on vigorous trees with strong roots. Cut the ends of these back by one-third.

Pruning Young Shade Trees

Pruning to establish a young tree's shape and branching pattern will help it grow into a graceful and long-lived shade tree. Pruning cuts made on small limbs are easier and safer to make, and they heal faster than cuts made on large limbs.

Selecting a well-shaped tree that is appropriate for its site is the first and most important step in obtaining a desirable shade tree. Ask plant nursery staff about mature sizes and growth habits, and then choose a tree that matches your needs. Most shade trees should have a single trunk, or central leader, surrounded by well-spaced side branches. Avoid those with multiple leaders, crowded, crossing branches, and narrow crotches where limb meets trunk.

After planting, prune off dead, broken, and rubbing branches that can strip the bark and provide an entrance for diseases and pests. Prune limbs flush to a series of ridges at the base of the branch, called a branch collar. Sharp cuts made flush with the outermost ridge of the collar heal most quickly.

Keep shade trees trained to a single trunk by removing any shoots that compete with the main trunk. (Double trunk, or forked, trees often suffer massive storm damage.) Also prune off root suckers that grow up from the base of the tree, as these will weaken the main trunk and limbs and detract from the tree's appearance. Water sprouts—vigorous, vertically growing branches—can also weaken trees and should be removed immediately. Remove lower limbs that interfere with mowing or other activities.

Except for trees that bleed sap heavily in the spring, such as maples, birches, and walnuts, you should prune young trees in late winter or very early spring before the buds begin to expand. Prune bleeders in late summer. And never remove more than one-third of the tree's live wood in any one year. ✿

HAVE ON HAND:

▶ Gloves

▶ Safety glasses

▶ Pruning shears

▶ Protractor

▶ Loppers

▶ Pruning saw

Wear gloves. Choose strongest, straightest trunk or leader. Remove competing leaders at branch collar. Do not leave stubs.

Remove water sprouts and suckers close to their base. The blade of pruning shears should be toward tree side of the growth being cut.

Measure crotch angles (where limb meets trunk) with protractor. Prune branches with less than a 45°crotch. Use loppers on larger limbs.

Eliminate any crossed branches that rub against each another. Prune out weaker ones or branches growing in the wrong direction.

Cut off low limbs that interfere with mowing or traffic areas. Use a pruning saw for limbs larger than 1 1/2 inches.

Thin out weak or crowded limbs, but do not remove more than 1/3 of tree limbs in any one year to prevent damaging, or killing, tree.

HERE'S HOW

PRUNING OLDER TREES

Trees that have been neglected, suffered damage, or outgrown their space may benefit from pruning to prolong their life and make them safer or more aesthetically pleasing.

Remove any broken, diseased, and dead limbs first. Reduce to a single trunk, if possible. Then, thin out suckers, water sprouts, and branches that rub against each other. Use a three-part cut to prevent bark tearing when removing heavy limbs (see Pruning Ornamental Trees, pages 160-161).

Complete the process over a period of several years so that no more than one-third of the limbs are removed in any one year. Contact a professional arborist if your tree is near power lines or buildings, or if it requires cuts that you cannot safely reach from the ground.

Pruning Ornamental Trees

Ornamental trees provide beauty in the landscape with their showy fruits, beautiful flowers, foliage, bark, and growth habits. Keep your tree's special features in mind and prune to emphasize its natural assets.

As with any tree, you should remove dead, damaged, and crowded branches and those that rub against one another. Beyond these basics, prune to maintain your tree's habit and vigor. Root suckers that grow from below a graft union of a crab apple, for example, can spoil the tree's appearance and weaken the more desirable limbs. Vigorous vertical growth on branches, called water sprouts, detract from the effect of trees with a cascading habit, such as weeping cherries or weeping European beech.

Some ornamental trees, such as dogwoods and birches, commonly grow in clumps. As the trunks increase in size, they may begin to crowd one another and should be thinned to eliminate the most unattractive and the weakest ones. Remove unwanted trunks while they are still small. This will help to maintain a clump's pleasing appearance.

Using a three-step cut is the safest way to remove large limbs and will help to limit the amount the bark is torn while you are cutting. This method, described opposite, avoids creating an unsightly wound that can weaken a tree by making it susceptible to disease and pests.

Most ornamental trees should be pruned in late winter or early spring, while they are still dormant. Trees that flower early in the spring, however, such as redbuds, should be pruned after they have finished blooming. Prune heavy sap bleeders, such as birches, in mid- to late-summer to avoid stressing the trees and causing stains on their bark. 🌺

HAVE ON HAND:

▶ Gloves

▶ Safety glasses

▶ Pruning saw for limbs over 1 ¾-inch diameter

▶ Pole saw for high limbs

▶ Loppers for branches up to 1 ¾-inch diameter

HEAVY LIMBS. *Wear gloves, safety glasses. Use pruning saw to cut 1/3 of the way through limb from underside, 1 to 2 feet from tree trunk.*

MULTISTEMMED. *Cut out weak or crowded trunks from small tree clumps. Remove close to ground and angle so stumps shed water.*

Next, saw limb from the top, 1 inch farther out on limb than the undercut. Support limb with free hand while cutting or have help. Remove.

Finally, remove the remaining branch stump, sawing from top to bottom at outer ring of branch collar. Make a clean, smooth cut.

HIGH LIMBS. Use pole saw to cut weak, crowded, and crossing limbs too high to reach. For safety, make all pruning cuts from ground.

SMALL GROWTH. Use loppers to cut smaller diameter branches, water sprouts, and suckers. Blade should be on trunk side of cut.

HERE'S HOW

MAKING THE RIGHT CUT

The main goals of pruning are to improve the health and appearance of shrubs and trees. With the exception of topiary and formally sheared hedges, good pruning doesn't show. Look your tree over carefully and decide before-hand what you are going to do, since cuts cannot be reversed.

Small pruning cuts heal faster than large ones. Prune the ends of small branches back to a healthy bud that points toward the outside of the plant or in the direction you desire growth. Cut about ¼ inch above the bud at a slight angle so that water will run away from the bud.

Prune to the branch collar anytime you remove a limb back to the trunk or another branch. Make sharp pruning cuts flush with the outside of the collar without leaving stubs.

Rejuvenating Ornamentals

SHRUBS

Shrubs that have become leggy and open or dense and tangled, have decreased flowering, or have outgrown their space may benefit from a renovation pruning. Some species can tolerate a drastic pruning, while others will need several moderate prunings over a period of time to achieve the desired results.

Deciduous shrubs that readily send up new shoots from their roots can be cut to within 6 inches of the ground in early spring before growth begins. Shrubs that tolerate such treatment include forsythia, privet, spirea, and hibiscus. As an alternative, you can prune out one-third of the oldest stems with basal cuts at the ground each year.

Less vigorous or single-stemmed shrubs can be rejuvenated with thinning cuts.

If you want to return a sheared shrub to its natural shape, first choose the branches that you will keep, selecting healthy ones that suggest the shrub's natural form. Next remove dead, damaged, and crossing limbs, and thin out remaining branches to let air and light into the center of the shrub. Complete this process over several years removing no more than one-third of the limbs in any one year.

Prune spring-flowering shrubs after they bloom, and summer-flowering ones in late winter before their growth resumes. ✿

HAVE ON HAND:

▶ Gloves

▶ Safety glasses

▶ Loppers for stems up to 1 ¾-inch diameter

▶ Pruning shears for stems up to ¾-inch diameter

▶ Pruning saw for stems over 1 ¾-inch diameter

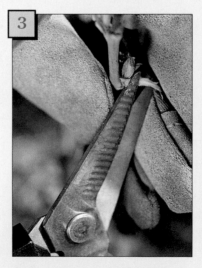

1 Use gloves, safety glasses. Late winter, cut ⅓ of weakest stems from root-suckering shrub close to ground.

2 With shears or saw, cut dead, damaged, and rubbing stems to healthy branch or trunk. Do not leave stubs.

3 Redirect growth by pruning stems to bud or branch. Cut flush with branch collar or within ¼ inch of bud.

4 The next winter, prune out ⅓ of remaining old, weak stems. Thin to prevent rubbing and crowding.

TREES

Long-neglected or storm-damaged ornamental trees may have lost the special character that made them so appealing. With careful pruning, you can restore a tree's natural shape, increase flowering and fruiting, and repair damage.

Dead, damaged, and crossing branches create a hazard and provide an entrance for diseases and pests. Remove these limbs whenever you see them. Grafted trees, such as crab apples, frequently grow root suckers from below the graft union. These shoots do not have the same ornamental characteristics as the top of the tree. Use pruning shears to cut them flush to the trunk or to the ground.

Water sprouts are upright branches that can weaken a tree and detract from its natural shape. Remove them and rub off new ones before they begin to lengthen. Next, look at the overall structure of the tree and identify the main framework of branches you want to keep. Prune out those that do not fit.

Rejuvenation of your tree might take a number of years, since you should never remove more than one-quarter to one-third of a tree's living wood in any one year. Prune spring-flowering trees after blossoms fade and summer-blooming trees in late winter. 🌺

HAVE ON HAND:

► Gloves

► Safety glasses

► Pruning saw for limbs over 1 ¾-inch diameter

► Loppers for limbs up to 1 ¾-inch diameter

► Pruning shears for limbs up to ¾-inch diameter

► Pole pruner or saw for high limbs

Wear gloves and safety glasses. Saw dead or damaged limbs off to the branch collar.

Lop off suckers flush with trunk or ground, blade on tree side of cut. Make sharp cut; do not leave stubs.

Prune or lop water sprouts flush with branch collars on limbs without leaving stubs. Rub off new sprouts.

Remove undesirable branches high in tree with a pole saw or pruner. Use a three step cut (see pages 160-161).

Staking Established Trees

Strong windstorms may loosen an established tree's hold on the earth and send it toppling. If the tree is not large or badly damaged, it can be returned to its upright position and secured until it becomes reestablished. Trees with trunks less than 3 inches in diameter, when transplanted or revived, need less secure staking than larger ones.

Staking—or guying—large trees involves attaching strong cables to the tree and to ground anchors or stakes. You can

HAVE ON HAND:

▶ Sledge hammer

▶ Three notched metal stakes

▶ Tape measure

▶ Wire cable, ⅛ to ³⁄₁₆ inch

▶ Cable cutters

▶ Six cable clamps, ⅛ to ³⁄₁₆ inch

▶ Three lengths rubber hose, 1 foot

▶ Screwdriver

▶ Mulch

▶ Ribbons or cloth strips

attach a cable to the tree either by looping it around the trunk above the lowest branches or by inserting it through screw eyes drilled into the trunk. Whenever you encircle the trunk with cable, be sure to cushion it by running it through a length of soft rubber hose. Use this method only for temporary guying since encircling cables will strangle a tree if left on for more than two or three seasons.

If you use screw eyes, however, they can be left in your tree permanently. They are useful when the tree is too large or does not have limbs well placed for encirclement. Always predrill the holes slightly smaller than the screw diameter and at the same angle as the direction of the pull. Stagger screws along the trunk to avoid weakening the wood at any one level. Eventually, the tree will grow around the screw eye, making the connection even stronger. Cut the cable when the guy is no longer needed.

Anchor your tree to the ground with either stakes or earth anchors. Stakes should have their notched side turned away from the tree before being driven in. To permanently anchor large trees, attach the wires to deeply buried objects, such as concrete blocks. Garden centers also offer a variety of other anchoring devices. ❧

Drive three notched stakes into ground around upright tree at a distance of 3 to 4 feet from its trunk. Angle the stakes away from the tree.

Slip two cable clamps onto long end of cable. Slide one up to fasten together two pieces of cable coming out of hose. Tighten clamp.

Measure from stake to tree's lowest limb. Add tree circumference plus 2 to 3 feet. Cut three lengths of wire cable to that measurement.

Loop hose to fit around trunk just above lowest limb. Thread cable through hose, letting end overlap cable entering hose by 8 to 12 inches.

Loop lower end of cable around notched stake and pull taut. Check tree trunk for straightness. Secure wire at stake with second cable clamp.

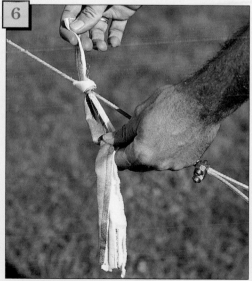

Repeat Steps 3, 4, and 5 for last two stakes, placing all three hose pieces above lowest limb. Attach cloth strips to cables for safety.

HERE'S HOW

LIFTING A FALLEN TREE

Trees growing in sandy or very wet soil may blow over in stormy weather. Young, recently planted trees that lean at no more than a 45° angle are good candidates for successful righting and anchoring. Larger trees and those that have fallen to the ground may have suffered too much root damage to survive replanting, although some do survive.

To pull a listing tree to an upright position and replant, dig under the dislodged roots so that the tree will remain at the original planting depth when righted. Prune exposed roots to fit into the planting hole. Anchor the tree securely with buried supports, such as earth anchors, and attach the cables to screw eyes in the trunk. Leave the tree anchored for several years. Water and fertilize the tree as you would a new transplant, until its roots become reestablished.

Designing for All Seasons

Part of the fun and reward of gardening is planning your garden for all-season interest. With your notebook (or camera) in hand, you can sketch, describe, and record plants that catch your interest in each season. Then replicate or adapt the projects and plant suggestions you will find on the following pages for your own attractive, year-round garden.

As you plan your design, use season-extending tricks of the trade. For instance, you can plant later-emerging plants or ground covers to camouflage fading spring bulb foliage. Or use a colorful annual bed to create a new garden every year. Take the opportunity to experiment with color, height, texture, and unusual plant varieties.

Know the mature size of the plants in your garden and resist the temptation to overplant at the outset. Your carefully planned design will hold its shape much better in seasons to come if you fill in a new perennial bed or border with bulbs and annuals until the permanent plants reach their mature size.

Don't feel you have to plant an entire garden for each season if you want year-round interest in one bed. A scattering of fall or winter plants in a summer bed or border will be enough to extend the season. If you want to do more, include bulbs for spring and fall, evergreen shrubs or shrubs with colorful winter stems, and perennials that have unusual seed pods for attention-getting beds and borders throughout the year. 🌿

Delicate Spring Wildflowers

THIS GARDEN THRIVES WITH

SUN
Full

WATER
Medium

SOIL
Average, well drained

Wildflower gardens have gained popularity in part due to their reliable, beautiful blooms year after year. The fact that this type of garden is easy to care for is an added incentive for you to begin your own. Choose flowers native to your region, where they have already adapted to the climatic conditions. You will find volunteer plants springing up during subsequent years.

These gardens can be as small as a patch in your yard or as large as a meadow. Small plots are the most manageable, allowing you to try scaled-down experiments with new plants and different combinations. Adding new wildflowers will make your garden more diverse, but avoid aggressive species as they may choke out other plants. When purchasing plants, buy from reputable nurseries that propagate from their own stock. Digging wild plants can destroy an entire colony, and the survival rate for removed plants is very low. It is also illegal to dig up any endangered wild species.

Wildflowers are attractive to wildlife. You will find butterflies and pollinating bees frequenting your garden, and birds will come for the seeds and insects. There's no better introduction to the workings of the natural world than this special kind of garden. ❧

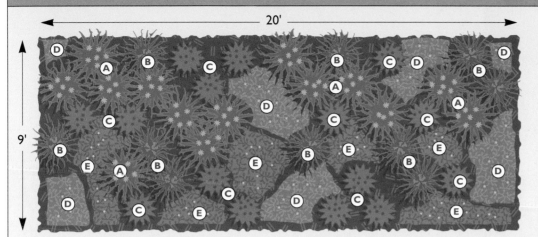

20'

9'

PLANT LIST

A. Wallflower, 14 yellow,
2 to 2½ feet tall

B. Beard-tongue, 10, 2 to 5 feet tall

C. Bachelor's-button, 15,
2 to 2½ feet tall

D. Corn poppy, 1 to 3 seed packets,
1 to 3 feet tall

E. California poppy, 1 to 3 seed
packets, 1 to 2 feet tall

1. Mark an area 9 x 20 feet. Remove sod, till soil, add 1 to 2 inches of compost, and retill the soil.

2. Rake the surface smooth so that the areas without plants will be prepared as a seedbed for the poppies.

3. One foot from the back, beginning 2 feet from the left side, plant 1 wallflower (A), 1 beard-tongue (B), 2 bachelor's-buttons (C), then 1 wallflower, 1 beard-tongue, 1 bachelor's-button. Plant 1 beard-tongue 2 feet from the right side.

4. Offset the second row beginning on the left side. Plant 3 wallflowers and 1 bachelor's-button. Leave a 4-foot space, then plant 2 wallflowers. Leave another 4-foot space, then plant 1 wallflower and 1 beard-tongue.

5. Offset the third row from the left, planting 2 bachelor's-buttons and 2 wallflowers. Leave a 4-foot space, then plant 1 bachelor's-button, 1 wallflower, 1 bachelor's-button, and 1 wallflower.

6. For the fourth row, offset beginning at left border, planting 1 beard-tongue. Leave a 4-foot space, then plant 1 beard-tongue and 1 wallflower. Leave a 4-foot space, then plant 1 beard-tongue. Leave another 4-foot space, then plant another beard-tongue.

7. Offset the fifth row, beginning 4 feet from the left side, planting 1 wallflower, 1 beard-tongue, 1 bachelor's-button. Leave a 6-foot space, then plant 1 bachelor's-button, 1 beard-tongue, and 1 more bachelor's-button.

8. Offset row six, beginning 5 feet from left side: plant 1 bachelor's-button; leave a 4-foot space, then plant 1 more bachelor's-button; leave a 4-foot space, then plant 2 bachelor's-buttons.

9. Mulch around plants and water them well.

10. Mark poppy (D) and (E) areas. Mix poppy seeds with finely pulverized soil or clean sand, then sprinkle on marked areas. Pat soil to ensure seed/soil contact. Do not cover with soil: seeds need light to germinate. Water lightly.

HERE'S HOW

HARVESTING WILDFLOWER SEEDS

Cut plants at the end of a sunny day. Place a paper bag around each seed head and secure with a rubber band. Hang plants upside down in a shaded, low humidity area. When seeds are dry, separate by shaking on a screen with mesh large enough to permit the seeds to pass through. Store in an airtight container in the refrigerator.

A Spring Bulb Garden

THIS GARDEN THRIVES WITH

SUN
Full to part

WATER
Medium

SOIL
Average to rich

Celebrate winter's end with the bright, welcoming colors of a spring bulb garden. Bulb gardens are daily indications of spring's progress, from the emergence of the first shoots to the opening of colorful blooms. For best results, choose bulbs that will perform well in your climate. In all climates, tulips will give the best show if new bulbs are planted each year.

Your spring bulb garden can be either geometric or free form in shape. As you are planning a bulb garden, lay it out with string and stakes or mark the area with lime to be certain the scale is appropriate for the surrounding landscape. A small garden may seem lost in a vast lawn area, for example, but can look spectacular located at the edge of your yard or near the entrance to your house. A large garden may need some space around it to have the most impact.

Locate your spring bulb garden where you will be able to enjoy watching its progress. Bulbs usually make their best show in large masses of a single color or drifts featuring a minimum of six to twelve bulbs. Keep this rule of thumb in mind in the fall as you prepare and plant for your spring color display. ❧

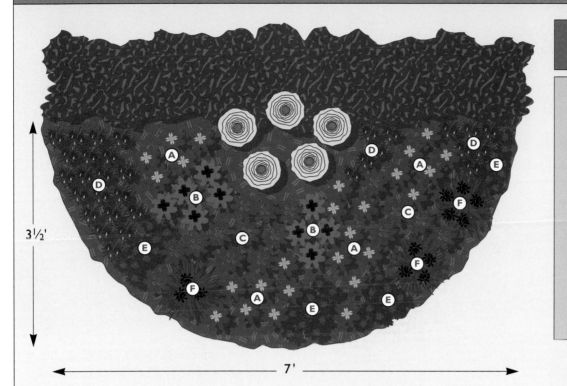

3½'

7'

1. In early fall, mark the edge of a half circle garden along a woodland border. Remove sod, taking care not to damage tree roots.

2. Mark bulb areas with lime. Lay bulbs on the ground in each area, spaced approximately as follows: tulips and iris 4 to 6 inches apart, bluebells 1 foot, and grape hyacinths 3 inches.

3. Use a bulb planter or shovel to dig holes for bulbs. Mix bulb fertilizer with soil at bottom of each hole, following directions on package label. Plant 5 yellow tulips (A) beginning in back and left of half circle center. Plant 5 maroon tulips (B), 11 pink tulips (C), 4 maroon tulips, 8 yellow tulips, 5 pink tulips, 5 iris (D), and 6 yellow tulips as you move from left to right, as shown.

4. Beginning at left again, plant 20 iris and 10 grape hyacinths (E) next to the iris.

5. Plant 1 bluebell (F), 7 yellow tulips, and 10 grape hyacinths in the front of the garden.

6. Continue on the right side with 9 grape hyacinths, 2 bluebells, and 6 iris. Plant 8 grape hyacinths along the edge next to the iris.

7. Water thoroughly and mulch the entire garden with 1 to 3 inches of light, organic mulch—preferably with shredded leaves from the overhead trees.

Vibrant Summer-into-Fall Color

THIS GARDEN THRIVES WITH

SUN
Full

WATER
Low

SOIL
Poor to average

This home's setting provided the inspiration for a vibrant border offering color from early summer into the fall. If your location is hot and sunny, this plan could work for you. Heat-loving plants screen sunny windows, offering shade as well as a garden view. Here, the informal, cottage style of the house is complemented by easy-care, old-fashioned plants.

Look at colors in and around your home to help determine the colors to use in your garden. Here, white trim on windows and fence is echoed in the cleome and summer savory, while spirited colors are offset by dark siding on the house. Note how the pink cosmos at the back separates the white of the window trim from the tall, white cleome blossoms. The dark green cleome foliage provides a backdrop for the carpet of yellow, pink, and orange along the stone walk.

Keep in mind when planting that dark or bold hues tend to draw more attention than paler hues, and that tall plants draw more attention than short ones. Balance your border by placing short, bold-colored flowers near the front and tall plants with large, light-colored flowers at the back. You can tone down large, imposing plants by placing plants with small, delicate foliage nearby. ❧

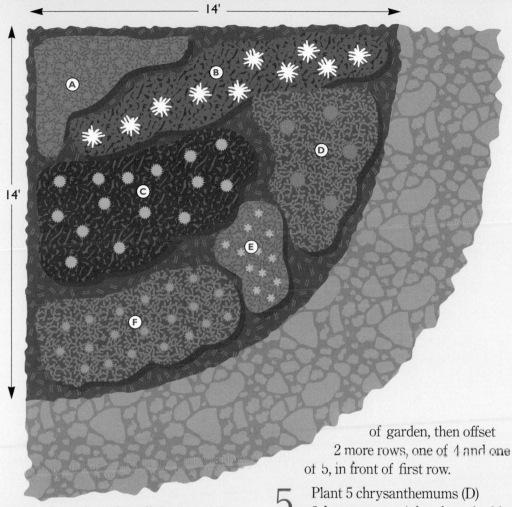

14'

14'

A

B

C

D

E

F

PLANT LIST

A. Cosmos, 17 pink, 4 to 5 feet tall

B. Cleome, 10 white, 4 to 5 feet tall

C. African marigold, 15 yellow, 2 to 3 feet tall

D. Chrysanthemum, 5 pink, 2 feet tall

E. Summer savory, 12 white, 12 to 18 inches tall

F. Zinnia, 20 orange, 14 inches tall

1. In spring after all danger of frost, mark off a 14-foot, quarter-circle garden (see Here's How). Remove sod, till soil, and spread a 3- to 4-inch layer of compost over area.

2. Plant 17 cosmos (A) 1 foot apart in the back left corner.

3. Plant 10 cleome (B) 2 feet apart, in a staggered row ending in the upper right corner.

4. Plant marigolds (C) 2 feet apart. Start with row of 6 from left edge of garden, then offset 2 more rows, one of 4 and one of 5, in front of first row.

5. Plant 5 chrysanthemums (D) 2 feet apart, to right of marigolds and 1 foot in front of cleome, coming forward as shown.

6. Plant 12 summer savories (E) 8 inches apart, in offset rows of 3, as shown.

7. Complete your planting with a grouping of 20 zinnias (F) 1 foot apart. Extend along front of border to meet the summer savories.

8. Mulch entire garden and water plants thoroughly.

HERE'S HOW

LAYING OUT A QUARTER-CIRCLE GARDEN

Mark back corner and front edge boundaries with three stakes. Attach a 14-foot-long string to the back corner stake. With string pulled tightly, walk in an arc between the other two stakes while marking the pattern on the ground with lime. Dig sod from the curve first to keep the pattern from being distorted.

A Sizzling-Hot Summer Border

THIS GARDEN THRIVES WITH

SUN	WATER	SOIL
Full	**Medium**	**Average**

The garden at left will provide you with color all summer long. These striking annual flowers in dramatic reds, lemony yellows, candy pinks, and rich purple-violets typify bright, sun-drenched summer days.

Locate your border along a wall, a fence, or in front of a shrub border where it will receive full sun all day. During the summer, when the sun is most direct, the colors will seem especially brilliant.

Place foliage plants in groups to form a background for bright colors and between strong colors as a buffer. Here, the dusty miller's silver foliage offsets the deep red of the geraniums and tones down the visual impact of neighboring yellow marigolds.

Keep similar colors together, rather than separating groups or scattering plants throughout the garden, for a bolder effect. The strongest colors, such as the geranium's red, are kept to the front, and darker colors, such as the salvia's purple-violet, serve as a backdrop. You can incorporate your own favorite summer flowers and colors for long-lasting summer sizzle. 🌺

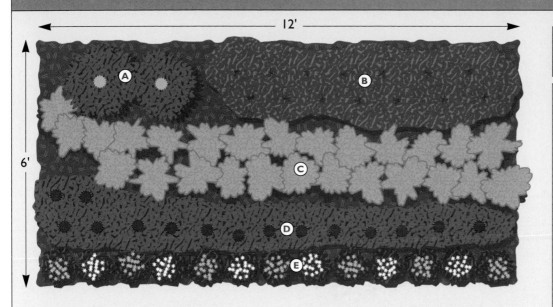

PLANT LIST

A. African marigold, 2 yellow,
   2 to 3 feet tall

B. Salvia, 14 purple,
   20 to 24 inches tall

C. Dusty miller, 26,
   20 to 24 inches tall

D. Geranium, 15 red,
   12 to 18 inches tall

E. Sweet alyssum, 6 pink, 7 white,
   4 to 6 inches tall

1. Measure an area 12 x 6 feet; remove sod and stones. Till soil 1 foot deep. Spread 4 inches of organic compost over the surface and till the soil again, 4 to 6 inches deep.

2. Beginning at the back left side of your border, plant 2 yellow marigolds (A) 2 feet apart, 18 inches from the back.

3. To the right of marigolds, 1 foot from the back, plant 2 rows, each with 7 salvia (B). Leave 1 foot between plants. Stagger the rows.

4. Plant a row of 13 dusty millers (C) 3 feet from the back of the border, 1 foot apart. Stagger a second row of 12 in front of first row. Plant 1 dusty miller 1 foot behind back row on the far left.

5. In front of the dusty millers plant 13 red geraniums (D) 1 foot apart. On the left behind this row, plant 2 red geraniums as shown.

6. In front of the row of geraniums, plant 1 row of 13 sweet alyssum (E), with plants 1 foot apart. Alternate pink and white plants, as shown.

7. Mulch your entire garden with a layer of organic mulch, such as compost or chopped leaves; water well.

HERE'S HOW

TAKE CUTTINGS FROM YOUR GERANIUMS

With a clean, sharp knife, cut 4- to 6-inch stems from healthy geranium plants. Remove flower buds and leaves on lower 2 inches. Push cuttings into sterile, well-drained growing medium. Water, and place container in a sunny, east window. Water every 3 or 4 days. Check for rooting with a light tug after 2 weeks. Cuttings are ready to replant when you encounter resistance.

Showy Annual Edging

THIS GARDEN THRIVES WITH

SUN	WATER	SOIL
Part	Medium to high	Average to rich

In the spring, before your ornamental shrubs bloom, enjoy the showy presentation of an early flowering edging. Choose a location where trees will provide filtered shade during the hottest part of the day, since the plants featured here will not tolerate direct sun for more than 2 to 4 hours daily over a long period of time. Plants in this garden will perform best in cool, moist areas of the country. In warmer areas, you may want to substitute heat-tolerant summer annuals. If this is the case, plant your edging in full sun.

This brightly colored edging creates visual interest and separation between the green lawn and the green foliage of the shrub border. To avoid clashes, choose flowers that complement the border colors already in place. The red, yellow, and blue flowers here serve to refine the vibrant pinks of the azaleas and rhododendrons when they are in bloom.

You may want to vary the width of your edging, as shown here, so it won't look lost in front of larger plants with coarse foliage. This border is 2 feet wide near smaller-leaved azaleas but widens to over 3 feet in front of the rhododendrons. You can adjust your own edging width to suit your style and situation.

1. In the fall, using a hose and lime, mark serpentine shape 10 feet long, increasing from 2 feet wide at the start to 42 inches at its widest, then decreasing to 3 feet wide at the opposite end. Remove sod, till soil to 1 foot deep, cover with 4 to 6 inches of compost, and retill the top 6 inches of soil.

2. Beginning at back left, plant 6 daffodils (A) 6 to 10 inches deep, 4 to 6 inches apart and 4 inches from the back edge.

3. In spring, plant 1 blue and 1 pink forget-me-not (B) left of daffodils, spacing plants 8 inches apart. Along front edge, plant 3 rows of forget-me-nots 8 inches apart, alternating colors as follows: Row 1—Plant as follows: blue, pink, blue, pink, white. (You will extend this row in Step 4.) Row 2—Alternate 1 blue, 1 white to the end of the row. Row 3—Plant 1 blue, 1 white, and 1 blue forget-me-not.

4. Plant the remaining 13 blue forget-me-nots along the outside garden edge, as the continuation of Row 1.

5. Plant wallflowers (C) in rows 1 foot apart, as shown. Begin with yellow and alternate colors (4 yellow, 4 red). In a second row, begin with 2 yellow wallflowers, then alternate colors, ending with 2 yellow (6 yellow, 3 red). Finally, for the third row, plant 1 yellow and 3 red wallflowers above the last blue forget-me-not.

6. Mulch your garden with composted organic matter, bark nuggets, or other organic mulch and water well.

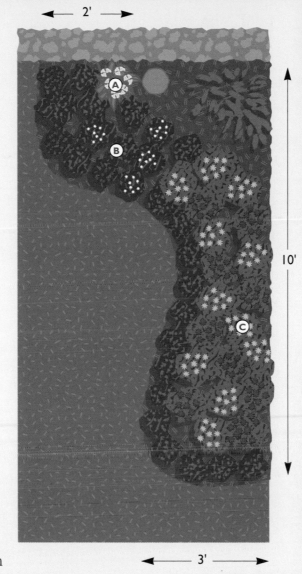

← 2' →

10'

← 3' →

PLANT LIST

A. Daffodil, 6, 14 to 18 inches tall

B. Forget-me-not, 20 blue, 4 white, 3 pink, 8 to 12 inches tall

C. Wallflower, 10 red, 11 yellow, 14 to 16 inches tall

HERE'S HOW

DIVIDING DAFFODILS

Six weeks or more after flowering, use a garden fork to lift daffodil bulbs after digging around clump 6 inches away from the foliage. Very gently, remove soil from bulbs, leaving roots attached. Split larger bulbs by pulling apart, gently untangling roots. Separate smaller bulbs if they come apart easily. Replant, spacing bulbs 4 to 6 inches apart, with pointed ends facing up.

A Garden for Winter Interest

THIS GARDEN THRIVES WITH

SUN
Full

WATER
Low to medium

SOIL
Average to rich

Creating any garden is, in part, an exercise in architecture. A satisfying winter garden, without flowers to consider, depends even more on form, structure, layout, arrangement, and plant attributes. Paths, walks, gates, or other permanent features take on increased importance. Lighting, whether natural or artificial, will also change the look of your garden at different times of day. Elements of climate, such as fog, frost, mist, and snow, can outline, define, change, and enhance forms and shapes. Even garden fragrances change with cold temperatures and moist or dry air.

Locate your winter interest garden where it will be seen the most, whether you spend time indoors or out. If you will see your garden mostly from a distance, then larger, coarser plants are called for. In this garden, for example, large, mature evergreens create a background for the other plants. The ornamental grasses offer long-lasting, colored foliage and interesting shapes for months on end. Your winter planting will also attract wildlife, such as birds and small animals, for your enjoyment. You may even want to set out a bird feeder, winterized birdbath, or other encouragement for winter wildlife visitors. ❧

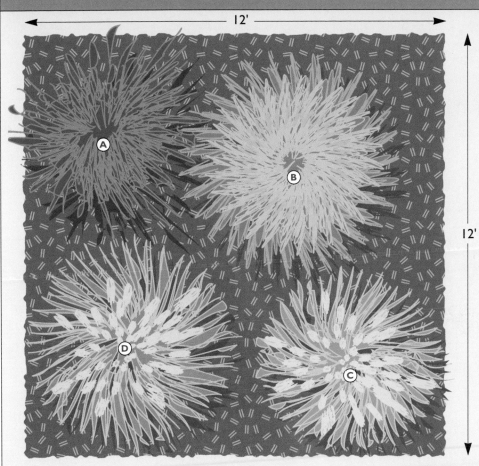

12'

12'

HERE'S HOW

CONTROL SPREADING GRASSES

1. In a sunny location with well-drained soil, as soon as soil can be worked, remove the sod from an area 12 x 12 feet. Till the soil 1 foot deep, add 4 inches of compost, and retill the soil to 4 inches deep.

2. Beginning at the back left-hand corner, plant a young Hill's red cedar (A) as deep as its rootball, 2 ½ feet from both the back and left side of garden. Stake (see Here's How, page 215).

3. Next, plant dwarf blue spruce (B) as deep as its rootball, 5 feet from both the back and right side of the garden. Stake as above.

4. Mulch the cedar and spruce with a 2- to 4-inch layer of shredded bark.

5. Plant the maiden grass (C) at the same depth it was planted in its container and 2 ½ feet from both the front and right sides of the garden.

6. Plant the pampas grass (D) at same depth it was planted in its container and 3 feet from both the front and left sides of the garden.

7. Mulch both grasses with 3 to 4 inches of organic mulch. Water entire garden thoroughly.

Keep aggressive grasses from spreading by planting them in a 10- to 15-gallon plastic pot with the bottom removed. (Make sure pot does not have side holes for drainage.) Dig a hole the same size as pot. Place pot into hole, keeping the rim 1 to 2 inches above the soil. Backfill around pot edges, then fill it with a mix of garden soil and organic compost. Plant your ornamental grass in the center and water well.

Designing with Color

Whether you envision a riot of color or a soothing green oasis, designing a garden with color in mind is a challenge well worth the effort.

Successful color combinations among plants are based on the principles of harmony and contrast. When flowers of one hue are grown next to different flowers of a complementary hue the result is an intensely brilliant combination. And the closer plants are on the color wheel, the more harmonious the effect. Color may also be used as an enhancing accent.

Red is the most dominant of all garden colors and is often used as a single accent. A cascade of red climbing roses on a trellis, for instance, can attract the eye and dominate a view. But the same vivid color brushstroked through a cottage garden can enliven the entire planting. Most garden reds appear as shades or tints that can be effectively combined. Reds do well under sunlight but show up less in deep shade, where white impatiens make a bright accent.

You can give your garden exciting depths by taking advantage of special effects. For instance, if you place the gray green foliage of dusty miller behind a bed of dark, low evergreens, your eye will be drawn past the evergreens to the light-colored dusty miller, creating the illusion of more depth in your garden. Foliage can also be a buffer between flower colors or can complement them. Although not as striking a design element as flowers, foliage is an essential element in your color scheme.

The designs in this section offer suggestions for contrasting as well as harmonizing the colors in your garden to create a balanced effect. Plan your own palette for striking seasonal or long-lasting color. ❧

A Cool Blue Flower Border

THIS GARDEN THRIVES WITH

SUN
Part or full shade

WATER
Medium to high

SOIL
Average to rich

In midsummer's heat, a border of flowers in refreshing shades of blue appears soothing and relaxing. Drifts of blue suggest tranquil shadows, calm water, and gentle shade.

This cool blue border needs a moist, partly shady area, but other blue borders can be grown in full sun or dry conditions. In moderate summer climates, a border like this one can tolerate more sun if large amounts of moisture are available. However, direct sunlight will affect the way in which blues and purples are seen, especially pastels or pale shades, which may look washed out or faded. In dappled sun or full shade, the same colors will appear more intense.

To choose harmonious hues for your blue border, avoid all brightly colored flowers. When small amounts of red or orange are used in a predominately blue garden, those colors will dominate, forcing blues into the background. Green and violet, both found along with blue on the cool side of the color wheel, create harmony because they both contain blue. Mixing dark and light hues of these colors will provide the variation you need for your cool border. In this garden, for example, color contrast is created by using lighter, purplish forget-me-nots and vivid, blue-violet bluebells.

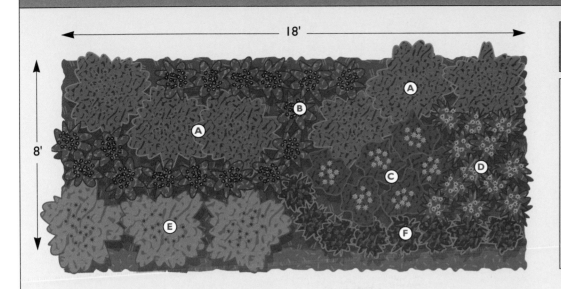

18'

8'

PLANT LIST

A. Blue hosta, 6, 3 feet tall

B. Royal blue forget-me-not, 16, 14 to 18 inches tall

C. Variegated hosta, 6, 2½ feet tall

D. Spanish bluebell, 12, 1½ feet tall

E. Gold hosta, 3, 2 feet tall

F. Bethlehem sage, 8, 1½ feet tall

1. In the spring, mark off an area 8 x 18 feet. Remove the sod, till soil, and then till in 3 to 4 inches of compost over the entire garden.

2. Plant 3 blue hostas (A) 3 feet apart starting in the back left corner and coming slightly forward, then 3 more starting from the back right corner.

3. Plant a staggered row of 2 forget-me-nots (B) along the middle of the left edge. Then plant 6 forget-me-nots along the back and 6 in front of the blue hostas on the left side, spaced 18 inches apart. Plant 2 more forget-me-nots between the groups of blue hostas.

4. Plant 1 variegated hosta (C) in front of the blue hostas on the right. In front of this one, offset 3 more variegated hostas 2 feet apart, then offset 2 more variegated hostas in front of the 3.

5. Plant 3 bluebells (D) on the right, in front of the blue hostas, then 3 staggered rows of 2 bluebells, and then 1 row of 3 in front of these.

6. Plant 3 gold hostas (E) along the left front of the garden.

7. Plant 6 Bethlehem sages (F) along the front on the right, and 2 more between the variegated and gold hostas.

8. Mulch entire garden and water plants thoroughly.

HERE'S HOW

DIVIDING HOSTAS

In early spring or late fall, dig up entire hosta crown. (In the fall, trim the leaves back to 2 to 3 inches.) Rinse the roots under running water to remove excess soil. Inspect the crown for natural divisions between the original plant and healthy new parts. Using a clean, sharp knife, separate the plant into pieces. Make sure shoots, crowns, and roots are all included in each new plant division. Reset pieces in the soil at the same depth as the parent plant.

A Brilliant Blue and Gold Border

THIS GARDEN THRIVES WITH

SUN
Full or part

WATER
Medium

SOIL
Average, well drained

Color contrasts make blue and gold borders popular, and are a great way to brighten up a drab, green hedge. Blue and gold choices include blues and purples, as well as ivory, yellows, and oranges. These basic garden colors are available in varying intensities, from soft pastels to deep, intense hues. In this garden, blue-purple beard-tongue and reddish purple ornamental onion offer subtle variations in blue, and intensities vary from the soft yellow of dusty meadow rue to the deep purple catmint.

Tall plants, such as the violet-blue goat's-rue and the dusty meadow rue, dominate the back of the border. Side by side, their contrasting colors form the backdrop for the border, bringing both color and structure to this area. The hedge behind the border accentuates the flower colors by providing a continuous band of green foliage.

When planning your border, choose plants that span the blue and gold color ranges from pale pastels to deep, dominant hues. Avoid concentrating light or dark colors together in one spot. Instead, spread them throughout. You will find that this will keep your border visually balanced and pleasing. ✿

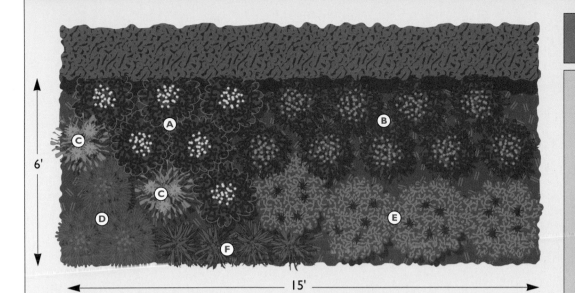

6'

15'

PLANT LIST

A. Dusty meadow rue, 6,
3 to 5 feet tall

B. Goat's-rue, 9, 3 to 5 feet tall

C. Red-hot poker, 2, 3 feet tall

D. Beard-tongue, 3, 2 to 4 feet tall

E. Catmint, 4, 2 feet tall

F. Ornamental onion, 4,
1 to 2 feet tall

1. In an area 6 x 15 feet, remove sod, till the soil, and add 3 inches of compost. Retill the soil, mixing in compost well.

2. In front of the hedge, starting on the left, plant a row of 3 dusty meadow rues (A) and 4 goat's-rues (B), spacing each plant 2 feet apart.

3. In front of this row, starting on the left, offset a row of 1 red-hot poker (C), 2 dusty meadow rues, and 5 goat's-rues. Space each plant 2 feet apart.

4. Offset a partial row in front of this row, starting on the left, by planting 1 beard-tongue (D), 1 red-hot poker, 1 dusty meadow rue, and 1 catmint (E) spaced 2 feet apart.

5. Offset the front row by planting from the left 2 beard-tongue, spaced 2 feet apart, and a line of 4 ornamental onions (F), spaced 1 ½ feet apart.

6. Continue the front row by planting on the right side 3 catmints, spacing plants 2 ½ feet apart.

7. Mulch the garden with a 3-inch layer of organic mulch such as wood chips or chopped leaves, and water well.

HERE'S HOW

CUT FLOWERS FOR ARRANGEMENTS

Any plant in this border will make a beautiful addition to a cut flower arrangement. Early in the morning or late in the evening, cut the flower stems 4 to 6 inches longer than the desired length for the arrangement. Cut the stems on an angle just prior to placing them in water and remove all lower leaves. Be sure to cut a variety of different shapes, such as rounded ornamental onions, spiky red-hot pokers, and feathery dusty meadow rues as fillers.

A Colorful Island

THIS GARDEN THRIVES WITH

SUN	WATER	SOIL
Full	**Medium**	**Average to rich**

An island bed, a garden surrounded by lawn or paving, can be a colorful or calm focal point in your home landscape. Islands can be as large or as small as you wish and in whatever shape that takes your fancy. But you may want to start with a small, easy-care island that you can enlarge over time.

Choose your location first, then select plants that suit your conditions. For example, for a fairly well-drained, sunny site, choose plants that tolerate heat well and need only moderate amounts of water. If your spot is shady and cool, look for shade-tolerant plants that like moisture, such as hostas and ferns.

Since island beds will be seen from many angles, you will generally want to locate taller plants near the bed's center and shorter plants around the outside. In the case of this colorful island, the tall cleome is used off-center but, since its stalks are slender and the plants are spaced apart, no view is obscured.

Consider a bed shape that can be mowed around easily, such as an oval or circle. Sharp corners may need to be hand-trimmed. Use of an edging will define your island bed and help prevent invasion by grass (see Here's How, page 187). ❧

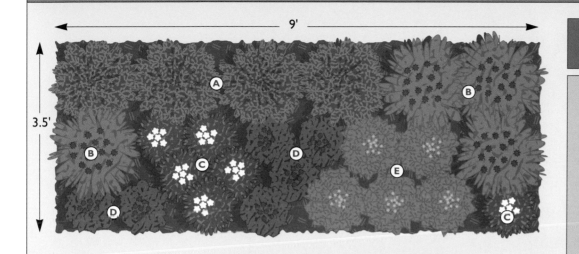

9'

3.5'

PLANT LIST

A. Salvia, 4 blue, 2 feet tall

B. Globe amaranth, 4 red, 2 feet tall

C. Petunia, 6 white, 14 inches tall

D. China pink, 6 red, 8 inches tall

E. Potentilla, 5, 1 foot tall

1. Mark an area 9 x 3 ½ feet. Remove sod, till soil, add 2 to 3 inches of compost, and retill the soil.

2. Begin at the back left side of garden: plant 4 salvias (A) in a row, spacing them 18 inches apart.

3. Plant 2 globe amaranths (B) 18 inches apart to the right of the salvias. Plant 1 globe amaranth on each side of the border.

4. Plant a row of 2 petunias (C), 1 foot apart, to the right of the leftmost single globe amaranth. Offset 2 and then 1 more petunia in front of these. Plant the last petunia in front of the globe amaranth on the right.

5. Plant 2 China pinks (D) 1 foot apart, starting at the left front row. Then plant 2 more pinks in the center, in front of the salvias and to the right of the petunias. Offset 1 pink in front of these, then plant 1 more offset pink in the front row.

6. Plant 3 potentillas (E) 18 inches apart in the front row. Then offset 2 more directly behind.

7. Mulch the garden with 2 to 3 inches of an organic mulch such as bark chips or compost; water thoroughly.

HERE'S HOW

SIMPLE METHODS TO STAKE PLANTS

Provide discrete staking for taller plants before they reach half their mature height. To create a simple structure, encircle the base of the plant with 1-inch-thick wooden or metal stakes up to approximately ¾ of the plant's mature height. Tie a series of strings connecting each stake every 3 to 6 inches of the stake's length. As the plant fills in, the support will become less noticeable.

A Complementary Color Border

THIS GARDEN THRIVES WITH

SUN
Full

WATER
Medium

SOIL
Poor to average

To brighten a monochromatic row of conifers, consider planting this complementary color border in front of it. Set against the soft, fine foliage of coniferous trees and shrubs, the border shown here combines two complementary colors to create a strong, eye-catching contrast.

Complementary color gardens contain combinations of colors that are opposite each other on the color wheel (see Here's How, page 191). Understanding color relationships will allow you to create inviting combinations in your garden plan. In this garden, fernleaf gold yarrow and daisy-like coreopsis are highlighted by the deep blue-purple spikes of salvia.

Use complementary color schemes in your garden to create a vibrant, intense design. True flower colors that are not pastels or mixes, such as bright yellow marigolds and dark purple salvias, create the strongest visual contrast. Use paler colors, such as lavender and creamy yellow, for a more subdued contrast. Before deciding upon your color combinations, think about the effect you want to create—subtle, bold, or something in between. With a little planning, color can add a punch to your garden and surrounding landscape.

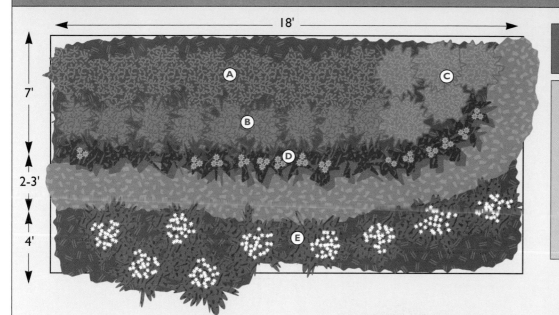

18'

7'

2-3'

4'

PLANT LIST

A. Fernleaf yarrow, 8, 3 feet tall

B. Salvia, 9, 2 feet tall

C. Artemisia, 5, 24 to 30 inches tall

D. Coreopsis, 19, 18 to 24 inches tall

E. Bumald spirea, 9, 2 to 3 feet tall

1. Remove sod from an area 7 x 18 feet in front of background plants, taking care to stay beyond their dripline to avoid root injury. Till the soil, add 4 inches of compost, and retill the soil 4 to 6 inches deep.

2. Beginning 1 foot from the back left side, plant 8 yarrows (A) in a row, spacing them 2 feet apart.

3. Plant 9 salvias (B) in a row 18 inches apart, 3 feet in front of yarrows.

4. To the right of the row of yarrows plant 3 artemisias (C) spaced 18 inches apart. Plant 2 artemisias staggered in front of this row, as shown.

5. Next, plant a row of 19 coreopsis (D) 1 foot apart, ending in front of the artemisias as shown on diagram.

6. If you don't have a ready-made garden path, remove a strip of sod 2 to 3 feet wide in front of this planting

bed, as shown. Cover with 4 inches of fine gravel, level with a rake, and compact with a roller, if possible.

7. On the other side of the path, remove sod to create an area 3 x 18 feet. Enlarge the first 8 feet of the left side by an additional 1 foot. Till the soil, add 4 inches of compost, and retill the soil 4 to 6 inches deep.

8. Plant 7 spireas (E) 3 feet apart, as shown. Plant the 2 remaining spireas in the enlarged left edge of bed, staggering them in front of the first 3 spireas on the left.

9. Mulch plantings with compost. Water well.

HERE'S HOW

USING THE COLOR WHEEL

The color wheel represents the spectrum of color that appears naturally in rainbows. The primary colors, red, blue, and yellow, are the starting points for every other color. To find a color's opposite or complementary color, draw a line from one color through the center of the wheel to the color directly opposite on the wheel.

Cascades of Color

THIS GARDEN THRIVES WITH

SUN
Full

WATER
Medium

SOIL
Average, well drained

An informal mix of flowers and foliage cascading from trellises and across your garden can accent a back door or shed, as they do here. Along with blooming vines, this planting features showy annuals for all-season color. The mixture of plants invites the use of many different hues simultaneously, including red, pink, yellow, purple, and orange. Bold green foliage and mounding plant forms also help this scheme succeed.

Repetition of its various colors keeps this planting cohesive. The red of the climbing rose is reflected in the petunias and echoed again in the nasturtiums and pansies. The purple clematis can be trained upright and then allowed to spill downward in a waterfall effect.

This plant assortment also provides textural contrasts. Coarse and fine foliage and flowers appear throughout the garden. Delicate pansy leaves and flowers, appropriately located along the front of the garden, are offset by the larger blooms of roses and clematis in the background.

Your cascading garden doesn't have to be planted from scratch. Start with just one or two cascading plants tucked into your permanent bed and add to your design each season.

A. Clematis, 2, 10 feet tall

B. Climbing rose, 1, 10 feet tall

C. Petunias, 14 mixed colors, 10 inches tall

D. Nasturtium, 8 mixed colors, 1 foot tall

E. Pansy, 10 mixed colors, 6 to 12 inches tall

1. In an area 4 x 5 feet on one side of your back door and another area 4 x 8 feet on the other side, remove sod. On left side of house, remove sod from 2- x 1-foot area connected to front bed. In all areas, till the soil, add 3 to 4 inches of compost, and retill the soil.

2. Install trellises on either side of the door and around the left corner. Install window box.

3. Plant clematis (A) 6 inches away from the front of left trellises.

4. Plant the climbing rose (B) 12 to 18 inches away from the front of trellis on the right side of the door.

5. Plant 4 petunias (C) in the window box on the right and 4 more petunias (not shown) directly under the window box, starting on the right side of the climbing rose and running along by the house to the right side of the large bed.

6. Plant the middle rows of both beds, spacing all plants 1 foot apart. Begin with 1 petunia, 2 nasturtiums (D), and 1 pansy (E). For the 8-foot middle row, begin on the bed's left and plant 3 pansies, 3 nasturtiums, then 2 pansies.

7. Plant the front rows of the garden with 2 petunias, 1 nasturtium, and 1 pansy. Then, in the bed on the right, plant 2 pansies, 2 nasturtiums, 3 petunias, and 1 pansy.

8. Mulch the entire garden. Water well until plants are established.

HERE'S HOW

CANDIED FLOWERS

For ornamental, edible candied flowers, cut pansy, violet, or nasturtium blossoms just after they have opened, leaving a ½-inch stem. Use flowers that haven't been sprayed with insecticide. Beat an egg white until fluffy and paint the blossoms with it, using a soft, clean paintbrush. Sprinkle the blossoms with extra-fine granulated sugar and allow to dry for 48 to 72 hours. Store in an airtight container. (Do not try with other flowers unless you are sure they are edible.)

Designing Around Features

Spectacular gardens are often created around unique garden elements such as water features, lighting, or specimen plants. To find a central focus for your garden, begin by assessing your walkways, entries, trees, mailboxes, lampposts, fences, and even rocks.

You can create a garden or landscape picture, for example, by using the principle of framing. Isolate an element in your garden—perhaps a venerable old tree—and give it star status. Special treatment might include encircling the tree with planting beds or benches, helping to make it a focal point in your garden. Contrast, another important design element, can be used to great effect as well. Lead the eye with a light-colored walkway in a shady area, for example, or enhance the light color of your front door with a planting of dark foliage.

Even problem areas can be transformed by clever treatment of special features. If you have too prominent a view of a neighbor's fence, emphasize a feature in your own landscape to direct attention where you want it. Or turn a rocky slope into an artful rock garden. Whatever your situation, use the ideas and projects in this section to create garden designs around your own property's unique features. ✾

A Textured Walkway

THIS GARDEN THRIVES WITH

SUN	WATER	SOIL
Part sun to shade	**Medium to high**	**Average to rich**

From the glossy, leathery foliage of Siberian bergenia to the silver-spotted leaves of Bethlehem sage, planning a textured walkway, such as the one shown here, will introduce you to another dimension of gardening. You can use the forms and colors of your plants and walkway materials as well as the light in an area to create a palette of exciting visual and tactile texture.

Vary leaf shape and surface quality, plant form, and flowers to provide a variety of sensations. Juxtapose large, coarse foliage against light and airy leaves to show each off to its best advantage. In this garden, the rounded, horizontal bergenia leaves contrast well with arching daylily clumps and spiky, upright ligularias.

By planting the edges of your path with plants whose colors contrast with the walking surface, you will add visual impact to both path and garden. For example, plant light-colored foliage or flowering plants next to dark surfaces and use light walkway surfaces for dark, shaded areas.

Low-growing plants work best placed immediately next to a walk. They help to define the walkway and provide a smooth transition from the surface of the path to taller plants at the back.

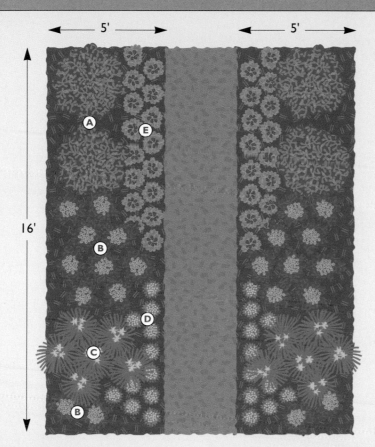

← 5' →   ← 5' →

Ⓐ   Ⓔ

16'

Ⓑ

Ⓓ

Ⓒ

Ⓑ

PLANT LIST

A. Ligularia, 4, 4 to 6 feet tall

B. Bergenia, 22, 1½ feet tall

C. Daylily, 12 yellow,
   3 to 4 feet tall

D. Cypress spurge, 22, 1 foot tall

E. Bethlehem sage, 32, 1 foot tall

HERE'S HOW

CONTROLLING SLUGS

Shady, moist gardens are an ideal habitat for slugs. Feeding at night, slugs devour leaves, stems, bulbs, and fruits, leaving slimy trails of mucus as evidence of their presence. Here are two proven methods of control:

Place a board on the ground in your garden. Slugs will congregate underneath it overnight. Pick them off in the morning.

Fill a shallow pan with beer; sink it level with the soil surface. Slugs will fall in and drown. Empty frequently.

1. Measure a 5- x 16-foot border on either side of your walkway. Remove sod, till soil, add 3 to 4 inches of compost, and retill the soil.

2. Beginning at the back left, plant 2 ligularias (A) 3 feet apart, one in front of the other. (The planting beds on either side of the path are mirror images of each other. Plant one side first, then repeat on other side.)

3. Plant 9 bergenias (B) in 4 staggered rows in front of the ligularias, spacing plants and rows 18 inches apart. Plant 2 bergenias in the first, second, and fourth rows, and 3 in the third row.

4. Plant 6 daylilies (C) 18 inches apart in staggered rows in front of the bergenias with 2 in the first row, 3 in the second, and 1 in the third.

5. Plant 2 bergenias in front of the daylilies in a staggered row.

6. Plant 11 cypress spurges (D) 1 foot apart to the right of the daylilies and bergenias, as shown.

7. Plant 16 Bethlehem sages (E) in two staggered rows of 8 to the right of the ligularias and bergenias.

8. Repeat planting directions for right side. Mulch the gardens and water well.

An Inviting Entryway Garden

THIS GARDEN THRIVES WITH

SUN
Full

WATER
Medium

SOIL
Average

The most public part of your yard is the entrance. Planting an inviting, attractive garden creates a warm atmosphere that invites visitors right to your door. Depending on the plants used, visitors may be greeted by an array of vibrant colors or sweet scents.

Entrance gardens should have a more formal appearance than backyard gardens. Along a stone walk, a garden mulch of light-colored stone chips is preferable to straggly, shredded bark. Stray stone chips can be quickly swept back into the garden. They will also protect the plants from splashed soil particles or loose mulch when your garden is watered.

Privacy fences are a common feature of entrance gardens. They both define your personal space and act as a backdrop for the public part of your yard. If your entrance doesn't have a privacy fence, a sturdy trellis or an arbor can be substituted. Cover it with a climbing rose, and this feature will become the focal point of the garden, defining the limit of public space to your visitors. Choose a climbing rose that will bloom all season long and provide you with fragrance as well. Regardless of the maintenance they require, roses are popular, beautiful, and rewarding to grow.

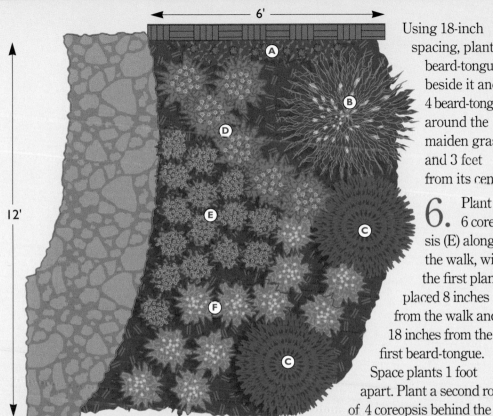

6'

12'

Using 18-inch spacing, plant 1 beard-tongue beside it and 4 beard-tongue around the maiden grass and 3 feet from its center.

6. Plant 6 coreopsis (E) along the walk, with the first plant placed 8 inches from the walk and 18 inches from the first beard-tongue. Space plants 1 foot apart. Plant a second row of 4 coreopsis behind the first row, staggering plants 1 foot behind and between the first 4 plants of the front row. Plant a third row of 3 coreopsis and a fourth row of 2 coreopsis.

7. Next, plant 2 Stokes' asters (F) 18 inches apart, at the back of bed and 18 inches between dwarf white pines. Plant 3 Stokes' asters 18 inches in front of first 2 asters. Plant remaining asters 18 inches to the left of the coreopsis, in two rows of 3 each. Stagger plants in each row for visual appeal.

8. Cover entire garden with 2 inches of compost. Cover compost with 2 inches of light-colored rock chip mulch. Water the garden thoroughly.

1. Clear an area 6 x 12-feet along your entrance walk. Till soil and spread 4 inches of compost over the surface. Retill the soil 6 inches deep.

2. Plant climbing rose (A) 10 inches from the fence and 3 feet from walk.

3. Plant maiden grass (B) 4 feet from the walk and 3 feet from the fence.

4. Plant 1 dwarf white pine (C) 5 feet from the fence and 5 feet in from the walk. Plant the other dwarf white pine 4 feet from the walk and 2 feet from the bottom edge of the garden.

5. Plant 1 beard-tongue (D) 1 foot from the fence and from the walk.

PLANT LIST

A. Climbing rose, 1, 8 to 10 feet tall
B. Maiden grass, 1, 5 to 6 feet tall
C. Dwarf white pine, 2, 3 to 8 feet tall
D. Beard-tongue, 6, 20 to 24 inches tall
E. Threadleaf coreopsis, 15, 18 to 24 inches tall
F. Stokes' aster, 11, 24 to 30 inches tall

HERE'S HOW

TRAINING CLIMBING ROSES

As your climbing rose grows, support the upper canes by training them to grow along a fence. You can purchase professional ties at a local nursery or use soft cloth or twine to fasten canes to the fence. Tie fasteners tight enough to support growing canes but not so tight as to strangle them. Never use wire or other rigid fasteners that can cut or sever canes.

A Petite Planting Around a Tree

THIS GARDEN THRIVES WITH

SUN	WATER	SOIL
Part sun to shade	Medium	Average, well drained

The right combination of plants can beautify the area surrounding a tree base with spectacular results. A little extra attention to planning and detail will give your landscape a finished look and provide an attractive focal point throughout the year. Creating a circular bed around a tree also eliminates the need to trim around the tree and will simplify lawn mowing.

The delicate, coordinated planting shown at left is only one part of this careful plan. In spring, lamium flowers enhance and balance this tree's pink blooms. Silvery lamium leaves will provide a distinctive contrast to the dark tree trunk all season as other plants bloom and fade. From early spring through fall, a succession of plants will appear.

Choose plants to match your growing conditions and to complement your tree's attributes, such as color and shape. If your climate is one with no snow cover, consider plants that are evergreen or have attractive seed pods for winter interest. Mulch and spreading ground covers can be attractive, low-maintenance alternatives to garden plants.

Ideally, you should install your garden around a tree when you plant the tree or shortly thereafter. It is difficult to cultivate or plant around established trees without damaging roots. ❧

12'

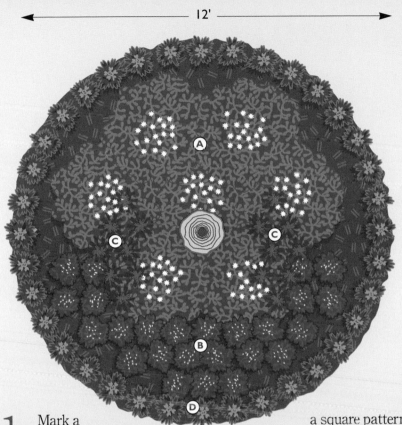

PLANT LIST

A. Lamium, 7, 4 to 10 inches tall

B. Lily of the valley, 25,
6 to 8 inches tall

C. Magic lily, 16, 2 to 3 feet tall

D. Hardy cyclamen, 36,
6 to 10 inches tall

1. Mark a circle 12 feet in diameter around a tree. Remove sod and till soil (be careful near roots). Add 2 inches of compost and till again.

2. Begin 2 feet in from the far edge and 3 ½ feet from the left side. Plant 2 lamiums (A) 3 feet apart. Closer to tree, offset a row of 3 lamiums 2 feet apart and, on the other side of the tree, another row of 2 lamiums.

3. One foot from the near side of garden edge, and 1 foot apart, plant a row of 3 lilies of the valley (B). Offset 2 rows of 6 and 8 behind this, spaced 1 foot apart. Plant 4 lilies of the valley in a square pattern on each side behind the end plants of the back row.

4. Plant the magic lilies (C) 4 inches deep and spaced 1 foot apart. Plant in 5 offset rows, beginning 4 feet from the far edge and 3 ½ feet from each side. Plant 1 in the first and last rows and 2 in the other rows.

5. Six inches from the edge of the bed, plant a ring of 36 cyclamens (D) 2 inches deep, spaced 1 foot apart.

6. Mulch the entire garden with 1 to 2 inches of organic mulch and water thoroughly.

HERE'S HOW

MICROWAVE DRYING PLANTS

Lily of the valley fragrance added to potpourri brings the scent of your garden indoors to last throughout the year. Prepare lily of the valley by cutting newly opened flowers just after the morning dew has dried. Place them between two sheets of paper towels and microwave on high for approximately 3 minutes, turning every 30 seconds until they feel dry and brittle. Store unused stalks in a covered glass jar.

A Fuss-Free Rock Garden

THIS GARDEN THRIVES WITH

SUN
Full

WATER
Low to medium

SOIL
Poor to average

Creating a rock garden can transform a bare slope or rock outcropping into a point of interest. Since rock gardens simulate alpine settings, they are uniquely suited to a slope or an embankment. An elaborate rock garden might contain features such as alpine shrubs, large boulders, waterfalls, or brooks. The fuss-free rock garden here can be built mostly by hand. If your site does not have large rocks, smaller ones can be positioned to look natural, especially when planted with tiny alpine flowers and shrubs.

Situate your rock garden on a sunny hillside or gentle slope. Or, place it near a stone patio or other permanent feature. Resist placing your rock garden under trees, where tree roots might be damaged or smothered.

Partially bury rocks to give the illusion of a ledge emerging from the soil. Expose more rock surface toward the garden front, which will create larger soil pockets for planting behind the ledge. Change elevation and tilt rocks for a more natural look.

Rock piles and larger stones of the same type are preferable to scattered rocks. Rocks with lichen and moss work best when placed weathered-side up. Rounded stones will give the illusion of a stream bed. ❧

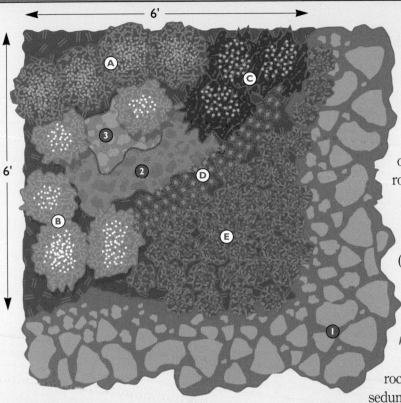

6'

6'

4. Plant 3 moss phlox (A) 1 foot apart, as shown, then 1 more, right of last phlox.

5. Plant 2 sedums (B), one on either side of rock area 3.

6. To right of phlox, plant 2 basket-of-golds (C) 1 foot apart, and 1 basket-of-gold offset 1 foot in front.

7. At front left corner of rock area 2, plant 3 sedums 1 foot apart as shown in diagram.

8. From front of rock area 2, extending to rock area 1 in a triangle, remove soil to 6-inch depth. In front of rock area 2, plant 3 rows of 16 tulips (D), as shown, with plants 4 inches apart. Mix soil with compost and carefully replace over the bulbs. Tamp with hands.

9. In remainder of triangle, with 6 inches between plants, plant rock cress (E) in front of tulip area. Offset rows back to front.

10. Using coarse rock chips, mulch the garden. Be careful not to injure small plants. Water well.

1. Choose a point at the top of the bank. Measure and mark a 6-foot square. Remove sod and soil to an 18-inch depth.

2. Beginning front left, construct stable rock area (1) along front and right sides. Place largest rocks outside, smaller rocks toward center. Construct two other, smaller rock areas (2 and 3) higher up, as shown in diagram.

3. Mix dug soil with coarse sand and gravel. Starting at front left, backfill behind rock area 1. Tamp and water soil every 4 inches to remove air pockets. Allow soil to settle 4 to 7 days, with final level 1 to 2 inches below area 1 rock surface.

PLANT LIST

A. Moss phlox, 4, 4 inches tall

B. Creeping sedum, 5, 2 inches tall

C. Basket of-gold, 3, 1 foot tall

D. Tulip, 48 pink, 15 inches tall

E. Rock cress, 35, 2 inches tall

HERE'S HOW

A LEVEL- AREA ROCK GARDEN

Excavate the measured area to a depth of 18 inches. Set rocks aside. Mix soil with coarse sand and gravel to obtain well-drained consistency. Place 6 inches of coarse gravel in bed, arrange rocks in desired pattern on gravel. Backfill soil areas in 4-inch layers, tamp, and water. Add extra soil over 4 to 7 days as settling occurs.

A Colorful Lamppost Planting

THIS GARDEN THRIVES WITH

SUN
Full

WATER
Medium

SOIL
Rich, well drained

Vertical features in your landscape, such as lampposts, mailboxes, signs, flagpoles, and lights, can be incorporated into your plantings to add interest and variety. By emphasizing your garden's horizontal lines, the height of vertical elements won't overwhelm their surroundings. The garden shown at left provides a good example. The plants do not obstruct light from the lamppost, but it becomes less prominent in the overall landscape design.

Repetition and contrast are elements often used in good garden design. Tall scarlet sage accents the repetitive white and purple color scheme along the front and side. Surrounding colors then subdue the sage's drama. Highlighted by the purple and white flowers in front, it is toned down by the reddish green leaves behind. The repetition of mounding plants, alyssum, and lobelia softens the pavement's edge, creating a graceful transition to the yard. The plants also flow onto the walk, reducing the straight division between garden and pavement.

Scarlet sage's vertical flower spikes mirror the upright lamppost while mounding alyssum and lobelia repeat the Japanese maple and mugo pine forms. Look for ways to use subtle repetition in your own lamppost or other plantings. ❧

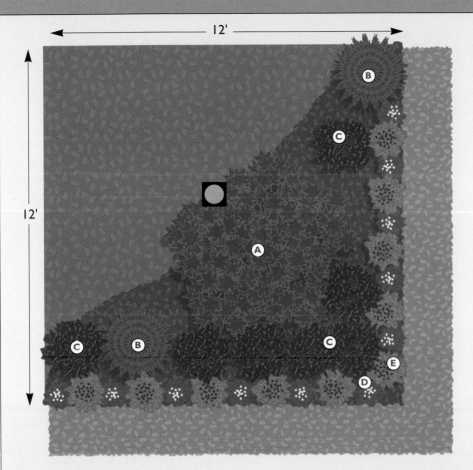

PLANT LIST

A. Japanese maple, 1, 6 to 8 feet tall

B. Mugo pine, 2, 3 to 4 feet tall

C. Scarlet sage, 7, 16 to 20 inches tall

D. Sweet alyssum, 11 white,
6 to 12 inches tall

E. Lobelia, 10, 8 to 12 inches tall

1. Remove the sod from a triangular area with two equal sides of 12 feet. Till the soil, add a 4- to 6-inch layer of compost, and till again to a depth of 6 inches. Plant at same depth plants were in their containers.

2. Plant the Japanese maple tree (A) 6 feet from both front and right side of walk. Stake as in Here's How, page 215.

3. Plant 1 mugo pine (B), 8 feet left of front right corner, 2 feet from walk. Plant other mugo pine 10 feet from right corner at back, 2 feet from walk.

4. To the left of each pine, plant 1 scarlet sage (C) 30 inches in from garden edge. To the right of pine at left, plant 4 more 18 inches apart in a row, 30 inches from the garden's edge. Plant 1 more sage 18 inches above the last.

5. Spacing plants 1 foot apart and 6 inches in from the garden edges, alternate planting 11 alyssums (D) and 10 lobelias (E) along the two sides, beginning and ending with alyssums

6. Cover the garden with 2 inches of compost. Top with 2 inches of shredded bark mulch. Water well.

HERE'S HOW

PLANTING A WINTER COVER CROP

Winter rye, oats, and vetch can grow in cold fall weather and add organic matter and nitrogen to the soil when turned under early in the spring. In fall, remove dead annuals, spread ½ inch of lime dust over the area, and till the soil 3 to 4 inches deep. Using a metal garden rake, level the soil and sprinkle with seed. Lightly rake the soil's surface with the rake's tines to set the seed. Till plants into soil in the spring when they are 2 to 3 inches tall, before seeds form.

A Moisture-Loving Garden

THIS GARDEN THRIVES WITH

SUN
Part to full shade

WATER
High

SOIL
Average to rich

Don't let the perpetually wet spots in your yard intimidate you. These areas can be transformed into spectacular, moisture-loving gardens. There are many plants that can tolerate or even require boggy conditions in order to thrive. If you do not have an area that is naturally wet but would like to grow plants that are moisture-loving, a marsh garden is easy to construct (see Here's How, page 207).

Moisture-loving gardens are best in areas that naturally retain water—miniature wetlands. In these wetlands, you can grow plants that won't thrive under other conditions, for instance the bog garden candelabra primroses. Bog gardens placed next to ponds can provide attractive transitions to the rest of the garden and, in late summer when other garden plants may not be at their most attractive, your moisture-loving plants will look delightfully fresh.

You will want to place a raised path, steppingstones, or rocks nearby from which to view your garden without crushing plants or stepping in water. Check water level regularly during the growing season, adding water if necessary. Marsh gardens are very difficult to overwater. ❧

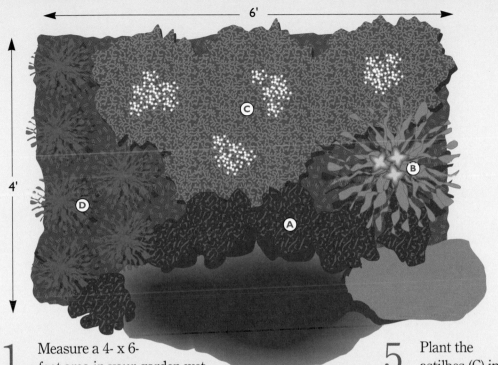

6'

4'

A. Candelabra primrose, 6,
2 feet tall

B. Siberian iris, 1, 2 ½ feet tall

C. Astilbe, 4, 2 feet tall

D. Japanese sedge, 6, 2 feet tall

HERE'S HOW

CONSTRUCTING A MARSH GARDEN

1. Measure a 4- x 6-foot area in your garden wetland. Remove sod and stones. In the wettest spot, dig a shallow depression 4 to 10 inches lower than the surrounding soil, to hold open water. Place a large rock at the garden's edge, next to the depression.

2. Till soil to a depth of 1 foot. Add 6 to 8 inches of compost to the surface and retill to a depth of 4 to 6 inches. Plants should be at same depth they were in their nursery containers.

3. Beginning near water as shown, plant 5 primroses (A) 1 foot apart near rock and along water's edge.

4. Plant 1 iris (B) 18 inches from the right garden edge and 2 feet behind the primroses.

5. Plant the astilbes (C) in a triangle, as shown, 2 feet apart and 1 foot from the back garden edge.

6. Beginning at the back left corner of the garden, plant 4 Japanese sedges (D) 1 foot apart in a row coming forward. Plant 2 more, 1 foot to the right of first row, and 1 foot apart, as shown.

7. Plant 1 primrose at left, between the Japanese sedges and the edge of the water.

8. Mulch the garden with 4 to 6 inches of compost and water well to settle plant roots.

Dig an area 18 inches deep in sun or part shade. Line with 2 inches of sand, and place a 40-mil black plastic liner (available from pond supply catalogs or garden supply stores) over the sand. Cut drainage holes in the liner 8 inches from top. Fill liner with soil high in organic matter. Make a depression in the soil to allow for a pool of standing water, if desired. Water until the soil is completely saturated and the low area is full of water. Set stones around edge for an attractive look.

Designing for a Special Style

How do you go about deciding on a personal garden style? The first step is to ask yourself why you want a garden—what will be its purpose? There are many possible answers. The designs in this section were chosen to help you find a style that satisfies your needs and expresses your preferences.

You will want to consider where your garden is going to be and make sure the style you have in mind can be adapted to your site. You may find that the architecture of your home or the character of your neighborhood is best suited to a specific kind of garden. A good garden design will create a unified outdoor atmosphere that will also fit your surroundings and mode of life.

Identify what makes a distinctive garden style appealing to you. Do you prefer the variety of a cottage garden, the hardiness of a native garden, or the fragrance of a rose garden? Gourmet cooks may want to plant an herb garden not only for its charm but also for its utility.

Think about what attracts you to a garden most: color, fragrance, shape? You can give distinction to a common style by incorporating your preferred variations. As you review the varieties of garden styles presented in this section, you will see that the possibilities are endless. You can adapt the garden projects here to develop your own particular theme. You will quickly discover the excitement of expressing your special style through garden design. ❧

A Classic Cottage Garden

THIS GARDEN THRIVES WITH

SUN
Full

WATER
Medium

SOIL
Average, well drained

Cottage gardens are informal, colorful medleys of annuals, shrubs, perennials, and sometimes herbs and vegetables as well. Originally grown for a family's medicinal and culinary needs, cottage gardens remind us of the country gardens of the past.

As you plan your cottage garden, consider any natural features already in place, such as large rocks, fruiting shrubs, vines, or trees. Trellises, birdbaths, swings, benches, and fences also can become a part of your cottage garden design. The plants at left grow through the railings and billow over the top of a picket fence for a natural, uncontrived look.

Cottage gardens are generally low maintenance, requiring only weeding and the removal of spent flowers to keep them looking their best. Choose a sunny location and prepare your soil well. Cultivate carefully around established perennials and volunteer plants that spring up from self-sowing annuals or perennials, such as pansies and foxgloves. Thin the seedlings but allow a few to grow randomly for a casual, cottage garden effect. ❧

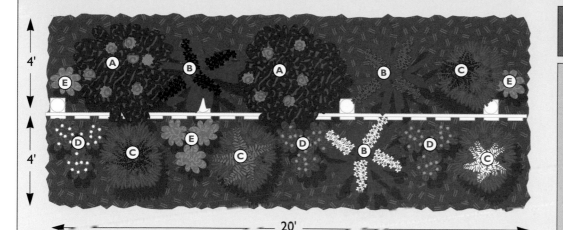

PLANT LIST

A. Hybrid tea rose, 2, 4 to 5 feet tall

B. Delphinium, 1 white, 1 purple, 1 pink, 4 to 6 feet tall

C. Foxglove, 2 purple, 1 pink, 1 white, 3 to 6 feet tall

D. Strawflower, 6 pink, 3 white, 1 foot tall

E. Dusty miller, 5, 1 to 2 feet tall

1. Remove the sod from areas 4 x 20 feet on both sides of a picket fence. Till soil, add 2 to 3 inches of compost, and retill the soil.

2. On the back side of the fence, plant 2 roses (A), one 3 feet from the left edge and the other 7 feet to the right of the first.

3. Plant 2 delphiniums (B), 1 dark purple between the roses and a pink one 3 feet to the right of the second rose.

4. Plant 1 purple foxglove (C) 2 feet to the right of the pink delphinium.

5. Plant 3 foxgloves in front of the picket fence: 1 purple 4 feet from the left, 1 pink 4 feet away from the purple, and 1 white 1 ½ feet in from the right side of the garden.

6. In front of the fence, plant the remaining white delphinium between the pink and white foxgloves.

7. Plant groups of 3 strawflowers (D) beginning on the left side with 3 white, then 3 pink between the pink foxgloves and the white delphinium, and another pink group between the white delphinium and white foxglove.

8. Plant a group of 3 dusty millers (E) between the purple and pink foxgloves, and 1 dusty miller behind the fence as shown.

9. Water thoroughly and mulch the entire garden with an organic mulch such as compost or wood chips.

HERE'S HOW

WIRING STRAWFLOWERS

Wire strawflowers for winter display by removing all but ½ inch of the stem. Using an 8- to 12-inch piece of florist wire, push it up through the stem and 1 inch above the flower top. Bend the 1-inch wire end to form a U (upside down) approximately ½ inch long and pull long wire back down until the U disappears. Hang upside down in a cool, dry, shady place until dry, then wrap the wire stem with green florist tape.

An All-American Rose Garden

THIS GARDEN THRIVES WITH

SUN — Full

WATER — Medium

SOIL — Average to rich, well drained

Roses have aptly been called the "Queen of Flowers." Their glorious blooms and extravagant fragrances have made them romantic favorites, cultivated for thousands of years and handed down from generation to generation. Settlers brought rose slips with them not just for their beauty but as a basic necessity of life. Household roses were used for sachets, to flavor cakes and jams, and even for medicinal purposes as they provided vitamin C with their rose hips.

More types of roses are constantly being added to old favorites, and recently emphasis has been on everblooming, large-flowered hybrid teas. This garden is planned with hybrid teas spaced in single rows to provide the air circulation that will keep disease and insect infestations to a minimum.

An edging of low-growing wax begonias hides the open bases of the hybrid teas. The begonias give a finished look to the beds and repeat the white color of the 'John F. Kennedy' rose. The color of the 'Mr. Lincoln' red is repeated in the striking floribunda roses planted in front of the arbor. Although at left you see a clematis climbing over the arches, for an even more spectacular entranceway you may want to plant a red 'Don Juan' climbing rose instead. 🌺

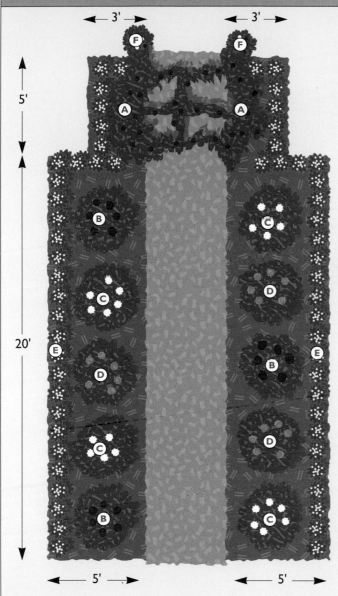

← 3' → ← 3' →

5'

20'

← 5' → ← 5' →

A. Climbing rose, 2 red,
12 to 14 feet tall

B. Hybrid tea rose, 3 red, 4 feet tall

C. Hybrid tea rose, 4 white,
3 feet tall

D. Hybrid tea rose, 3 pink, 4 feet tall

E. Wax begonia, 60 white, 1 foot tall

F. Floribunda rose, 2 red and white
striped, 3 to 4 feet tall

3. Plant a row of hybrid tea roses 2 feet in from the walk and spaced 4 feet apart: 1 red (B), 1 white (C), 1 pink (D), 1 more white, and 1 more red.

4. Plant an opposite row of hybrid tea roses: 1 white, 1 pink, 1 red, 1 pink, and 1 white—again planting them 2 feet away from the middle walk and spacing them 4 feet apart.

5. On each side of the rose beds, along the outside edges, plant 20 wax begonias (E) behind the hybrid tea roses and a row of 6 wax begonias behind the climbing roses. Plant 2 wax begonias between these two rows, and 1 in front of the ends of each row of 6, as shown.

6. Plant 1 floribunda rose (F) on each side of the arbor entryway.

7. Mulch the entire garden with 2 to 3 inches of organic mulch, such as wood chips, and water thoroughly.

1. Mark and prepare areas 5 x 20 feet on both sides of the walk and 3 x 5 feet on both sides of the arbor. Remove sod, till the soil, add 4 to 6 inches of compost, and retill the soil.

2. Plant 1 climbing rose (A) centered on each side of the arbor and 1 foot away from arbor.

HERE'S HOW

PROPAGATING ROSES BY LAYERING

Select a flexible, healthy cane 1 foot or longer. Remove foliage from the bottom half. Three to four inches up the stem, cut a 1-inch-long, ¼-inch-deep slit. Leave stem intact, wedge the slit open with a toothpick and bury it in a trench 2 to 4 inches deep. Next spring, separate cane from original plant, dig up the newly rooted stem, and transplant to its permanent location.

A Native Plant Garden

THIS GARDEN THRIVES WITH

SUN	WATER	SOIL
Full to partial	**Medium to high**	**Average to rich**

Interest in native plant gardens has grown dramatically over the past few years. What began as a search for a more environmentally friendly—as well as a less work-intensive—approach to landscaping and gardening has developed into a rediscovery of the beauty and variety that native plants have to offer. Native plants are easily cared for because they flourish in their local habitats—an added incentive to explore your own native garden possibilities.

Conditions in your landscape and garden will help you decide which plants to choose. Start by determining which areas of your garden are sunny, shaded, exposed to winds, sheltered, low and wet, or high and dry. Test your soil to determine type and water content.

With this information in mind, observe natural areas in your region and note plant associations. The alumroot and wild bleeding heart in the garden shown here are both native to eastern North America.

You will find your native plant garden fits beautifully into your surroundings and needs very little maintenance. It also will be relatively free from pests and diseases, attract wildlife, and afford you long-lasting pleasure.

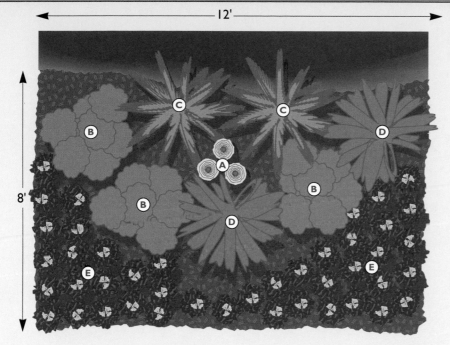

|← 12' →|

8'

PLANT LIST

A. River birch, 1, 50 to 75 feet tall
B. Alumroot, 3, 2 to 3 feet tall
C. Christmas fern, 2, 2 to 3 feet tall
D. Grecian foxglove, 2, 3 feet tall
E. Wild bleeding heart, 43,
      12 to 18 inches tall

HERE'S HOW

STAKING A YOUNG TREE

1. Select your site and as soon as soil can be worked in the spring, measure off an 8 x 12-foot area. Remove sod and stones and till the soil 1 foot deep. Add 4 to 6 inches of organic compost and till again, 4 to 6 inches deep.

2. Dig a hole 8 to 12 inches wider than the rootball of a balled-and-burlapped river birch (A) 3 feet from the back and 4 feet from the left side of the garden. Make a small mound of soil in the bottom of the hole for roots. Remove plastic and metal; leave burlap around rootball. Plant so that the top of the rootball is level with soil surface.

3. Backfill the hole, tamping the soil every 6 inches and watering to remove air pockets. Stake tree to prevent it from blowing over until roots grow to anchor it (see Here's How, on this page).

4. Beginning in the back left corner, spacing everything 3 feet apart and planting at same depth as they were in their containers, plant 1 alumroot (B), 2 ferns (C), and 1 foxglove (D) across the back. Next, plant 1 alumroot on either side of the tree. Plant 1 foxglove in front of the tree.

5. Plant bleeding hearts (E) as shown, 1 foot apart, beginning at the left edge of garden coming forward. Continue as shown in the diagram above. Remember to stagger the plants for a more natural look.

6. Mulch the garden with organic material, and water well.

Drive two 6-foot stakes 18 inches into the soil on either side of tree. Cut old rubber hosing into two 1-foot sections. Thread guy wires through the two pieces of hose. Wrap one end of wire around top of one stake and around tree trunk at approximately the same height, with hose-covered wire against the tree. Wrap other end of wire around the same stake. Repeat on opposite side of the tree.

In areas of high wind, especially when planting in sandy soil, use three evenly spaced stakes. Remove stakes and wires the following spring.

A Wildlife Garden

THIS GARDEN THRIVES WITH

SUN
Full

WATER
Medium

SOIL
Average

Fragrant, brightly colored native flowers attract birds and insects to a wildlife garden. Most native flowers have abundant pollen and nectar, providing food for insects and birds. By encouraging insects, you will also increase the bird population visiting your garden, and insects will help to pollinate fruiting shrubs and trees nearby.

Locate your wildlife garden near trees and open fields where habitat will be available for the kind of wildlife you wish to attract. Plant flowers in the large drifts, or masses, that wildlife prefers, rather than in spotty plantings. Wildlife numbers will increase over the coming years, so plan to locate the garden where it is possible to expand its size, but make your first garden small and easy to care for.

Never use pesticides or insecticides in or near the wildlife garden. Even biologically engineered viruses, such as Bt which infects all caterpillars, can injure desirable wildlife. Chemical pesticides can drift or run off from other areas, killing plants and wildlife. Invest in a reliable resource to identify good and bad caterpillars and handpick them off rather than spray.

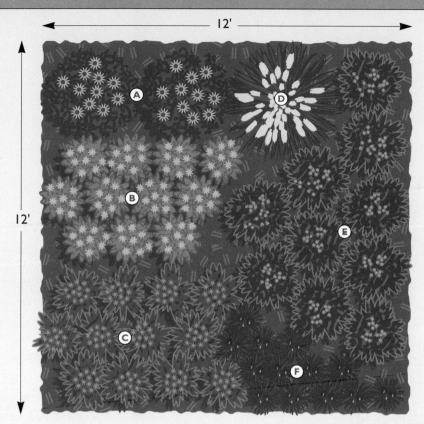

12'

12'

PLANT LIST

A. Black-eyed Susan, 2,
4 to 6 feet tall

B. Pincushion flower, 11,
2 to 2 ½ feet tall

C. Aster, 12, 2 to 3 feet tall

D. Eulalia grass, 1, 4 to 6 feet tall

E. Butterfly weed, 10, 2 feet tall

F. German flag, 13, 2 to 4 feet tall

1. Mark an area 12 x 12 feet and remove sod, till soil, add 3 to 4 inches of compost, and retill the soil.

2. Along the back, plant 2 black-eyed Susans (A).

3. Plant a row of 4 pincushion flowers (B) in front of the black-eyed Susans; then plant a second row of 4 pincushion flowers offset in front of the first row, and then a third row of 3 pincushion flowers offset in front of the second row. Space plants and rows 16 inches apart.

4. Plant 3 offset rows each of 4 asters (C) in front of the pincushion flowers, spacing plants and rows 16 inches apart.

5. At the garden back, 2 feet to the right of the black-eyed Susans, plant 1 eulalia grass (D).

6. Plant a row of 5 butterfly weeds (E) along the right side of the garden. To the left, plant 2 offset rows of butterfly weed, as shown.

7. Plant a row of 5 German flags (F) along the front on the right, and offset 3 rows behind it of 4, 3, and 1, as shown.

8. Mulch the garden and water all plants thoroughly until the garden is well established.

HERE'S HOW

BARREL PLANTING FOR WINTER BIRDSEED

Fill a half barrel with garden soil enriched with compost. Plant six common sunflower plants evenly spaced. Use a 3- to 6-foot variety, such as *Helianthus annuus* 'Velvet Tapestry' or 'Sunspot', which will set large flowers and seed heads on sturdy stems. In the fall, loosely tie individual stems together to keep them upright in the winter. Sunflower seeds are a favorite of winter songbirds.

An Informal Herb Garden

THIS GARDEN THRIVES WITH

SUN
Full

WATER
Low

SOIL
Poor

Herbs have been cultivated since the earliest civilizations, and for good reason. Herb gardens were vital components of everyday life, often depicted in manuscripts, drawings, and tapestries.

Today, growing your own herb garden can satisfy your personal interests whether they be herbal remedies, natural plant dyes, culinary pursuits, or, of course, garden design. Herbs provide a vast array of foliage colors and textures, flowers, and fragrances from which to choose. They have been planted in many styles, from casual kitchen gardens to formal, geometrical knot beds designed around monastic or Shakespearean themes. The garden shown at left features an array of herbs in a sunny, informal border.

Hardworking herbs often do double duty in annual and perennial beds, grown for both beauty and utility. They serve landscaping purposes as hedges (lavender, for instance) and are used as ground covers (sweet woodruff). They also make good companion plants in the vegetable garden. Herb flowers attract pollinators, such as bees and butterflies, and can help repel garden pests that prey on other plants.

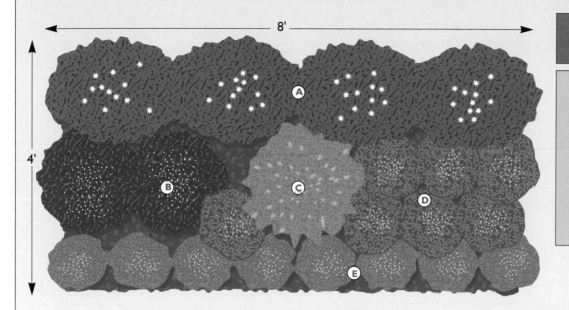

8'

4'

PLANT LIST

A. Feverfew, 4, 3 feet tall

B. Basil, 2, 2 feet tall

C. Sage, 1, 2 feet tall

D. Santolina, 7, 18 inches tall

E. Thyme, 8, 1 foot tall

1. Measure a 4 x 8-foot area and remove sod and stones. Till the soil to a depth of 1 foot. Spread 3 to 4 inches of compost over the garden surface and till again, 3 to 4 inches deep. Plant all herbs at the same depth they grew in their containers.

2. Beginning at the back left corner of the garden, plant the 4 feverfews (A) 2 feet apart across the back.

3. Returning to the left side, 2 feet in front of the feverfews, plant 2 basils (B) 18 inches apart. Plant 1 sage (C) 2 feet to the right of the basils.

4. Two feet to the right of the sage, plant 2 rows of 3 santolinas (D), each 1 foot apart. Plant the first row 14 inches in front of the feverfews. Stagger the second row 1 foot in front of the first. Plant the final santolina between the sage and basil as shown.

5. Plant 8 thymes (E) 1 foot apart along front edge of the garden.

6. Water plants well and mulch with 2 to 4 inches of compost.

HERE'S HOW

DRYING HERBS

Cut herbs in the morning after the dew has dried and just before they come into bloom. Remove any damaged leaves. Tie stems together in 1-inch-thick bunches with cotton string and hang upside down at least 6 inches apart in a warm, dry place out of direct sun. A dark, well-ventilated attic is ideal. In dusty areas, place herbs in a paper bag and secure the top. When crispy dry to the touch, package in airtight containers. Pack whole leaves when possible and crush just before use.

A Tasteful Mixed Border

THIS GARDEN THRIVES WITH

SUN	WATER	SOIL
Full	Medium	Average

Mixed borders are gardens that contain shrubs, perennials, and annuals often located in front of a fence, wall, row of trees or other shrubs. They can be tucked into an area devoid of foliage and flowers or planted in front of a backdrop of shrubs or evergreens. The existing pieris shrub border in this garden, for example, has interest added by the colorful flowers planted in the semi-enclosure of the shrubs as well as all along the border front. Annual and perennial flowers, framed by the shiny, deep green pieris leaves, brighten the space and create additional interest in the planting.

Choose a design for your mixed border that will coordinate with existing plantings. The yard and garden surrounding this border are rather formal and so the symmetrical layout shown works well. If your yard has more random plantings, use a more informal, asymmetrical design. Also, keep your mixed border planting in scale with its surroundings. If your border fronts a row of large conifers, you may want to add a background grouping of shrubs so that small annuals don't look lost.

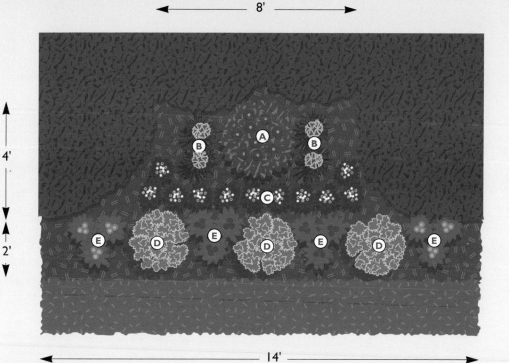

8'

4'

2'

14'

PLANT LIST

A. Zinnia, 1 red, 3 feet tall

B. Canna, 4 yellow, 5 feet tall

C. Cape marigold, 11, 1 foot tall

D. Variegated wintercreeper, 3, 4 to 5 feet tall

E. Geranium, 6 pink, 6 red, 10 inches tall

1. Prepare an 8 x 4-foot area in front of shrubs or trees, with an additional 2 x 14-foot-long strip in front, by removing sod or other ground cover, tilling the soil, adding 2 inches of compost, and retilling.

2. At back of border, plant 1 zinnia (A) in the center.

3. Plant 2 cannas (B) on each side of the zinnia, one in front of the other.

4. Plant a row of 9 Cape marigolds (C) in front of the cannas and the zinnia, and 1 more offset behind each end of the row.

5. Plant 3 variegated winter creepers (D) spaced 4 feet apart in front of the Cape marigolds.

6. Between the wintercreepers, plant 4 groups of 3 pink or red geraniums (E). Within each single-color trio, place 2 in the back and 1 offset in front.

7. Mulch your garden and water it thoroughly.

HERE'S HOW

CANNAS FOR INDOOR BLOOMS

Choose dwarf canna varieties for indoor blooms. In late winter or early spring, select a pot that has drainage holes and fill it to 3 inches from the top with a moisture-retentive potting mix. Place the rhizomes on the soil surface, then cover with 2 inches of soil mix. Place the pot in a bright, sunny window and keep rhizomes moist. After sprouting, continue to keep the soil moist.

Adding Accents for Design

A SIMPLE TRELLIS

Trellises are upright structures that can support climbing vines and will provide an attractive focal point in your garden even when standing alone. A trellis can also be used to create shade and to separate one kind of garden space from another.

Trellises come in a variety of shapes, sizes, and materials. Use the overall character of your garden, the desired plant, or a specific location to help you choose a trellis style. Vase-shaped trellises are appropriate for climbing roses, for example, because the canes can be easily trained to grow along the fan-shaped form. Rectangular trellises provide a wide base for climbing annuals, such as morning glories. An overhead arch will frame the entrance to your yard or gardens, as well as create a tranquil nook for rest or reading.

The amount of maintenance required by your trellis will depend on the material used. Common trellis materials include fiberglass, plastic, wood, and metal. Fiberglass and plastic require little in the way of care and maintenance. Natural wood, depending on the finish, may need only simple maintenance or repair. Painted trellises will have to be sanded and repainted every few years to keep them looking their best.

Once you have your trellis, position it where the vines you plant will receive proper sunlight. Unless your plant needs shade, place the trellis to the plant's north side. ❧

HAVE ON HAND:

▶ Trellis

▶ Tape measure

▶ Wooden mallet

▶ Stakes

▶ Wrench or pliers

Place two stakes on the north side of the planting area, the same distance apart as the trellis supports.

Replace stakes with trellis anchors. Check distance apart; sink anchors until 6 inches remain above ground.

Slide side supports into anchor bases and secure with supplied hardware. Tighten. Check stability.

Plant climbing plant(s) on south side of trellis and 12 to 18 inches from base for ease of maintenance.

A BEAUTIFUL BIRDBATH

A birdbath can act as a focal point in your garden while attracting beneficial birds to your yard. Place it in a sunny, open location near trees or shrubs, birdfeeders, or plants with berries or seed pods so birds can watch for predators, seek refuge, and find food all in one area.

A birdbath located near a water faucet or convenient to a hose will enable you to provide clean, fresh water all year round. You can announce its availability by letting a hose drip into the birdbath or by purchasing an aerator to splash water. You can also use the mist setting on a hose nozzle as a bird shower. If you do this every day at the same time, birds will appear specifically for this special treat.

There are some things to consider before and after you buy your birdbath. Pedestals should be no less than 3 feet high to protect birds from predators. The basin should be shallow since most birds don't like deep water. And, if you're contemplating a one-piece birdbath, take into account that a two-piece model will be easier to empty.

You may want to buy a submersible water heater to keep your birdbath from freezing in winter. Never introduce chemicals to keep the water from freezing or to kill algae; birds could be harmed as well. Spraying or using chemicals nearby can also be toxic to birds. ❧

HAVE ON HAND:

▶ Birdbath

▶ Tape measure

▶ Scissors

▶ Stake and string

▶ Lime for marking

▶ Shovel

▶ Decorative gravel

▶ Metal garden rake

Cut string to ¹/₂ basin diameter plus I foot. Drive stake into center of area; attach string; mark circle.

Use a shovel to remove sod and excavate the soil to a depth of 4 inches, keeping bottom even.

Fill depression with gravel. Tamp with rake to remove air pockets and to settle soil and gravel.

Rake the gravel until level. Measure to center of circle, place birdbath, and check level again before filling.

Basic Landscaping Projects

The parts of your landscape you use most often tend to be close to the house or along a well-traveled path. Improving those areas by paving walkways with stone or expanding your patio makes outdoor living more enjoyable and adds to the value of your home. Your choice of materials will help set the tone for the rest of your yard. When deciding how you will enclose your planting beds, or when choosing the type of surface for your patio, think ahead to your long-term plans for your landscape so that the different elements will work together harmoniously.

Whether you are installing a watering system or turning a washed-out path into a walkway, take accurate measurements so you can correctly estimate the amount of materials you will need for each project. Heavy lifting is required when excavating soil or working with stone. To prevent possible injury to your back, make lifting with your legs a habit. Take your time with these projects, and set your own pace. You will have less lifting to do if you have mulch, lumber, or other materials delivered close to where they will be used. While large projects are in progress, cover your materials with a plastic tarp to keep them clean and dry. ❧

Installing Drip Irrigation

Adrip irrigation system is the most efficient way to water your garden, in terms of both your effort and water use. Drip irrigation systems use a porous soaker hose or, in more expensive systems, a series of delivery hoses attached to emitters that slowly release water at the plants' roots where it is needed. Drip irrigation avoids problems associated with overhead sprinklers, which waste water, require time and effort to move, and can promote plant diseases by drenching leaves.

Install your system in early spring so you are ready to water by the time dry weather hits. Setting the hoses out early in the season saves effort since it is easier to move around in the garden before plants grow big. Also, you can see clearly how to space the soaker hoses for the maximum benefit of all the plants in your garden. If possible, design drip irrigation systems so the soaker hoses can be left in place all season. You may wish to hide the hoses under a loose mulch such as bark chips.

You will probably need one or more ordinary hoses to connect the soaker hose(s) to a distant faucet. Measure the distance from the faucet to the nearest point of each growing area so you can purchase the shortest connector hoses needed Plan to remove the connecter hoses between waterings if they cross areas of heavy traffic or lawn that needs mowing.

If you wish to run more than one hose from a faucet, purchase a splitter, which attaches directly to the faucet. Each branch of the splitter has its own on- and off-valve, giving you more flexibility.

Another way to enhance your drip irrigation system is by using a timer. The added expense is well worth it if you need to be away or have a tendency to forget to turn off the water. Timers allow you

HAVE ON HAND:

▶ Tape measure
▶ Ordinary garden hose
▶ Soaker hose
Optional
▶ Splitter attachment
▶ Timer

to program the system to go on and off at certain times and for a specific duration without your having to be there. Timers are available at any garden center and come with easy instructions.

The right frequency of watering depends on weather, soil type, and needs of specific plants. The goal is to keep garden soil evenly moist but not soggy. Watch your soil and plants for signals. Puddling and runoff are signs of overwatering. Too much water will cause leaves to yellow and plants to rot. Not enough water will cause leaves to droop.

Water deeply to encourage good root growth. Plants that are deeply rooted are well anchored and better able to withstand fluctuations in temperature or rainfall, and they can reach deep down into the soil to get nutrients. Adjust water pressure until water soaks in slowly rather than runs off the surface. ❧

Early in spring, measure distance from faucet to garden to find number and lengths of hoses needed.

Attach splitter (and timer) to faucet; connect ordinary hose(s) to lead from faucet to growing areas.

Snake soaker hoses along rows in vegetable gardens and between plants in flower beds and borders.

Attach soaker hoses to connector hoses and test system to be sure it delivers water at the right rate.

Installing a Simple Patio

A properly installed patio located just outside your back door serves as an outdoor room—a place for relaxation, eating, entertaining, and working on projects that are too messy for the kitchen table. As a transition area between the house and the rest of the landscape, a patio has the feel of the outdoors with the tidiness of indoor space.

Determine the size of your patio by considering your available space, its relationship to the scale of your house, and the furniture and equipment it needs to hold. For example, to accommodate a standard picnic table with benches, a barbecue grill, and two lawn chairs with a small table, you will need an area at least 12 feet on each side, or 144 square feet.

Paving slabs of natural or reconstituted stone, plain concrete, bricks, or block pavers can be used for your patio floor. Bricks and concrete pavers are relatively inexpensive to use. When set in a properly prepared bed, they can mold themselves to the slight shifts that develop in the subsoil—common around a new house. When deciding whether to dry-lay your paving materials in sand or stone dust—very fine, crushed gravel—or set them in a concrete base, consider your site, design preferences, and climate. 🌿

DRY-LAID BRICK

This 12 x 12-foot patio is large enough for both grilling and dining. The basket-weave pattern shown here is a simple way to position bricks into a smooth surface that drains quickly. If your soil has poor drainage, lay down a bed of gravel before adding stone dust and sand. ✿

HAVE ON HAND:

- ▶ Tape measure
- ▶ Twelve marker stakes
- ▶ Hammer
- ▶ String
- ▶ Shovel
- ▶ Metal rake
- ▶ Stone dust
- ▶ Water
- ▶ Landscape fabric, 12 x 12 feet
- ▶ Four 8-foot landscape timbers and four 4-foot timbers
- ▶ T-square
- ▶ Spikes
- ▶ Carpenter's level
- ▶ Clean sand
- ▶ Kneeling board
- ▶ Bricks, approximately 650
- ▶ Wheelbarrow
- ▶ Broom

Choose site. Hammer two stakes at each corner and three stakes along the outermost edge of each side. Tie string to stakes to create square.

Remove large rocks or other items from area. Use shovel to clear area to a depth of 10 inches. Level the area with a metal rake.

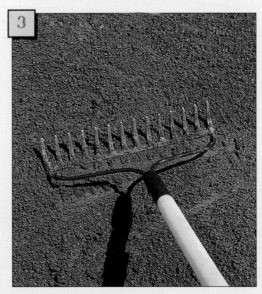

Add a 4-inch layer of stone dust to the excavated area. Distribute with rake to make a level bed for patio. Water thoroughly so it settles.

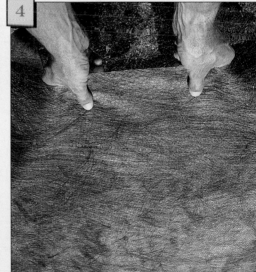

Place landscape fabric over level stone dust. This will prevent weeds from growing up between bricks in the future. Stretch edges to each side.

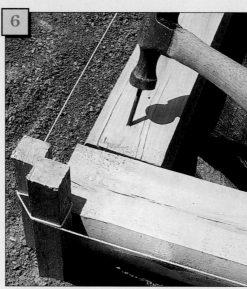

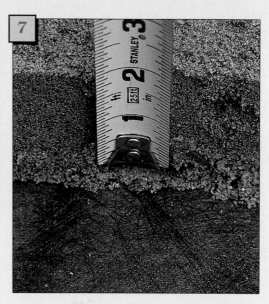

Place a 4-foot and an 8-foot timber along each edge, just inside the stakes. Hammer stakes in so they hold timbers firmly in place. Level area.

Use a T-square to ensure corners are square. Nail corner timbers together with spikes. After all corners are nailed, check with level.

Add 2 inches of clean sand on top of stone dust. Water layer well to settle the sand, tamp and smooth with a rake when dry enough to work.

Arrange bricks on top of the sand, tapping into place with a hammer handle. Kneel on a board as you go to avoid making sand base uneven.

Keep the surface of the bricks you are placing even. Use a level to check each section or row and add sand to even surface as needed.

To keep bricks in place and give a finished look to your patio, add a thin layer of sand to patio surface, and sweep to fill spaces between bricks.

Alternatives

INTERLOCKING PAVERS

Interlocking pavers are formed from durable concrete material. They are easy to work with and provide clean, straight edges because they are uniform. Pavers are also very stable, providing a hard, even surface that is easy to clean and to maintain with either hose or broom. Because they are available in a variety of colors and shapes, it's easy to choose a paver that complements your home and garden as well as one that offers an interesting, finished geometric pattern to your patio area. Because of its contemporary look and feel, a surface made with pavers is especially suited to modern surroundings.

Preparation for paver installation is similar to that of brick. If your soil drainage is poor, first put down a level bed of gravel. Then, fit the pavers together tightly and evenly; with the more informal look of brick, this is not as important. Use a heavy rubber mallet to knock on the side of each paver after it is placed. Remember to make sure the crevices between the pavers are uniform for a finished, formal look.

GRANITE

Granite is an excellent natural surface for your outdoor patio. This exceptionally durable material provides a naturally beautiful texture and color and is suitable for use in almost any landscape. Although more expensive than other pavers, granite paving stones are long lasting and easy to maintain; they don't become slippery when wet and they're easy to clean with water or a broom. You can plan a design that is made completely with the same size granite stone or you may want to combine sizes (and even colors) to create a unique and personal look. If you have a stone foundation, consider building your patio up against your house. The patio will then look like a natural and permanent extension of your home.

You can place your granite patio stones on stone dust or concrete with a 2- to 4-inch layer of crushed gravel. Lay it as you would loose bricks, or allow 1- to 2-inch crevices between the stones. Fill these crevices with a mixture of equal parts of sand and weed-free compost and plant with creeping thyme, sweet woodruff, or other small plants with aromatic foliage. In very damp settings, you might also plant plugs of native moss in the crevices.

Installing a Garden Walkway

Establishing a garden walkway will add interest and definition to your landscape. Your walkway might serve as the shortest distance between two well-traveled points, or lead strollers to meander through special parts of your garden. It can also serve as a focal point and be a destination in its own right.

A path directs the way you move through the landscape, serving as a means of traffic control. A well-placed garden path can protect your beds and large areas of ground cover from being trampled. Install pathways to replace or prevent worn tracks in your lawn. If possible, make them 3 to 4 feet wide, so that two people can walk side by side. And consider making your walkway of stone. Stone paths are well worth the effort they take to install as they delight the eye and last for many years.

To enhance the character of a stone walkway, try planting low-growing perennials between the stones. Ground-hugging herbs with fragrant foliage, such as creeping thymes, Roman chamomile, and Corsican mint, are popular choices; they release their delightful scents when crushed underfoot. In moist, shady spots, native mosses are perfect for growing between stones.

FIELDSTONE PATH

Flat pieces of unfinished stone, called fieldstone, are often sold by masonry supply companies. For a walkway 4 feet wide and 20 feet long, plan on using a ton of fieldstone. If fieldstone is not available in your area, you can use the same procedure to install a walkway made of concrete pavers or any type of flat stone. 🌺

HAVE ON HAND:

- ▶ Marker stakes (two per each 3-foot length of walkway)
- ▶ Twine
- ▶ Small sledgehammer
- ▶ Tape measure
- ▶ Fieldstone
- ▶ Shovel
- ▶ Pick or mattock
- ▶ Metal rake
- ▶ Landscape fabric
- ▶ Stone dust
- ▶ Clean, coarse sand

Use stakes and twine to mark outline of walkway. With a sledgehammer, drive stakes into ground at 3-foot intervals along walkway sides.

Measure walkway length and width and multiply to get square footage. Use this figure when ordering fieldstone.

Pile fieldstone or have it delivered as close as possible to site to save extra hauling. The pile may kill grass if left for more than two weeks.

Excavate the soil from the walkway area with a shovel. Remove soil to a depth of the fieldstone's thickness plus 4 inches.

With pick or mattock, remove any large stones you encounter. Smooth excavated walkway with a metal rake so base appears roughly level.

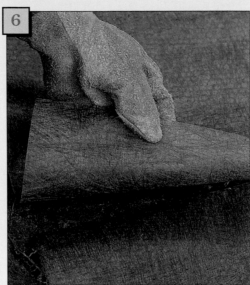

Spread landscape fabric over entire base to keep the walkway free of weeds. To join pieces, overlap edges by a few inches.

Spread a 3-inch layer of stone dust evenly over landscape fabric. Rake it level. Tamp down and smooth with the back of the metal rake.

On top of the stone dust, spread an inch of clean, coarse sand. Tamp and level with rake to form a firm foundation for your stone walkway.

Arrange all stones on top of the sand. Then use the wooden handle of the small sledgehammer to level each stone and settle it into the sand.

After all the stones are settled in place, fill in the cracks between stones and along the edges with additional coarse sand.

Alternatives

A MULCH WALKWAY

A walkway made of shredded bark mulch or bark chips is ideal for woodland walks, informal garden paths, and utility paths for garden carts and other equipment. Bark is also quiet to walk on and blends nicely with natural surroundings.

A mulch path is quick and easy to install. First, clear the path of eye-level branches and other obstructions. Remove rocks with a pick and rake the area smooth before applying a 3- to 4-inch layer of mulch. Spread mulch evenly over the entire area and rake it smooth. If the path is surrounded by lawn, install edging on either side to help keep mulch in place. Check the depth of the mulch every year and renew as needed.

Several kinds of bark mulch are available either bagged or in bulk from garden centers. Avoid the very large, chunky materials, which make an awkward walking surface. A standard bag of bark mulch is approximately 40 pounds. This amount of mulch can be expected to cover an area of 2 square yards to a depth of approximately 2 inches. To cover a large area, it is more economical to buy mulch in bulk (by the truckload). ❦

A GRAVEL WALKWAY

Gravel paths are easy and inexpensive to install, and they provide a clean, durable surface that makes a pleasant sound when crunched underfoot. Because gravel packs well, carts and wheelbarrows move easily over it, and its fine texture makes it especially useful for small or narrow places.

Choose a color that blends well with your surroundings. A very pale gravel will look right at home in a desert environment or by the sea, while a darker gravel will look more natural in wooded areas. Choose a gravel diameter smaller than 1 inch for comfortable walking. Small, rounded pea gravel or pea stone makes a particularly nice surface.

Begin by clearing the path of any obstructions. Install landscape fabric to minimize weeds, keep gravel from disappearing into the soil below, and keep it clean. Secure the landscape fabric and keep gravel in place by edging on either side. You can use bricks set on end, treated 2 x 4 lumber, landscape timbers, or commercial edging strips. For maximum longevity, install gravel over a 3-inch base of crushed stone. After applying each wheelbarrow load of gravel, smooth it over with a metal rake. ❦

Building a Raised Bed

Raised beds, where garden soil sits above ground level, are an attractive addition to your landscape as well as an easy way to solve garden problems. A raised bed allows you to create ideal soil conditions for specific plants, from adequate drainage to the appropriate nutrients. With the right soil in place you can include more plants closer together for a beautiful display or a more productive harvest. In addition, planting can begin earlier since the soil in raised beds warms faster in the spring—a good reason to consider building and filling your raised bed in the fall of the year.

Convenience is another advantage of the raised bed. A 4-foot-wide bed can be planted, weeded, and watered from the bed's perimeter. Soil compaction is avoided, and the loose soil is easy to work. If you are planning to build more than one raised bed, keep wheelbarrow and garden-cart access in mind, and mulch paths between beds with shredded bark or sawdust to keep weeds under control.

Whether your bed contains flowers, vegetables, herbs, or shrubs, match the scale of its plants to the scale of the bed. It will add an orderly and appealing element to your landscape or garden. 🌿

A WOODEN BED

Wooden raised beds are economical, and no special equipment or expertise is needed to build them.

Use air- or kiln-dried lumber where edible plants are grown. Pressure-treated lumber, though more durable, may leach toxic metals into garden soil. Do not use creosote-soaked timbers for edibles.

You may want to drive stakes at set intervals along the bed's exterior to reinforce the frame against soil pressure. 🌿

HAVE ON HAND:

- Tape measure
- Four marker stakes
- String
- Garden spade
- Metal rake
- Three 2 x 4s, 8 feet long, one cut in half
- Eight 3-inch wood screws
- Screwdriver
- Four 4-inch L-brackets
- Carpenter's level
- Sixteen 1-inch wood screws
- Wire mesh, 4 x 8-foot piece
- Wire cutters
- Two dozen 1-inch roofing nails
- Hammer
- Soil and compost
- Water

Optional
- Eight stakes, 1 x 1 x 18 inches

Mark off intended site with stakes and string. Position bed to receive maximum sunlight by orienting long sides north to south.

Remove sod and any large stones from bed area. Till the soil to a depth of 3 inches. Level with back of rake head.

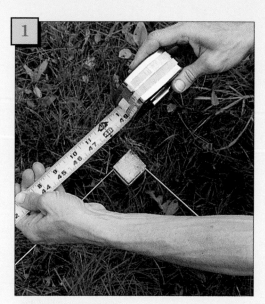

Arrange lumber around bed's edges. Drill pilot holes for 3-inch wood screws. Fasten frame with two screws in each corner.

Reinforce box corners by attaching a 4-inch L-bracket to the inside of each corner using 1-inch wood screws.

Position the box over your site and check to see that it is level. If not, dig shallow trenches at bed perimeter to level it.

Unroll wire mesh. Use wire cutters to remove a 2-inch square from each corner. Fold the 2-inch edges up 90 degrees. Line bed with mesh.

Attach mesh to sides with 1-inch nails at 1-foot intervals. Make sure nailheads overlap mesh. Your bed is now safe from burrowing rodents.

Fill the bed with a mixture of 90 percent soil and 10 percent compost to within 2 inches of the top of the frame. Do not overfill.

Smooth the soil with the back of rake head to create a level planting surface. Water the bed thoroughly to settle soil.

Revisit your new bed the next day and add soil to low areas where settling may have occurred. Water any amended spots before planting.

Alternatives

A TIMBER RAISED BED

Landscape timber, a heavy-duty yet attractive lumber cut to a standard 4 inches by 4 inches, is an excellent choice of material for a long-lasting raised bed. Ideal for jobs where a large amount of soil needs to be supported, it is a vast improvement over the massive, creosote-soaked railroad ties that have been used for raised beds in the past. Landscape timbers are readily available at most home and garden centers.

The sturdy, rustic-looking lumber is easy to stack, making it possible to build your soil to whatever depth you choose. Support, however, is needed to keep the timbers in place over time. As with other wooden beds, you can attach L-brackets to the inside of each corner and drive in wooden or metal stakes along the exterior of the bed to secure the timbers against soil pressure. Better yet, use heavy-duty bolts to fasten the corners.

Building your raised bed with landscape timbers has another benefit. Once your bed is tilled and work in the garden is under way, the timbers' width provides a convenient place to sit, reducing the amount of bending required to plant, weed, and harvest. ❧

A FREESTANDING RAISED BED

The freestanding bed, a raised bed with no built structure to contain it, offers many advantages. It is the fastest and the easiest design to build. In addition, it is the least durable—a distinct advantage when shape, size, and use for your bed may change from one year to another. In a vegetable garden, for example, it's important to rotate types and placements of crops in order to avoid diseases and soil depletion. And if you're not certain you'll like a raised bed in a particular spot, its impermanence makes it the easiest type to move or eliminate.

A freestanding bed could be your best choice if space is limited. You can increase planting area and yield by sowing crops across the top and sides of the bed. Though the sides of freestanding beds will naturally erode from rain and routine watering, a layer of straw mulch will lessen the impact of water hitting the soil surface. Planting the sides of the bed also helps hold the soil.

You can build freestanding raised beds up to a level of 8 inches without having to contain the soil. Keep in mind that these beds are less tidy than other types and should be used where a little soil in the walkways is acceptable. ❧

Edging Your Driveway

THIS GARDEN THRIVES WITH

SUN
Full

WATER
Medium

SOIL
Fertile

The first part of your landscape that people see is your driveway. Finishing the edge of your driveway with naturally neat plants will make your entire front yard look more polished and will serve practical purposes as well. The soil along driveway edges tends to wash away, but a narrow, mulched border of deeply rooted plants can help prevent this problem. Edging your driveway also helps eliminate the weeds that often grow in the transition area between a lawn and any paved surface.

When designing an edging for your driveway, make sure you allow ample room for people to get into and out of their cars. Also avoid having your edging interfere with traffic patterns or play areas. The end of the driveway closest to the street usually has more room for creative landscaping than the areas closer to the house.

Your driveway edging can be a thin ribbon of a single plant or a narrow bed planted with several different plants in a repetitive pattern. Try to include small evergreens to give the edge form and definition during the winter. Between your cultivated plants and adjoining swaths of lawn, install a strip of hard plastic, stone, or brick edging to stop lawn grass from creeping toward the driveway. ❧

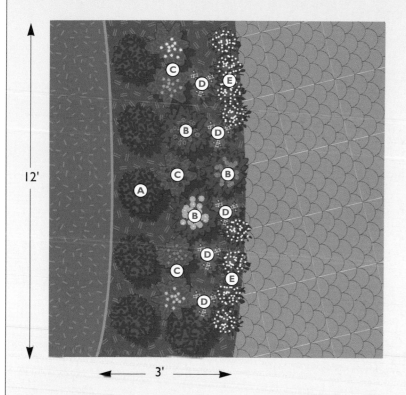

12'

3'

PLANT LIST

A. Edging boxwood, 6, 1-3 feet tall

B. Miniature rose, 3, 16 inches tall

C. Stock 'Brompton Dwarf', 5, 18 inches tall

D. Pansy, 15, 9 inches tall

E. Sweet alyssum, 8, 6 inches tall

HERE'S HOW

WINTER DE-ICING

In areas with cold winter climates, avoid using driveway de-icing compounds that contain rock salt or sodium chloride. Instead, use those made with calcium chloride or urea, which won't damage edging plants.

1. Remove sod from a 3-foot-wide strip along the driveway. Use a spade to cut horizontally beneath the grass so that 1 inch of soil remains attached to grass roots. Roll up sod in sheets and transplant to another part of your yard. When the sod has been removed, cultivate the soil and work in a 3-inch layer of compost.

2. Plant five container-grown edging boxwoods (A) along lawn side, 2 feet apart. Plant one more, 1 foot from driveway edge, as shown, to establish pattern. Plant miniature roses (B) in a triangular group to become a focal point in the edging bed.

3. Plant stocks (C) 2 feet apart down the center of the bed to form a broken line for the length of the bed.

4. In groups of three, plant pansies (D) 1 foot from driveway side of the bed. Space each group of pansies 30 inches apart to form an irregular line down the length of the bed.

5. Plant sweet alyssum (E) 8 inches apart along the driveway side of the bed. Thoroughly water all plants. Cut a clean edge where the bed meets lawn, and install a hard edging. Mulch the bed with 2 inches of shredded bark or another attractive mulch.

Designing to Conceal

Every yard has objects or views that would be better unseen. The projects in this section show how you can use design techniques to reduce or hide undesirable views, call attention to desirable ones, and flatter the best features of your house and yard.

When landscaping to conceal certain features or views, the challenge is to hide problems without having your improvements call attention to the problem itself. To accomplish this trick, use the design principle known as repetition. For example, if you use a fence or hedge to conceal a piece of machinery and that is the only hedge or fence in your yard, it tends to draw attention to itself. However, if you repeat the same hedge or fence in other parts of your yard, the features you are trying to conceal will blend into the overall design.

Other projects in this section show you how to use specially designed beds to draw attention away from a foundation that is too high or too low. You will also learn how to use arbors or trees to frame views that lack depth or interest, as well as techniques for concealing unattractive views in your landscape. In these situations, designing to conceal is often a simple matter of using plants and structures to balance horizontal or vertical lines that are a little too strong. ❦

Creating a New View

Frame desired features, conceal unwanted ones, or simply add a beautiful element to your landscape by installing an arbor such as the one shown here, or by planting a border of evergreens or native plants that grow vigorously in your area. There are virtually hundreds of ways to enhance the best features of your landscape, screen less pleasant views, and add value to your property.

Arbors are traditional architectural features that support climbing plants and add vertical accents. Your arbor can act as a beautiful gateway to a garden path, separate one area of your landscape from another, and allow you to frame a view in the most attractive way possible. Most home and garden centers carry prefabricated arbors that can be set in place quickly.

Screening and defining a view can also be accomplished with plants alone. The classic evergreen hedge is a handsome, year-round feature that can screen unattractive features and define your landscape. Many juniper and arborvitae species are well suited to this task.

For a less formal approach, native plant species will provide variation and natural good looks, as well as attract birds and butterflies to your garden. 🍃

INSTALLING AN ARBOR

If the arbor you choose is made of wood, a treatment with wood preservative or a good coat of paint will add years to its life.

When you prepare the holes in which your arbor will be set, take note of the length of its legs to be certain it will stand at the appropriate height.

Match climbing plants to your arbor's strength and consider the conditions they need for growth. Plant 8 to 12 inches from outside of arbor to allow maintenance without disturbing plants. ❧

HAVE ON HAND:

- ▶ Prefabricated arbor
- ▶ Four marking stakes
- ▶ Hammer
- ▶ Posthole digger
- ▶ Five gallons of gravel
- ▶ Carpenter's level
- ▶ Tape measure
- ▶ Topsoil

Optional
- ▶ Mulch

Place arbor in your chosen location. Check its position from both sides for the best aesthetics. Mark position of each leg with a stake.

Use a post-hole digger to make 1-foot-deep holes where stakes are placed. Reserve soil for use in Step 7.

Pour a bed of gravel in each hole that the arbor legs will rest on. Add gravel so that arbor stands straight and at the height you want.

Place arbor legs in holes and fill around them with gravel. Use a carpenter's level to check that the structure is plumb and level.

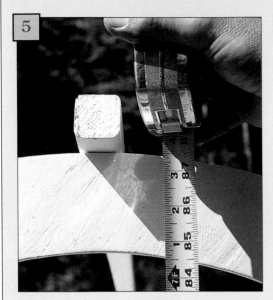

Measure clearance height through the arbor. The height should be at least 7 feet. Make necessary adjustments, recheck plumb, and level.

Fill each hole with remaining gravel to within 2 inches of the soil surface, making certain that arbor stays in place and is level.

For a better appearance, use soil from Step 2 to finish filling each hole; tamp down firmly. Use mulch or other material under arbor if you wish.

Plant a climbing vine 8 to 12 inches outside each arbor leg. Water thoroughly and mulch. Train vines to arbor as they grow.

HERE'S HOW

PLANTS FOR ARBORS

Your standing arbor will be an invitation to grow flowering vines that will curl around and cascade over it, enhancing the effect of your arbor.

Use such annuals as morning glory or hyacinth bean for fast, seasonal cover. For a more permanent effect try clematis. The hybrid Jackmanii, for example, offers mid-season, purple bloom. Avoid plants with thorns—climbing roses can snag clothing and scratch the skin.

Alternatives

AN EVERGREEN BORDER

Evergreens in an easily created border or hedge can work wonderfully either to conceal or to frame any spot in your landscape. A single-species border will function as if it were a uniform and solid hedge. A border made of mixed species or varieties of plants will have a less formal feeling and create an interesting view from a distance. For tight spots, a single-species hedge is most effective.

When choosing your plants, consider the ultimate size you want your border to be. Junipers, arborvitae, boxwoods, and yews all make excellent choices for a border that can be maintained at or will grow less than 12 feet high.

Where a taller screen is desired, you can use pine, blue spruce, Norway spruce, taller hemlocks, or arborvitaes and yews left untrimmed. Check with your local garden center for plant recommendations for your specific area. Ensure your success by using plants that will do well in your design. Single specimens of large evergreen trees such as hemlocks or pines work well for framing attractive views or for screening out undesirable ones. 🌺

A LOCALLY ADAPTED SCREEN

Plants indigenous to your region, or to another part of the world with a similar climate, make the sturdiest and most reliable screen of all. Perfectly adapted to their climate and environment, they can withstand fluctuations in temperature and moisture that other species cannot. For example, lavender and rosemary, two plants originally from the Mediterranean region, both thrive in the similar climate of California, as shown here. The use of locally adapted plants will enhance your feeling of harmony with the surrounding landscape.

Because native plants grow best in their "home zones," make sure the ones you choose are native to your local climate. Visit area nature trails and arboretums to get acquainted with pretty native plants, particularly those that might provide food and habitat for birds or other wildlife while framing or screening special views.

As native plants have become more popular in home landscapes, it has become easier to buy nursery-grown specimens. It is illegal to dig many native species, so always buy your plants from a reputable nursery or from a catalog specializing in nursery-grown native plants. 🌺

Concealing A/C and Pool Machinery

There is nothing attractive about the appearance of heat pumps, air conditioners, propane gas tanks, swimming pool pumps, or other machinery. You can conceal them by building or planting a screen that blends with the rest of your landscape. To make sure that the screen does not interfere with the operation of machinery, allow at least 2 feet of clearance all around and pay close attention to the location of buried utility lines. With heat pumps and air conditioners, you will also need to plan for the drainage of the condensation they produce.

You can create a screen by using lattice panels, shrubs, fencing, or a combination of these materials. Blend the screen into your landscape by making it match or coordinate with other structures. For example, you might paint a lattice panel to complement your house's siding or trim. Or, you could use a section of wood fence that matches other fencing used in your yard. Arrange outdoor seating so it faces away from the screened machinery. Also, locate ornamental features, such as a water garden or attractive statuary, where they will draw attention away from less attractive objects.

INSTALLING A TRELLIS

A framed trellis will let air circulate freely around your machinery. This 4-foot-wide panel stands 4½ feet high, but you can make it any size you like. 🌿

HAVE ON HAND:

- ► Tape measure
- ► Two wood stakes
- ► Hammer
- ► String
- ► Carpenter's level
- ► Posthole digger
- ► Shovel
- ► Two 6-foot-long 2 x 4s (posts)
- ► Pencil
- ► Saw
- ► Lattice panel 4 x 4 feet
- ► Box of ½-inch galvanized nails
- ► Four 45-inch-long 1 x 2 fir strips
- ► Two 4-foot-long 1 x 2 fir strips
- ► Fine-grade sandpaper
- ► Damp rag
- ► Exterior paint
- ► Paintbrush

Drive stakes 46 inches apart where posts will be located. Tie string between stakes. Use level to make sure it is straight.

Dig post holes 18 inches deep. Set posts in holes and refill halfway. Check with level again to make sure posts are straight. Firm soil.

Mark posts 54 inches from ground. Run a string between marks and adjust to make it level. Mark string line on posts with pencil.

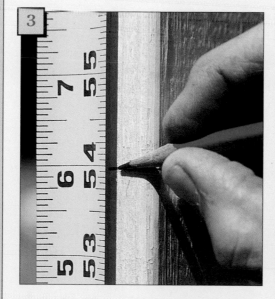

Fill holes, checking again to make sure posts are straight and tops are level. If top of the post projects above 54-inch mark, trim it to length.

Nail 45-inch-long fir strips to outside edges of lattice panel at top and bottom, leaving a 1½-inch margin on each side. Repeat on back.

Nail top corners of lattice panel to top fronts of posts. Check to make sure panel is horizontally level. Nail panel bottom to posts.

HERE'S HOW

CUTTING LATTICE PANELS

Lattice panels are usually sold in 4 x 8-foot pieces. Because they are so large and flimsy, the panels can be difficult to cut by yourself. Some stores will cut the lattice panels for you, provided you buy the whole panel. If cutting a lattice panel at home, get two helpers to support the ends of the panel as you cut. When working by yourself, try placing long pieces of scrap lumber under the panels to support them while you saw.

Nail fir strips to lattice panel sides and posts, spacing nails 8 inches apart. Sand lightly to remove splinters.

Clean panel with damp rag. When dry, paint the panel and posts or finish with sealant, stain, or polyurethane varnish.

Alternatives

HEDGE

If you already have a foundation planting close to machinery or anything else you want to hide, an easy solution is to extend the planting that already exists. In the photograph on the left, a possibly unattractive house foundation is concealed by arborvitae. This foundation planting of small evergreens can easily be extended as a hedge, and arborvitae is a good choice as it provides year-round concealment and can be kept to desirable height by clipping. Plants for screening purposes should not be so tall that they block more attractive views. Upright hedges require less space than mixed plantings, which explains their popularity in small, cottage-type gardens.

If a pathway or open area lies between your existing plants and, for instance, machinery, you can still use this approach and have the result look natural by making the area in front of the machinery into a planting bed. The key is to plant the screening bed with evergreens or shrubs that are used in other parts of your yard so that it looks like a part of your overall design. If nearby areas of your yard include a formal, clipped hedge, you can continue that element as your screen. ❧

FENCING

You can instantly hide machinery from view by erecting a fence. As with other types of concealing screens, you can avoid calling attention to the fence by using the kind that appears in other parts of your yard, or by matching the fence to nearby colors and textures. For example, if the machinery is located near a wood deck, natural wood fencing that mimics the style of the deck would work well. Near swimming pools where there are concrete surfaces, a low fence or wall made of perforated concrete might make an attractive screen.

Where fences are not already present in the landscape, you can still use a panel of fence to hide unattractive machinery if you keep the fence low and plant shrubs in front of it to make the fence less noticeable. Vertical slat fences, made from narrow boards nailed to top and bottom rails, are especially useful since their strong vertical lines draw the eye up and away from the fence. In addition, if you wish to make an attractive and useful enclosure in a small yard, add fencing at a right angle to the fence that is meant to conceal. ❧

Screening a High Foundation

THIS GARDEN THRIVES WITH

SUN
Full sun to part shade

WATER
Medium

SOIL
Average to acidic

Plants grown around the foundation of your house help frame the building by nestling it into the site. If the distance between the bottom of your windows and the ground is more than 4 feet, foundation shrubs will meld the house and grounds together gracefully while hiding less attractive features such as weep holes, crawlspace vents, and concrete block masonry.

Place the tallest plants at the back of your foundation bed. They need not be heavy bloomers, for an important part of their job is to serve as a backdrop for more colorful plants in the foreground. Include some evergreens to keep your foundation screened year round. Variations in form and texture among foundation shrubs add interest, but repeating the same combination of shrubs on both sides of the front door helps maintain a sense of unity within the landscape.

When fully grown, foundation shrubs should not crowd windows. Shop carefully for cultivars that will grow to appropriate heights and widths for the places where they will be planted. Also, plan for water runoff from gutters and downspouts. If you have drainage problems, install perforated drainage pipes under plantings as you prepare the soil.

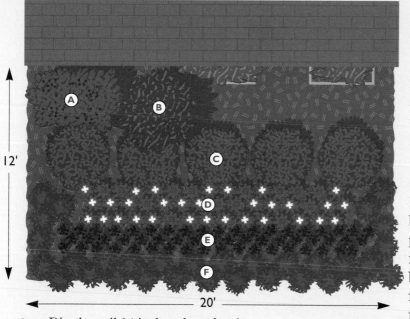

12'

20'

4. Plant boxwoods (C) the same as photinia, 6 feet from the house. Make sure they are upright and evenly spaced.

5. Excavate tulip bed 1 foot deep. Mix bone meal or high phosphorous bulb fertilizer into the bottom of the bed, following manufacturer's instructions. Set tulip bulbs (D) in a three-tiered arrangement as shown, with pointed ends of the bulbs facing up. If you are using two colors of tulips, mix the two colors in all three tiers, with a few more of the darker-colored tulips in the back tier and the lighter-colored ones in the front tier.

6. Rake soil smooth in remainder of bed, and set forget-me-nots (E) in an offset, three-tiered arrangement, as shown. Mulch all plants with a 2-inch layer of shredded bark.

7. Set English ivy (F) in foreground of bed, cultivating the soil slightly if it became compacted when you installed the larger plants. Mulch lightly and water well.

1. Dig the soil 14 inches deep for the foundation bed. Remove debris. Work in a 4- to 6-inch layer of soil amendments, including equal parts compost, peat moss, and composted manure. Don't cultivate the soil within 15 inches of your house. Mulch over this strip with shredded bark or pine needles.

2. Dig planting hole for photinia (A) 3 feet from corner end of the house. Set plant in hole, spread out roots, and check planting depth so that the highest roots will be covered with 1 inch of soil. Refill hole halfway, flood with water, and finish filling hole with soil.

3. Plant azalea (B) the same way, but set it higher in the planting hole. As you refill the hole, layer in 2 inches of soil, then 1 inch of peat moss. Flood the hole with water. Repeat layers until the top roots barely show through soil.

PLANT LIST

A. Chinese photinia, 1, 10 to 30 feet tall

B. Azalea, 1, 10 feet tall

C. Dwarf boxwood, 5, 4 feet tall

D. Darwin tulip, 45, 24 to 30 inches tall

E. Forget-me-not, 55, 8 inches tall

F. English ivy, 32, 8 inches tall

HERE'S HOW

WINDOW BOXES

Window boxes with colorful annuals such as pansies can be enjoyed from inside and outside your house. Allow a 1-inch recess between the top of the box and the soil line to keep the soil from splattering. To replenish, replace the soil every year and periodically water with liquid fertilizer.

Masking a Low Foundation

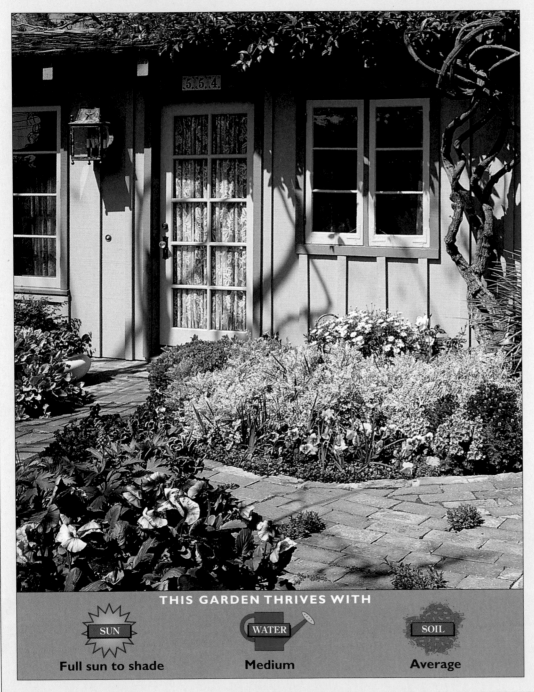

THIS GARDEN THRIVES WITH

SUN	WATER	SOIL
Full sun to shade	**Medium**	**Average**

If your home sits very low to the ground, you can make it seem taller by layering plants into foundation beds that gently slope away from the house. Crowding the foundation beds with massive shrubs would make the house look smaller. A spreading bed that skirts the foundation has the opposite effect. It pulls the frame forward, so the house appears tall and airy.

For the health of your house and your plants, the first step is to grade the site so that the house sits a few inches higher than the adjoining parts of your yard. Houses where the ground has not been graded away from the house may suffer water damage to sills or siding. Make necessary repairs before you begin any landscaping project. You can hire a landscape contractor to grade the site or do it yourself with a spade, rake, and a truckload of good topsoil.

Since small houses all too easily appear cluttered, try to keep your design lines simple and use walkways and edgings to create a neat and spacious look. Choosing light colors for your house and flowers will make each element appear larger. Using bright colors as accents will add interest to your flower beds as they conceal your foundation. ✿

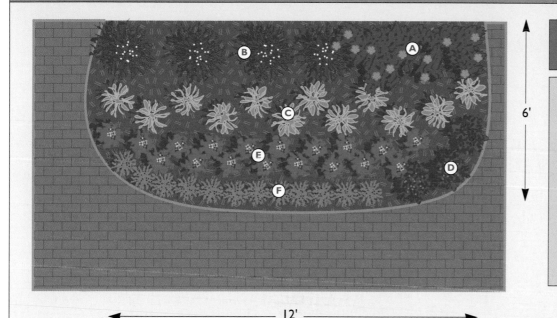

PLANT LIST

6'

A. Trumpet vine, 1, 30 feet tall

B. Shasta daisy, 4, 3 feet tall

C. Artemisia, 12, 3 feet tall

D. Butterfly flower, 3, 18 inches tall

E. Pansy, 18, 9 inches tall

F. Bugleweed, 12, 6 inches tall

12'

1. Amend the soil in your new bed by digging in a 3-inch layer of humus, such as a mixture of compost and peat moss, and two cups of 10-10-10 or other balanced fertilizer. Unless your soil is sandy, also mix in 50 pounds of sand to help the soil drain well.

2. Rake cultivated soil so that the part of the bed 2 feet closest to the house is 3 inches higher than the rest of the bed. Pave walkway with bricks or stones (see Installing a Garden Walkway, page 232).

3. Plant the trumpet vine (A) 15 inches from the house. Drive a 6-foot wooden stake into the ground midway between the house and the base of the vine. Tie the vine to the stake with cotton twine.

4. Standing on a board placed in the middle of the bed, plant the shasta daisies (B) 2 feet apart at the back of the bed. Remove the board.

5. Plant artemisias (C) 2 feet apart, offset as shown, in front of the shasta daisies. Plant pansies (E) spaced 1 foot apart, and also offset, in front of the artemisias.

6. Plant a group of butterfly flowers (D) 2 feet apart in a curve on the right. Plant an edging of bugleweed (F) at front 6 inches apart.

7. Water the entire bed and mulch between plants with a layer of shredded bark.

HERE'S HOW

ANNUAL VINES

You can use an annual vine as a vertical accent for a low foundation bed, and train it up a simple string, wire, or wooden trellis attached to stakes in the ground. Try climbing nasturtium, morning glory, scarlet runner beans for bright red blooms, or hyacinth bean for a touch of purple.

Hiding Utility Boxes and Wellheads

THIS GARDEN THRIVES WITH

SUN
Full sun to part shade

WATER
Medium

SOIL
Average

Utility equipment such as gas meters, wellheads, and electrical switch boxes are functional but unattractive landscape features. Their job is to keep your house comfortable, and it's up to you to make these awkward objects blend into your home landscape.

Several practical matters must be considered when concealing utility equipment. Digging near buried pipes or wires can have disastrous results, so find out where these lines are before beginning this project. If you do not know the location of underground lines, ask your local utility companies for this information. If utility equipment is located in a defined easement, which means the space is under the legal control of the utility companies, it's wise to limit your investment in any landscaping projects there.

In many cases, utility equipment can be camouflaged quickly and inexpensively by painting it a dark color and surrounding it with plants. Or, build a simple wooden box, paint it dark green, and place it over the equipment. When concealing gas or water meters with a box, include a hinged door so that repair people and meter-readers have easy access. And be sure any shutoff valves remain within easy reach. ❧

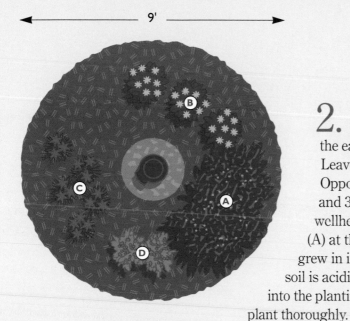

9'

C B A D

PLANT LIST

A. Lilac, 1, to 20 feet tall

B. Chrysanthemum, 3, 2 feet tall

C. Asiatic hybrid lily, 5, 3 feet tall

D. Dwarf astilbe, 2, 1 foot tall

2. Select the side of the wellhead with the easiest access. Leave this side open. Opposite the open side and 3 feet from the wellhead, plant one lilac (A) at the same depth it grew in its container. If soil is acidic, mix ½ cup lime into the planting hole. Water plant thoroughly.

3. Plant chrysanthemums (B) 2 feet from the wellhead, barely covering the roots with soil. Water and mulch. On the opposite side of the wellhead, plant five lily bulbs (C) in a clump, allowing 10 inches between bulbs. Cover lily bulbs with 4 inches of soil. Plant astilbes (D) 1 foot from the lilies.

1. If your wellhead has not been serviced recently, consider having it inspected before completing this project. If the wellhead is in good working order, proceed to clean and paint it, if needed. Dark green or brown are the best colors for outdoor camouflage. Finally, mulch around the wellhead with pebbles, bark, or another clean material. Spread the mulch in a 1-foot-wide collar around the wellhead.

4. Water all plants thoroughly, and spread 2 inches of organic mulch such as shredded bark beneath lilac and chrysanthemums. Mulch lilies and astilbes after they show vigorous new growth.

HERE'S HOW

WIRE BASKETS FOR BULBS

In many areas rodents are likely to dine on lily bulbs. To prevent rodent damage, loosely wrap individual lily bulbs in baskets made of ½-inch wire mesh before you plant them. Leave the top open, but have the chicken wire extend at least 2 inches above the bulb top.

Enhancing Difficult Terrain

Some of the most challenging places in your landscape can become its most dramatic features. Sweeping slopes, gnarled tree roots that lie at the soil's surface, and areas that receive heavy shade all have great potential. But rather than trying to change their nature, it's best to meet problem sites on their own terms. Before you decide on changes, let yourself imagine what the site might look like if nature had a century to work its wonders. Perhaps an eroded slope created by bulldozers would turn into a craggy stone outcropping. Maybe a dark, shady spot would become a moss-covered glen. The best way to landscape difficult spots is to mimic and accelerate the ecological changes that would occur naturally over time.

Difficult sites often hold hidden surprises underground, so spend time studying your problem area before you begin an improvement project. If you suspect that solid rock lies beneath a thin layer of soil, pound a thin metal rod into the ground to check the soil's depth. This is also a good way to find suitable planting pockets among large tree roots. As you make plans for enhancing your difficult site, eliminate natural hazards by filling in sunken holes or sawing off dead tree limbs. It's easier to see the potential in a problem area after it has been cleaned up and made safe. ❧

Transforming a Slope

A slope that's too steep to mow is frequently too steep to maintain as a garden. Although some sturdy plants will survive on a bank, most will need some help from stone, contoured terraces, or another device to hold the slope and restrain or channel the water following heavy rains. Managing the flow of rainwater is your biggest challenge, since unrestrained water will erode an incline as it rushes downward toward lower elevations.

In addition to reducing erosion, thoughtful landscaping of your slope will make it an easier place to work. In newly developed areas, the smooth banks left behind by bulldozers make for treacherous footing. Build some level terraces into your slope so that you will have solid places to stand and work. Be sure to choose low-maintenance plants that are suited to your site. Ground cover is useful in controlling erosion, as is a stone wall planted with easy-care rock garden plants. Weeding or pruning on a slope requires a certain amount of climbing and balancing, which you'll want to keep to a minimum. Make the lower parts of your slope as sturdy as possible so that you can use them as platforms when the higher tiers need your attention. ❧

CREATING A ROCK GARDEN

Since rocks tumble naturally down a hill, a low rock wall that restrains the bottom of a slope looks as if it belongs there. If you build a dry wall without bonding cement, you can plant phlox, sedums, and other rock-garden plants in carefully prepared pockets. The materials below will make a 20-foot-long wall 18 inches high. You can reduce the materials proportionally for a smaller area. Have landscaping stone delivered close to the site. 🐾

HAVE ON HAND:

- ▶ Five 12-inch wooden stakes
- ▶ Hammer
- ▶ String
- ▶ Shovel
- ▶ Wheelbarrow
- ▶ 200 pounds gravel
- ▶ Sturdy work gloves
- ▶ Landscaping stones, 1 ton
- ▶ 80 pounds dry peat moss
- ▶ 50-pound bag sand (if needed)

Use stakes and string to mark the location of your wall. Make it as straight as possible. Unnecessary contours will weaken the wall.

Use a shovel to dig a 14-inch-deep shelf into the slope. Set aside topsoil, rocks, and infertile subsoil in separate piles.

Dig the base by excavating 4 inches of soil from the bottom of the shelf. Make the front of the base 2 inches higher than the back.

Spread a 3-inch layer of gravel on the excavated shelf. Contour gravel if needed to keep the lip 2 inches higher than the back.

Set your largest, flattest stones on gravel, slanting them backward so the fronts are slightly higher than the backs. Set firmly in place.

Mix equal parts of topsoil and peat moss to make planting mixture. Add sand to clay soil. Pack mixture firmly into crevices.

Place plants in largest crevices. Cover roots with planting mixture. Water well to dampen roots and planting mixture.

Repeat Steps 5-7 to complete wall. Use long stones for second layer. Set stones so the wall tilts back slightly toward the slope.

Mix equal parts of small stones or gravel with the planting mixture. Firmly pack into pockets left between wall and slope.

Set plants in the bed you have created between wall and slope. Water thoroughly. Mulch with a 2-inch layer of small stones and gravel.

Alternatives

GROUND COVER

Many of the best ground-cover plants for slopes become invasive when grown in less rugged situations. However, the rigors of growing on sloping land act as a restraint on such rapid spreaders as English ivy and periwinkle. You can use ground covers such as these alone, in combination with bulbs, or you can flank them with low evergreen shrubs, such as creeping junipers. Large swaths of the same plant will give a slope the most natural look.

If the bank is badly eroded and consists mostly of rocks and subsoil, dig planting pockets twice as large as the rootballs of your plants and fill them with high-quality topsoil. Thoroughly dampen your plants before you remove them from their pots. Plant them slightly deeper than they grew in their containers.

As you set out your ground-cover plants, also install a fabric or straw mulch to control weeds and erosion while the plants are getting established. Landscape fabric covered with a decorative mulch of pine needles suppresses weeds and allows rain to soak into the soil beneath it. However, avoid using it if your ground cover grows by putting down surface roots. ❧

TERRACE

A terrace is a nearly level plateau built into a slope. Since water flows more slowly over a level surface, a terrace or series of terraces reduces erosion by slowing down rushing water. If your house is built on steeply sloping land, consider building a terrace to expand your usable outdoor space and help channel the flow of water around your house. Consult a professional first; this can be a big job.

The best place for a terrace is on the low side of your house. When planning, keep in mind that the area just below the terrace will receive copious amounts of water following heavy rains. To avoid creating an erosion problem, rock-lined conduits for water runoff can be built, either by you or by a contractor.

You may need stones to hold the edges of reinforcing timbers in place. Concrete retaining-wall blocks that are made to look like stone are easy to install and are also effective. To stabilize terrace edges with landscape timbers, they must be anchored into the slope with a perpendicular tie, called a deadman. This is best done by an experienced contractor. ❧

Masking Tree Bases

With a little planning and preparation, you can create a beautiful carpet of plants at the bases of your mature trees that will look great all season long. Shallow soil, too much shade, or competition for water and nutrients may have discouraged plants from getting established under your trees in the past. Working with these conditions, not against them, is your key to achieving the lush, finished look you want.

Since the area under your trees' canopies will be shady for a good portion of the day, choose plants that thrive in a shady location. Consider also that shade from different kinds of trees can vary. Evergreen trees, for example, cast deep shade all year round. Deciduous trees create varying amounts of shade. A large-leaved tree, such as a magnolia, will shade the area beneath it almost completely for most of the day. A tree with small, finely cut leaves, such as a Japanese maple, will create dappled shade beneath it.

Whether your choice is a planted ground cover, a moss bed, spring bulbs, or mulch, masking the bases of some of your trees will add unexpected interest to your landscape. ❦

INSTALLING GROUND COVER

Ground covers are used to create a carpet of lush green foliage and flowers. Many plant species work well in this capacity. Some excellent choices include hosta, ivy, pachysandra, ferns, bergenia, and periwinkle.

Follow the closest spacing requirements for the plants you choose, and fill the area with plants to create a dense ground cover. Plants need only enough room to grow and flourish; close planting will give you the best visual effect and will also conserve water and discourage weeds by completely shading the soil surface. ❧

HAVE ON HAND:

- ▸ Grass rake
- ▸ Topsoil (if needed)
- ▸ Balanced 10-10-10 fertilizer (nitrogen, phosphorus, potassium)
- ▸ Hand spade
- ▸ Watering can or garden sprinkler
- ▸ Edger

Rake away dead leaves, remove stones and debris from the area to be planted. Try not to disturb tree roots that may be near the surface.

Add topsoil to the area if the soil is shallow (less than 3 inches) at the base of the tree. Level soil with back of rake.

Broadcast a slow-release, balanced fertilizer such as 10-10-10 to nourish your developing plants as they begin to take hold.

Begin planting close to tree base, working out toward edge of bed. Use a hand spade to dig holes, moving slowly so as not to damage roots.

5

Set the young plants just below the surrounding soil surface so that a water-collecting depression is created around the plant base.

6

Plant in a triangular pattern for the best effect and maximum coverage, keeping recommended spacing in mind as you work.

7

Once your plants are in the ground, mulch and water them thoroughly to help settle the soil around plant roots without disturbing them.

8

Spreading lime or flour, mark bed's perimeter evenly, then follow with a long-handled garden edger to tidy appearance.

HERE'S HOW

HOW MANY PLANTS?

You can easily calculate the number of ground-cover plants you will need for a given area. Begin by measuring the bed to be planted. Next, calculate the bed's square footage. Then divide that number by the individual square footage requirements of the plants you intend to use. For example, some hostas require 2-foot spacing. To determine how many hostas you need, divide the total square footage of your bed by two. The number you arrive at is the number of plants needed to fill the area completely.

Alternatives

MOSS

Nothing rivals the serenity of an emerald green carpet of moss. Establishing a moss garden at the base of a mature tree takes prior preparation but, once established, it is virtually trouble-free. Moss is a good solution for an area under a tree where there is not enough topsoil because tree roots grow close to the surface.

Moss needs acid soil, so test the pH of the area where you will plant it; add gypsum or sulfur if the soil is not acidic. Because moss is not available in plant nurseries, look for it growing in your area. You can collect moss from its natural habitat as long as you leave some behind so the bed can reestablish itself. Lift it in sheets and keep it moist by wrapping in damp newspaper until you can plant it in your yard. Then place the moss on clean, cleared ground and press into the dirt with the palm of your hand. Don't be gentle; you want the moss to make solid contact with the soil surface so it won't dry out. The key word in moss gardening is water—and plenty of it.

Water your moss garden every day for a few weeks. Don't allow it to dry out completely. Maintain by removing leaves that fall upon it in autumn. 🍀

BULBS

Planting bulbs at the base of a tree in your landscape creates a beautiful splash of color and contrast, often before other plants in the garden have gotten started for the season. Spring bulbs emerge early, before deciduous trees have leafed out, and so get plenty of the direct sunlight they need.

For best results with your bulbs, add a phosphorus-rich fertilizer to the soil, such as bone meal or any of the commercial formulations recommended for bulbs. This increases the longevity of the planting and ensures that your bulbs will return year after year.

When planting spring-flowering bulbs in the fall, resist the temptation to form a perfect ring around the tree. Instead, scatter them unevenly among the tree's roots, taking care not to damage the roots. Doing this will give the planting a more natural appearance.

The list of bulbs you can use is nearly endless. Familiarize yourself with the wide assortment of tulips, daffodils, hyacinths, crocus, and scillas available from nurseries and garden catalogs. All do well in most soil types. Also, try some of the more unusual bulbs such as fritillaria, anemone, and cyclamen for a satisfying spring garden at the base of your tree. 🍀

Designing for a Wet Site

THIS GARDEN THRIVES WITH

SUN	WATER	SOIL
Sun to shade	**High**	**Average**

A wet spot in your landscape presents an opportunity to grow and enjoy a number of beautiful plants that you can't grow in ordinary, well-drained garden soil. Some species not only tolerate poorly drained soil but actually need the constant moisture in order to thrive. By planning your design around such plants, you can turn a potentially challenging area into a beautiful landscape asset.

When choosing plants for a wet site, keep in mind that some need full sun while others prefer a shady location. Check the amount of sunlight available in all parts of your wet site before deciding on your plant list. For the most attractive effect, include a mixture of different flowers, plant forms, and foliage shapes or textures. Placing such bold, upright plants as irises next to graceful, mounded plants, such as hostas, shows each off to its best advantage.

Other landscape features can be incorporated into this design for added interest. If your site does not already have standing water for much of the year, you can easily install a pond liner to create a shallow pool. Large rocks are a natural accompaniment to water features and lush, moisture-loving plants. Carefully chosen, weatherproof sculptures can also make attractive garden accents. ❧

8'

12'

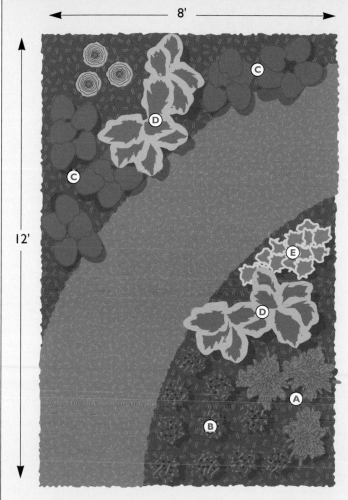

PLANT LIST

A. Astilbe, 3, 30 to 36 inches tall

B. Sweet violet, 10, 6 to 8 inches tall

C. Hosta 'Elegans', 5, 2 feet tall

D. Hosta 'Frances Williams', 4, 3 feet tall

E. Hosta, 'Shade Master', 1, 18 inches tall

3. Dig planting areas 14 inches deep on both sides of pathway, working around large tree roots. Mix a 4- to 6-inch layer of peat moss, compost, or other organic matter into the planting areas. Rake smooth.

4. Place boards on top of prepared soil and stand on them while planting three astilbes (A) 18 inches apart in the section of bed farthest from path.

5. Stand on boards if necessary to plant 10 sweet violets (B) 8 inches apart. Set violets at least 6 inches in from edge of the pathway.

6. Plant all hostas (C, D, E). Space hostas 2 feet apart and set them at least 1 foot in from the edge of the pathway. Water and mulch all plants.

7. Bury edges of the landscape fabric and mulch over pathway with pine needles, shredded bark, or light-colored pebbles.

1. Open the overhead canopy by pruning away low tree limbs and trimming nearby bushes. Rake area clean of fallen leaves and debris.

2. Fill in any low spots in pathway that may retain water after heavy rains. Rake center of pathway level, allowing a slight grade on the sides to improve drainage. Lay porous landscape fabric over the pathway.

HERE'S HOW

LAYING GRAVEL PATHS

Pathways paved with light-colored pebbles help brighten up shady places. They are also less likely to host slugs, a common leaf-eating pest in damp, shady situations. Line the bottom of your path with landscape fabric and bury the edges before adding pebbles. For firmer footing, place flat stepping-stones on the fabric and surround them with pea gravel.

Tackling the Elements

You can alter fundamental characteristics of your yard to make it more comfortable for you and your family. Blocking excessive wind, adding shady pockets to sun-drenched areas, or installing barriers to make your outdoor space more private enhance the value of your property by making your land more usable and attractive. Adding shade or windbreaks can also reduce the costs of cooling and heating your home.

Before you begin any of these projects, take some time to study the problem you are trying to solve. Refer to your landscape map to make sure the changes you make fit logically into the ways you plan to use your outdoor space. Plan ahead for pathways, play areas, and special gardens you may want to add later. Preserve the most desirable views, and make sure any structures you add are properly scaled to the size of your house and other large features in your landscape.

Whether you are bringing shade to sunny areas or slowing down the wind as it sweeps across your yard, the changes you make will create new environments for different types of plants. This diversity can strengthen the health and appeal of your landscape by attracting a vast assortment of birds, butterflies, and other wild companions. ✤

Creating Shade

Cool pockets of shade improve a landscape's appearance, provide comfortable spots to relax, and create places to grow plants that would rather not spend their days in full sun. Shady areas near the south or west sides of your house, where sunlight is most intense, can also make your home easier to cool in the summer.

The most natural way to create shade is to plant a tree, but some years must pass before a young tree will grow large enough to provide significant shade. Meanwhile, you can create a shady nook or passageway by building a pergola, an arbor with an open horizontal roof supported by columns or posts. This type of structure can be made from many different materials, including tree timbers, sapling poles, bamboo, split logs, or precut lumber. Unlike gazebos and other structures with roofs, pergolas allow rain and filtered sun to reach the plants growing beneath them.

In terms of landscape design, a pergola can work as a visual accent by itself, or it can link the house to special landscape features such as a colorful border or pond. It's also a great way to cool a sunny pathway that connects different gardens within the same yard. ❧

VINE-COVERED PERGOLA

This structure, built from standard lengths of lumber, can be painted for a formal look, or you can stain and seal it to create a more rustic mood. A bench can be built into the side of the pergola, or you can enjoy the filtered shade with portable seating.

Good plant possibilities for your pergola include climbing roses, clematis, grapes, honeysuckle, and trumpet vine. 🌿

HAVE ON HAND:

- ▶ Tape measure
- ▶ Four 1-foot-long stakes
- ▶ Hammer
- ▶ Posthole digger
- ▶ Shovel
- ▶ Four posts: 10-foot-long 4 x 4s
- ▶ Carpenter's level
- ▶ String
- ▶ Pencil
- ▶ Two lower side supports: 44-inch-long 2 x 4s
- ▶ Box of 16d galvanized nails
- ▶ Saw
- ▶ Two upper side supports: 48-inch-long 2 x 4s
- ▶ Two rafters: 8-foot-long 2 x 4s
- ▶ Nine top strips: 4-foot-long 2 x 2s

Mark the positions of the two back posts with stakes spaced 80 inches apart. Place stakes for front posts 42 inches from back post stakes.

Measure between diagonal corners to make sure the stakes create a perfect square. The two diagonal measurements should be the same.

Dig holes for posts 18 inches deep. Set posts in holes. Partially refill holes, using level to be sure uprights are straight. Finish refilling post holes.

Run a string around posts 16 inches from the ground, leaving front open. Check to be sure string is level and mark line on inside of posts.

Position lower side supports inside posts along level marks, checking again to make sure posts are straight and supports are level. Nail in place.

Run a level string between the tops of the posts as in Step 4. Saw tops of posts even. Run another level string 6 inches from tops of posts. Mark.

Attach upper side supports as in Step 5. Center the rafters atop the ends of side supports, on the outside of the posts. Nail rafters to posts.

Lay top strips across rafters, with end strips 1 inch inside ends of rafters, and others evenly spaced about 1 foot apart. Nail in place.

HERE'S HOW

SET POSTS IN CONCRETE

Even if you use treated wood, posts that are set in the ground eventually will rot. In addition, some soils are so light that they will not hold the posts firmly upright, even when they are set very deeply. Setting posts in concrete solves both of these problems.

Vibrations from nailing and sawing can ruin concrete footers, so use pieces of scrap lumber to brace poles in place while you are building your pergola, and fill the holes with concrete when your structure is complete.

Alternatives

USING TREES

The best shade trees, maples and oaks for instance, are deciduous: They will provide shelter from the sun in summer but allow the winter sun to filter through after they drop their leaves. Oaks grow steadily; several kinds may grow as much as two feet per year. Different kinds of maples have various growth rates. Check with your local nursery or Cooperative Extension Service for expert advice on shade trees appropriate for your area and their rates of growth.

Avoid planting trees such as hickories or mulberries that drop nuts or fruit. Their fallout may encourage animals or stain your walkways. However, some people enjoy the birds that are attracted to mulberry trees. Also, think carefully before planting pines, cedars, or other evergreen trees. Some are fast growers and will do a wonderful job of screening quickly but eventually cast so much shade that it is often impossible to grow anything in their shadows.

Planting shade trees is best done in late winter or early spring. Give your transplanted trees extra water their first year. Cover root zones with a mulch to discourage weeds and grasses and to eliminate the need for close mowing that might damage the main trunks.

USING YOUR HOUSE

You can create a delightfully shady spot just outside your house by building a modified pergola that extends the line of your roof over a patio and uses the side of your house as a windbreak. In addition to creating a comfortable bower from which you can enjoy the outdoors, a pergola will add to the permanent value and attractiveness of your home.

Shade can also be created in small courtyards, patios, and pool areas by attaching a canvas overhang to the eaves of your house. Canvas shades are usually taken down and stored during the winter even if you choose a fabric that is relatively rot- and mildewproof. You can make shades appear more permanent by securing them in summer to sturdy posts, perhaps of painted wood or iron, and attaching the canvas corners with the help of hooks and grommets. A local company that makes custom draperies might be able to help you with this sewing job.

A pergola constructed with treated wood will last a great deal longer than canvas shades and can be made into a charming extension of your garden. You can choose plants to grow overhead, perhaps climbing roses or wisteria, to create a beautiful, shady bower to enjoy all season long.

Installing a Decorative Barrier

The decorative barrier at left brings visual structure to an artful grouping of flowers and shrubs and helps frame the rest of the landscape at the same time. Installed in a corner of your garden or along the edge of your property, a short section of rustic fence defines boundaries while imparting a relaxed, pastoral mood. If your landscape looks a little too formal, a corner framed in weathered wood will lend a feeling of cozy warmth. This landscaping trick creates the illusion of enclosure while also preserving the impression of spaciousness.

Decorative barriers can fulfill practical landscape purposes, too. A short section of ornamental fence will direct the flow of foot traffic around delicate perennials, which should not be trod upon while they are dormant. Fencing can also serve as a secure trellis for prickly plants such as climbing roses. Perennial vines that need regular pruning to keep them well behaved, like trumpet vine or wisteria, are ideal candidates for fencepost planting. If a low-maintenance plan is more to your liking, flank your fence with a symmetrical group of junipers or other elegant evergreens for year-round drama and beauty.

WOODEN FENCE

This 16-foot-long, post-and-rail, angled corner fence can be built using precut materials purchased at building supply stores. The rail pieces come in 8-foot sections. Try to find posts and rails made from cedar, which resists termites and weathers to a light gray color. If you wish, you can use these instructions to make a longer, straight fence instead of an angled-corner one. 🐾

HAVE ON HAND:

- ▶ Three 1-foot stakes
- ▶ Hammer
- ▶ Four horizontal rails
- ▶ Posthole digger
- ▶ Tarp
- ▶ One corner post
- ▶ Two end posts
- ▶ Three heavyweight garbage bags
- ▶ Six thick rubber bands
- ▶ Shovel
- ▶ Carpenter's level
- ▶ 50-pound bag gravel
- ▶ Scissors

Drive a stake into the ground where the corner post will be placed. Lay two rails on the ground at right angles from the stake.

Drive stakes into the ground where the end posts will be placed. Remove the side rails from your work area.

Dig the hole for the corner post 2 feet deep and 1 foot wide. Set the excavated dirt on a tarp for use in later steps.

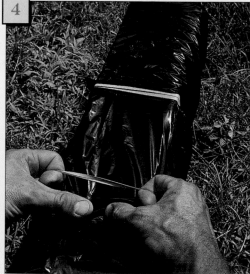

Place plastic garbage bags around post bottoms. Secure the bags to the posts with rubber bands placed 8 and 18 inches from the bottoms.

Place the corner post in the hole, turning it so the side holes face the end posts. Refill the hole with enough soil to hold the post straight.

Check location of end posts again by holding opposing side rails in place. Dig holes for the end posts, as in Step 3.

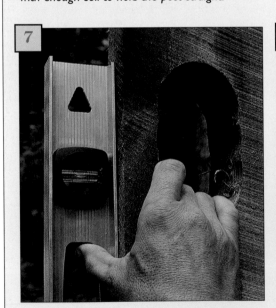

Assemble all pieces. Use the carpenter's level to make sure posts are straight. If needed, level side rails by adjusting the depth of end posts.

Refill holes with soil and gravel. Pack soil firmly around the posts with the handle end of your shovel. Trim off exposed edges of plastic bags.

HERE'S HOW

FINISH UNDER THE FENCE

If parts of your wood fence are anchored in grass, plan ahead to avoid tedious mowing and weed trimming around the bases of the posts. Before grass has a chance to grow around the posts, circle them with rounds of landscape fabric. You can also use a strip of landscape fabric to cover the area under the fence that is not used for ornamental plants. Mulch over the fabric with shredded bark, pine needles, or pretty stones. Small ground-cover plants such as ajuga and liriope can also be used as attractive, low-maintenance finishes under your fence.

Alternatives

HEDGE

The formal look of a hedge makes a lovely decorative barrier for many older homes. Historically, hedges have been used to emphasize boundaries between public spaces and private ones, and to create walls for outdoor rooms. If you are restoring an old house or cultivating a look of classic elegance for a new one, you may be happiest with a hedge.

Study hedge plants that do well in your area, and check with local nurseries to find the best cultivars. Many of the newer hedge plants resist common diseases and stop growing at specific sizes, so they require much less care than older cultivars.

When installing a new hedge, buy extra plants and keep them growing in large pots through the first winter. That way, if a plant from your original planting fails to grow or becomes badly damaged, you will have an exact match to plug into the space left in your hedge.

To shape your hedge, angle the sides out slightly so that the base is a little wider than the top. This will enable light to reach the lowest branches. The result will be more even growth.

WROUGHT-IRON FENCING

Small courtyards, patios, and other limited areas where every detail is important are ideal spots for elegant wrought-iron fences. While wrought iron is most familiar as an architectural detail, it can also be used very effectively as an ornamental accent in your landscape. You can also use small panels of wrought-iron fencing to create a lovely barrier along a narrow walkway in your side yard. Or dress up a modest entryway by edging its approach with a low run of decorative wrought iron.

Wrought iron is heavy and must be set in concrete if it is to hold up well to wind and wet weather. In addition to having an assistant help as you set the fencing in wet concrete, you will need to build a temporary reinforcing frame from inexpensive pine lumber to hold the wrought iron in place for two or three days, or until the concrete dries hard.

Ornamental vines make beautiful partners for wrought iron, but they must be able to withstand severe pruning from time to time, when the iron needs repainting. Especially in warm, damp climates, wrought iron can be counted upon to need some kind of maintenance every two or three years.

Establishing a Windbreak

THIS GARDEN THRIVES WITH

SUN	WATER	SOIL
Full	**Medium**	**Average**

If you live in a region where strong winds blow persistently, you can screen and protect your house and landscape by planting a windbreak. Wind increases the effects of high or low temperatures and robs plants of much-needed water in summer and winter. A windbreak reduces stress on landscape plants and makes your garden a more comfortable place for you and your family.

Since most windbreaks are situated where they will soften winter winds and block blowing snow, small- to medium-sized evergreen trees are the best plants for the job. You can space evergreen trees closely together to form a solid green wall that blocks an unwanted view, or you may want to allow more space between the trees so that they filter strong winds and frame a panoramic scene. Avoid using brittle trees such as tall, top-heavy pines, which are likely to split as they mature.

Planning will make your windbreak more effective. Determine prevailing winds by tying ribbons to several 4-foot-tall stakes on your property. A windbreak should buffer the wind at approximately a right angle to wind direction, but you can adjust the placement so that it not only buffers wind but also works well with the rest of your landscape. ❧

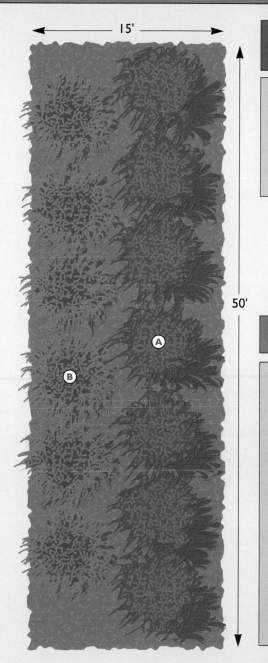

15'

50'

1. Choose a location for your wind-break at least 25 feet upwind of the area you wish to protect. Place stakes in the ground at the center and at both ends of a 50-foot line along your planned windbreak. Tie taut string between stakes. Tie short pieces of ribbon or cloth strips to the string at 8-foot intervals to mark planting holes for arborvitae.

2. Dig planting holes for the arborvitae (A) as deep as the plants' rootballs and twice as wide. Place plants in the planting holes and remove wires and wrapping material. Adjust soil beneath the plants as need-ed to make them stand straight at the same depth they grew in the field. Backfill with soil halfway; flood the holes with water and wait for it to seep in. Finish backfilling with soil. Mulch with a 3-inch layer of wood chips.

3. Plant 6 creeping junipers (B) in a line 10 feet in front of the arborvitae. Center the junipers in the spaces between the arborvitae. Install a sheet mulch of perforated plastic or landscape fabric on both sides of the junipers. Cover the sheet mulch with a 3-inch layer of wood chips.

PLANT LIST

A. Arborvitae, 7, 6 to 25 feet tall

B. Creeping juniper, 6,
6 to 20 inches tall

HERE'S HOW

DRIP WATER FROM JUGS

To create a slow water drip to your windbreak plants, make two small holes in the sides of plastic milk jugs, 2 inches from the bottoms of the jugs. Fill with water and place above root zones of the plants. The water left in the jugs below the holes will keep them from blowing away.

Improving Important Spaces

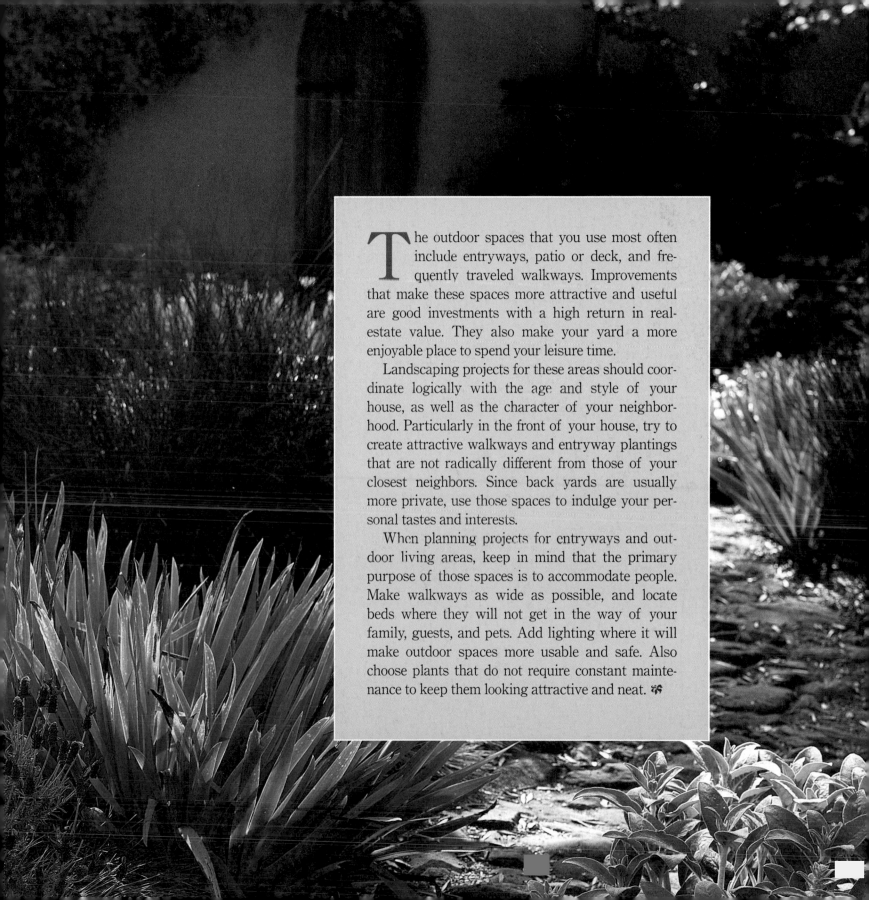

The outdoor spaces that you use most often include entryways, patio or deck, and frequently traveled walkways. Improvements that make these spaces more attractive and useful are good investments with a high return in real-estate value. They also make your yard a more enjoyable place to spend your leisure time.

Landscaping projects for these areas should coordinate logically with the age and style of your house, as well as the character of your neighborhood. Particularly in the front of your house, try to create attractive walkways and entryway plantings that are not radically different from those of your closest neighbors. Since back yards are usually more private, use those spaces to indulge your personal tastes and interests.

When planning projects for entryways and outdoor living areas, keep in mind that the primary purpose of those spaces is to accommodate people. Make walkways as wide as possible, and locate beds where they will not get in the way of your family, guests, and pets. Add lighting where it will make outdoor spaces more usable and safe. Also choose plants that do not require constant maintenance to keep them looking attractive and neat. ❧

Lighting Your Way

Outdoor lighting lets you stroll safely after dark. Light can also help deter prowlers. And, since most people work during the day, lighting greatly expands your opportunities for outdoor living when you come home from work.

To have the intense light needed for a basketball hoop or an outdoor workspace, you can mount spot floodlights on the eaves of your house. A relatively bright light at the front door makes sense for security reasons, but softer lights do a better job of illuminating steps, walkways, and special landscape features. Small, soft lights are easy to hide from direct view among shrubs or near stonework and can be positioned so they won't shine in your eyes. Most home supply stores carry a wide assortment of easy-to-install landscape lights.

Although solar-powered light fixtures are available, most outdoor lighting still runs on electricity connected to the electrical system in your house. Wiring for modest projects, such as lighting for a deck area and steps, can usually be connected to the circuits you already have. However, running an elaborate light system for a large landscape and pool will probably require a new circuit and fuse box. Unless you are skilled at wiring, hire a licensed electrician for this job. 🌼

WALKWAY LIGHTING

The steps on a deck can be illuminated with low voltage deck lights mounted flush against the posts that support the steps. Kits that include a power pack, cable, and six or more 7-watt bulbs in weather-resistant fixtures generally cost under $100 and use less electricity than one 60-watt, household light bulb. Study the kit's instructions before you begin the project. If you do not have an outdoor grounded electrical outlet to service your deck lights, have one installed by a licensed electrician. ❧

HAVE ON HAND:

▶ Lighting kit

▶ Tape measure

▶ Small flat head screwdriver

▶ Small Phillips head screwdriver

▶ Pencil

▶ Power drill and ⅟₁₆-inch bit

▶ Box of 1-inch cable staples

▶ Hammer

Obtain a suitable kit. Measure the cable's route from nearest outdoor electrical outlet to location of deck lights. Count number of lights desired.

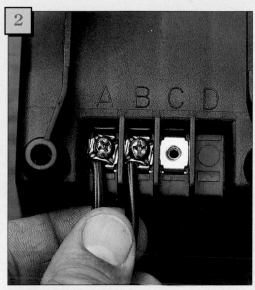

Attach cable wires to power pack from kit according to manufacturer's instructions. Screw connections down tightly.

Hang power pack on the wall within 1 foot of grounded electrical outlet and more than 1 foot above the ground.

Stretch cable along route where lights will be installed. Leave some slack. Allow 10 feet of cable between power pack and first light.

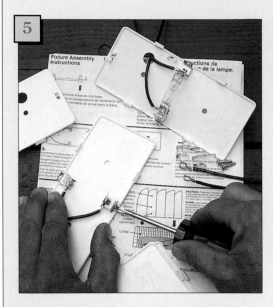

Following manufacturer's directions for lighting fixtures, attach wires to terminal posts or clamps on bases of fixtures. Install bulbs.

Mark holes for mounting screws. Drill guide holes. Screw bases in desired locations for lights. Snap on light covers.

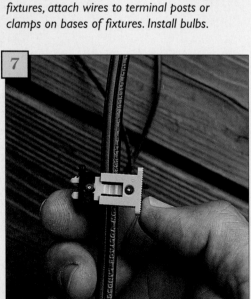

Connect cable to lights according to instructions. Plug in power pack and turn on. Check to see that all lamps light properly.

Secure cable to underside of deck with staples. Do not hit cable with hammer or compress cable with staples. Secure cover on power pack.

HERE'S HOW
UNDERGROUND WIRING

Even if you hire an electrician to install new wiring for outdoor lighting, you can save money by preparing the trenches for buried cables yourself. Buried cables are protected from moisture by a plastic covering, but it's up to you to make sure they will never be sliced by a shovel. Dig trenches 4 inches deep, and cover cables with any rigid material that will not rot, such as strips of fiberglass, PVC pipe, or even an old garden hose, before refilling the trench. Also, record the location of the new wiring on the base plan of your home so that you will always know where you should not dig.

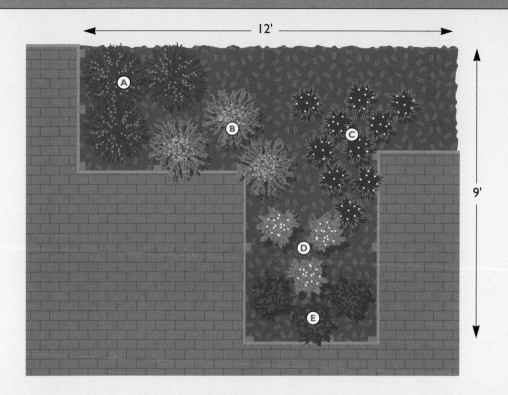

12'

9'

A. English lavender, 3, 2 feet tall

B. Santolina, 3, 2 feet tall

C. Alpine strawberry, 10,
6 inches tall

D. Golden marjoram, 3,
1 foot tall

E. Garden thyme, 3, 8 inches tall

1. To keep your patio free of spilled soil, spread a tarp or an old blanket over the bricks or other patio surface. Reinforce edges of patios made of unmortared bricks with 1 x 4 boards, held in place with wooden stakes. In areas where subterranean termites are common, use recycled plastic lumber or brick as an edging instead of wood.

2. Cultivate the soil in the bed 14 inches deep, and remove 4 inches of loose soil. Use a wheelbarrow to move this excess soil to another part of your yard. If your soil is sandy, work a 4-inch layer of humus into the bed. If your soil type is clay, mix a 2-inch layer of sand and a 2-inch layer of humus into the bed. Rake the bed smooth, mounding the soil slightly in the center if the soil level of the bed is higher than the surrounding patio.

3. Set English lavender (A) and santolina (B) in the rear of the bed, spacing the plants 18 to 24 inches apart to form triangles. Plant alpine strawberries (C) 6 inches apart with their crowns just above the soil line. Plant golden marjoram (D) and thyme (E) in the front, spacing the plants 1 foot apart in a triangular formation.

4. Add individual herb plants you like to open areas in the bed. Water well and mulch lightly.

HERE'S HOW

PROPAGATE HARDY HERBS

You can pot cuttings taken from hardy herbs in late summer and grow them indoors until the following spring. Cut a 4-inch-long piece of stem and remove the leaves from the bottom 2 inches. Plant the cuttings in small pots filled with a sandy potting soil mixture. Keep constantly moist until new growth appears.

Enhancing Your Front Walkway

THIS GARDEN THRIVES WITH

SUN
Full to partial

WATER
Medium

SOIL
Average

You can enhance the appearance and value of your property by planting an attractive border in front of your house next to the walkway, where it can be easily admired.

Front walkway beds work best if prominent plants are repeated often to create a clear and continuous pattern of color and texture. Choose flower colors that complement the colors of your house, and use plants that won't litter the walk with fallen leaves, berries, or other debris.

The fragrance of roses is a welcome addition to a walkway border as long as they are planted where their thorny stems won't be a nuisance to people using the walk. In general, steer clear of any shrubs or trees that grow so large they might crowd your windows or shade out neighboring plants. However, a carefully placed small tree, used as an accent, can help dramatize your entry. To keep the walkway from feeling cramped, flank the side of the walkway opposite the bed with lawn grass or a low ground cover, such as creeping juniper. As a finishing touch, bathe the walkway in soft light from fixtures hidden in the bed (see Lighting Your Way, page 286).

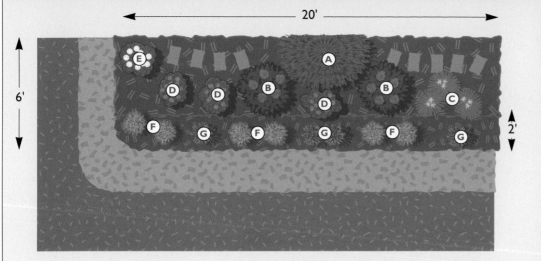

PLANT LIST

A. Japanese black pine, 1, 15 to 80 feet tall

B. Tree peony, 2, 4 to 6 feet tall

C. Daylily, 3, 2 to 3 feet tall

D. Rose 'The Fairy', 3, 2 to 3 feet tall

E. Rose 'Iceberg', 1, 3 feet tall

F. Blue salvia, 6, 3 feet tall

G. Coral bells, 4, 2 feet tall

1. Plant the pine tree (A) in a hole slightly larger than its rootball. Make sure the pine will not block the view from windows.

2. Before planting tree peonies (B), amend 18 inch-deep planting holes with weed-free compost or humus and set the peonies above the enriched soil. Cover the tops with no more than 2 inches of soil.

3. Plant daylilies (C) in a triangle 4 feet from the peony on the right. Lay stone pavers behind these plants for easy access.

4. Plant 2 'The Fairy' roses (D) on the left in front of the stone pavers and 1 in front of the Japanese pine. Plant the 'Iceberg' rose (E) to the far left as shown. Set pavers to right of 'Iceberg' and behind 'The Fairy'

roses. Dig all planting holes for roses 18 inches deep, and amend the soil with one part bagged humus to three parts soil. Refill holes with 8 inches of amended soil. Spread out rose roots and cover them with 3 inches of soil. Flood with water, then finish refilling the holes.

5. Cultivate a 2-foot-wide strip at the front of the bed. Amend the soil with a 4-inch layer of compost, peat moss, and rotted manure to improve its texture. Rake soil smooth, grading it so that the bed slopes away from the walkway. Plant blue salvias (F) and coral bells (G) in a repetitive pattern. Thoroughly water and mulch the bed.

HERE'S HOW

CREATE A FINISHED LOOK

Mulch the interior of your walkway border to suppress weeds, conserve moisture, and neaten the bed. Define the bed's edges with stone, brick, or landscaping timbers. To keep mulch from spilling into the walkway, use broad stones or make an edging that is slightly higher than the bed itself.

Fashioning a Dooryard Garden

THIS GARDEN THRIVES WITH

SUN — Full to partial shade

WATER — Medium

SOIL — Average

A front door framed with attractive plants is a welcoming sight. One of the most common ways to achieve this warm feeling in a dooryard garden is to use the "funnel effect," gradually narrowing the approach to your house. At the same time, try to keep your front door landing as wide as possible, so that two people can walk to the door side by side.

You will want to make your dooryard beds colorful and interesting without letting the area become cramped. In order to do this—since bed space is usually limited—try using only a few different kinds of plants. Layering them according to height will make the entryway appear elevated. Plants with fine-textured leaves usually work better than broad-leaved plants, which can overpower small spaces.

Match the mood of your house when designing your dooryard garden. Symmetrical layers of plants appear formal, a cottage garden style is more relaxed. Use colorful, low-maintenance annuals in containers or hanging baskets near your entranceway, and change them with the seasons for continuous color.

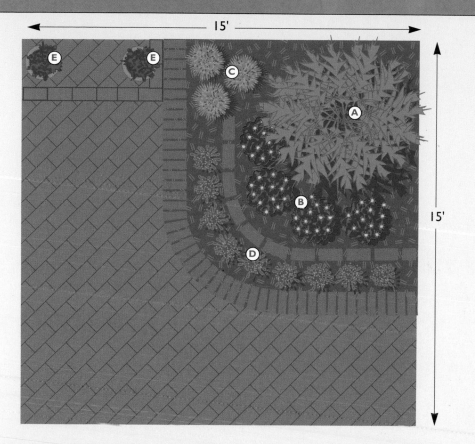

15'

15'

PLANT LIST

A. Tree fern, 1, 20 feet tall

B. Four-o'clock, 4, 3 feet tall

C. Mealycup sage, 3, 3 feet tall

D. Rosea ice plant, 9, 6 inches tall

E. Browallia, 2, 18 inches tall

1. Design and finish the hard surfaces of your entryway. Make sure the walkway is firm and comfortable under foot. It should be slightly angled so that rainwater will drain quickly.

2. Amend the soil in dooryard beds with a 4-inch layer of humus. If your soil is clay, also add a 1-inch layer of sand to improve drainage. To create the planting effect shown, rake the cultivated soil into two tiers so that it is 4 inches higher at the top than at the bottom of the bed. If desired, install a row of retaining bricks to hold soil in place.

3. Plant the tree fern (A) 3 feet from the foundation of the house. Cover the root area at the base of the plant with 2 inches of shredded bark or other organic mulch.

4. Plant four-o'clocks (B) 15 inches apart near the edge of the top tier of soil. Plant mealycup sage (C) in a tight clump on the entry side of the bed. Edge the front of the bed with rosea ice plants (D), spaced 6 inches apart. Thoroughly water the bed.

5. Install hanging baskets planted with browallia (E). Make sure they are low enough to get ample light, yet widely spaced so they do not block the entryway.

HERE'S HOW

HANGING BASKETS

Hanging baskets are usually suspended from metal hooks screwed into the eaves of the house. To adjust the height of the baskets, attach appropriate lengths of chain between the hooks. Position the baskets slightly above eye level where the bottoms and sides can be clearly seen yet allow you to reach the tops to provide water.

Accenting Your Landscape

Special features that personalize your landscape can include statuary, a water garden, cozy garden rooms, collections of special plants, or many other design touches that emphasize what you find most satisfying about the world outside your doors. When thinking over creative projects that will become strong visual accents, pursue the ones that will help develop the theme and tone of your landscape. Knot gardens and topiary usually impart a formal feel, while ponds and shady nooks work best in more relaxed, informal settings. Also choose accents that work well with your climate. Where winters are long, features that remain dramatic when shrouded in snow, such as hedges or sculpture, are especially desirable. Where summers are hot, cool shady spots often become favorite garden places. Garden accents can also help attract birds and butterflies to your property, which bring exciting color and motion to any outdoor scene.

Make sure you can easily reach the focal points in your landscape via walkways or mulched paths, and arrange seating so that you and your family can comfortably enjoy these special places. Also consider factors such as street noise and wind when developing a unique niche within your yard. Familiarize yourself with outdoor lighting, which enhances the appeal of many garden accents. ❧

The Allure of Water

Water gardens add a tranquil touch to the landscape, and they are surprisingly easy to build and maintain. Most water gardens include plants and fish, plus a few snails or frogs for added interest. The size of your water garden, which can be as small as a half-barrel, will be determined by a number of factors, including where it will be placed and which features will be included. An ideal depth ranges between 15 and 30 inches, depending on your climate. Make the pond deeper if you live in a very hot or very cold climate so that fish can take cover in the depths during extreme weather.

Ponds larger than 10 x 10 feet usually require a pump to keep the water circulating, but you can also create a small water garden in which plants and fish work together to keep the water in balance (see Here's How, page 300).

Choose a site that can be seen clearly from your house and gets at least the six hours of sun needed daily to keep your aquatic plants healthy. For a more natural effect, add plants around the outside edges. Since visiting your water garden will probably be a daily activity, you may want to include a hard-surfaced or mulched area nearby for a small garden bench or chairs. ❧

A PREFABRICATED POOL

Rigid fiberglass preformed ponds for water gardens come in many different shapes and depths. Some models are made to be combined into a series of small pools and waterways. This project uses a 3 x 4-foot preformed pond 18 inches deep, which allows enough room for several types of plants and three or four small goldfish or koi. If you run into large rocks or other problems while digging the hole, switch to a flexible plastic liner. Flexible liners cost more than preformed ponds, but they do not require a perfectly excavated hole. ✿

HAVE ON HAND:

▶ One preformed pool

▶ Three 50-pound bags of sand

▶ Tape measure

▶ Shovel

▶ Wheelbarrow

▶ Straight board 4 feet long

▶ Carpenter's level

▶ Stones and plants for landscaping pond edges

Set the pool form on your selected site. Trace around the top rim to define the digging area. Mark the edge with sand.

Dig the hole 1 inch deeper than the depth of the pool. Put excavated soil in a wheelbarrow and move it elsewhere in your yard.

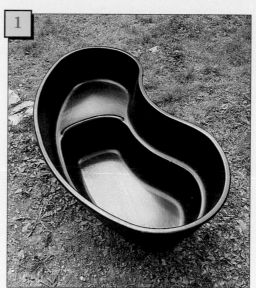

Put a board across the hole and place a carpenter's level on the board. Adjust the soil, making sure the top edges of the hole are level.

Level the bottom of the hole. Set the preformed pond in the hole so that its rim is even with the dirt. Check rim of pond form with the level.

5

Remove pond form and adjust depth of hole as needed to make the pond rim level. Prepare area around pond for stones and plants.

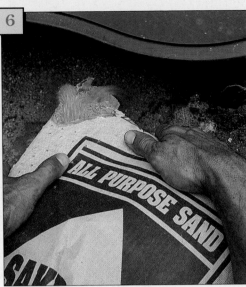

6

Spread 1 inch of sand in bottom of hole. Set pond form in hole. Add more sand to support curved edges on bottom of pond form.

7

Run 4 inches of water into pond. Pack soil to this level behind pond sides. Repeat until pond is full. Place stones and install plants around edges.

8

Wait three days before introducing aquatic plants. After another week, introduce fish and snails. Expect cloudy water for a few weeks.

HERE'S HOW

CHOOSING AQUATIC PLANTS

You can keep the water in your pond clear and oxygenated by stocking it with a mixture of aquatic plants. In a small water garden, when a pump is not used, at least half of the water's surface should be covered with plants. Floating plants such as water hyacinth, parrot feather, and water lettuce will keep water healthy for fish. (Be aware that water hyacinth is invasive and is not recommended for warmer regions.) Grow water lilies and lotus in submerged pots. Bog or shallow-water plants, such as cattails and rushes, fit nicely on ledges constructed along pond edges.

Alternatives

A SIMPLE FOUNTAIN

A submerged pump can bring the music of falling water to your pond. Pumps with filters also help keep the water clear of excessive algae and debris. You can add a pump after your pond is built. Its output can be piped over stones at the pond's edge to create a waterfall, or you can top the pump with a fountainhead to create bubbling or spraying effects. Check with pond suppliers for equipment that is the right size for your pond.

In a small pond, the turbulence caused by a fountain can disturb aquatic plants, but in larger ponds you can simply place plants around the pond's edges where water movement is slow. Submerged pumps must be set up above the pond's bottom, usually on bricks, so the intake valve does not become clogged with debris. When a pump is run without a filter, you will periodically need to remove the material that accumulates on the screen just outside the intake valve. For safe operation, the pump must be plugged into a moisture-proof outlet with a ground-fault circuit interrupter. This outlet can also be used for outdoor lighting around your pond. ❀

TUB WATER GARDEN

Even if your space is limited, you can make a water garden in a container. You will need a half-barrel, plastic tub, or large fiberglass flowerpot that will hold at least 10 gallons of water and two or three aquatic plants. Most container water gardens can only hold one submerged planting pot, but you can plant a miniature water lily and an upright plant, such as a water iris, together in the same pot. Add a floating plant, and you have a miniature water garden capable of keeping itself in natural balance. A 10-gallon tub garden can also accommodate two small goldfish, called comets.

Without fish to control mosquitoes and other insects, keep water moving in your tub garden by installing an aquarium-sized pump. Make a hole in the bottom of the container large enough for the pump's waterproof electrical cord and plug to pass through. Leaving 6 inches of cord inside the container (and the plug outside), seal the hole around the cord with silicone. When sealant is dry, set the pump above the bottom of the container on bricks. Wood barrels need to be lined with a plastic liner to control seepage. Liners that fit wooden half-barrels are available from water-garden suppliers. ❀

Visually Appealing Verticals

Landscape features that direct the eye upward create drama and excitement and are important parts of the framework, or bones, of a landscape's design. These features, called vertical accents, can make any scene more attractive.

Adding vertical architectural features to your landscape will provide height and varying levels of visual interest. Pergolas and arches improve otherwise bland sites. Tall, potted evergreens placed on either side of an entryway can give the illusion of height. Consider a trellis with fragrant, beautiful roses, a distinctive single specimen tree, or perhaps a free-standing pillar that can support climbing plants. These are some of the best ways to add balance to your landscape's design.

The tall trellis of climbing roses pictured here coaxes the eye upward with its vivid splash of color. However, be careful not to let vertical accents become so overwhelming that your house seems small and squat by comparison. In very small enclosed spaces, a pillar covered with vines will achieve the same effect as this rose-covered trellis. The best vertical features are properly scaled to their site. ❧

INSTALLING A HINGED TRELLIS

A hinged trellis is functional as well as attractive, since it can be moved away to paint the wall or to make pruning a plant less awkward. ❧

HAVE ON HAND:

- ▶ Two 50-inch-long 2 x 2 studs
- ▶ Two 8-foot-long 2 x 4 posts
- ▶ 4 x 6-foot heavy-duty lattice panel
- ▶ Exterior enamel paint and brush
- ▶ Four 2-inch hooks and eyes
- ▶ Pencil
- ▶ Carpenter's level
- ▶ Power drill with wood, masonry bits
- ▶ Four 3-inch lag bolts w/lead anchors
- ▶ $^7/_{16}$-inch wrench
- ▶ Screwdriver
- ▶ Saw, power or manual
- ▶ Two $1^1/_2$ x 4-inch strap hinges
- ▶ Posthole digger
- ▶ Two flat stones
- ▶ Hammer
- ▶ Four 1-inch nails
- ▶ Six 1-inch galvanized wood screws
- ▶ 50-pound bag, concrete mix
- ▶ Wheelbarrow
- ▶ Shovel
- ▶ Compost
- ▶ Two climbing roses
- ▶ Mulch
- ▶ Cotton twine or jute

Paint studs, posts, and lattice panel and let them dry. Screw a hook into each stud 1½ inches from top and bottom ends.

Mark level horizontal lines on wall 50 inches long, 78 inches and 42 inches from ground. Drill 1-inch holes in wall and studs equally far apart.

Attach studs to brick wall with lag bolts. Make sure studs are level and ends are plumb before you screw in lag bolts.

Saw off posts 72 inches from tops. Reattach the sawed-off pieces using hinges. Screw eyes on other side of posts 1 inch from top of post.

Dig post holes 20 inches deep. Place flat stones in bottom of holes. Set posts in holes with hinges on the outside. Hook at top to studs.

Adjust posts to make them perfectly plumb. Screw eyes into posts to match hooks in lower horizontal stud. Attach.

Position lattice panel on posts. Attach panel to posts with four nails. Secure panel to posts with six galvanized wood screws.

Mix concrete with water in wheelbarrow. Fill post holes. Let dry at least 48 hours. Wash wheelbarrow immediately after pouring the concrete.

Dig planting holes for roses at least 18 inches from trellis base. Amend soil with compost. Plant roses and water well. Mulch.

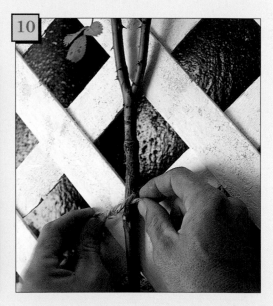

As rose canes grow, tie them to trellis with cotton twine or jute. As you tie, allow room for the stems to thicken.

Alternatives

A SINGLE TREE

Professionally designed home landscapes tend to have one thing in common—a small- to medium-sized ornamental tree placed a few yards from a front corner of the house. It may act as the vertical anchor for a large bed of low-growing shrubs, or it may stand by itself in the lawn. If the tree's purpose is to emphasize the vertical lines of a two-story house, it is usually narrow and tall, such as a column-shaped juniper. In the landscape of a ranch-style house, the tree is more likely to have branches that spread sideways into layers, as do dogwoods and Japanese maples. Flowering cherry, crab apple, and pear trees often are used as vertical accents, too. The best ornamental trees offer something extra in terms of form, flower, fruit for birds or people, or bold fall color.

If your yard is a size that will accommodate only one tree, make the most of it. Surround your tree with a grouping of dwarf shrubs and perennials, or perhaps a blooming ground cover. Finish with a border of edging plants, stonework, or a brick mowing strip.

A PILLAR

Vertical accents that are scaled down to fit small spaces are often called pillars. They function the same as larger vertical structures by making the eye stretch upward while giving the scene more depth. Because the entryway may be the first thing a visitor sees of your yard or landscape, pillars present a great opportunity to refocus attention there.

Gateposts, with or without an attached gate or fence, are classic pillars for defining the entry to a home. In small city yards, the gateposts can be painted to match the front door, which unifies the two elements. Along the entry to a rural property, large stone pillars make a strong statement in the wide-open spaces.

In suburban settings, vertical accents for your entryway might include tall concrete urns spilling over with petunias or verbena, or a pair of tight evergreen shrubs shaped like columns. Single, column-shaped shrubs can become vertical anchors in beds too small to accommodate a tree. In a bed that borders your driveway, use a lamppost as a pillar that also provides outdoor lighting. A birdbath on a thick concrete stand or a bird feeder on a straight black post make attractive, functional vertical accents for your backyard.

Planting a Knot Garden

THIS GARDEN THRIVES WITH

SUN	WATER	SOIL
Full	**Moderate**	**Very well drained**

If your taste tends toward the intricate and refined, sculpting selected plants into shapes and patterns can be tremendously satisfying. Knot gardens, topiary, and espalier were invented to be special features in European "pleasure gardens" in centuries past. All are garden elements that look best in formal landscapes where bold symmetrical lines have been incorporated into the design. Swaths of manicured lawn or handsome stonework make perfect matches for these living sculptures.

Knot gardens emphasize pattern and texture and are best located where they can be viewed from above. You might place a sundial, birdbath, or other ornament in the center, where it will be especially visible in winter when the pattern of your knot is outlined in snow.

The steps at right show the traditional way to mark and plant a knot garden, but there is a modern twist you might consider. If you expect persistent weeds to be a problem, cover the prepared soil with landscaping cloth or fabric weed barrier, and bury the outside edges. Mark the pattern on the fabric mulch, and cut x-shaped holes for your plants. Cover the fabric with a decorative mulch when you are finished. ❧

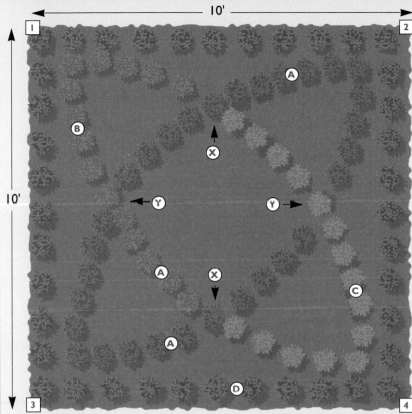

10'

10'

A. Germander, 30, 15 inches tall

B. Green santolina, 15, 22 inches tall

C. Silver santolina, 15, 22 inches tall

D. Dwarf Korean boxwood, 40, 2 feet tall

1. Measure a 10 x 10-foot-square site. Cultivate soil, remove weeds, add soil amendments as needed, and rake smooth.

2. Drive 1-foot stakes into the ground at corners and center. Check measurements to make sure you have a perfect square. The distances between diagonal corners should be the same.

3. Tie taut string between corner stakes. Fill an empty milk jug with dry sand. Mark the line under the string with the sand.

4. Tie one end of a 10-foot length of twine to stake at corner 1, and the other end to the handle of the jug filled with sand. Mark an arc with sand between corner 2 and corner 3. Swing arcs from other corners to form ellipses.

5. Plant the ellipses by placing plants 9 inches apart on the sand line. Where ellipses cross, place plants to create an over-and-under effect. Make the germanders (A) a continuous line at the X points. Use the santolinas (B and C) in a line at the Y points, which will break the line of germanders.

6. Plant boxwoods (D) 10 inches apart on the perimeter sand line. Remove stakes and strings, and water all plants thoroughly. Mulch the spaces inside the pattern with 3 to 4 inches of mulch.

7. When the interior plants show new growth, shear them to a uniform height. Shear boxwoods in midsummer so new growth will harden off before winter.

HERE'S HOW

ADDING GARDEN EDGING

You can play up the formal character of your knot garden and make it easier to groom by surrounding it with a brick edging. Dig a trench as deep and wide as your bricks. Level the bottom with ½ inch of sand, set bricks in place, and fill crevices with additional sand.

Creating Enclosures

THIS GARDEN THRIVES WITH

SUN	WATER	SOIL
Part shade	**Regular to high**	**High organic matter**

There are few outdoor areas more inviting than an enclosed garden designed for comfort and coziness. Whether its walls are made of plants, fencing, or stone, an enclosed garden space provides a tranquil oasis from everyday noise and activity. To adults, garden enclosures are private spots for reading, reflecting, and resting. To children, outdoor rooms are secret places that set the stage for hours of creative play.

When planning your enclosed space, think about what the site has to offer and what you will do in the space once it is complete. Decide what kind of seating, tables, or other furnishings you want to have and sketch a floor plan in the same way that you would if you were creating an indoor room.

To make your enclosure more livable, pave the ground with pebbles, gravel, or other clean mulch material. Whether you are opening up a wooded spot or creating an enclosure in a sunny area, leave one side open to keep it from feeling cramped.

Since you will probably want to use your outdoor room as a place to relax, you may want to choose plants that require little care or cleanup. Most of the plants in the design for this enclosure are permanent and require minimal attention. 🌸

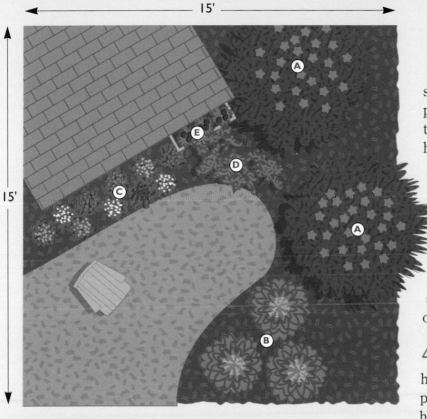

15'

15'

PLANT LIST

A. Rhododendron, 2, 2 to 12 feet tall

B. Hosta, 3, 3 feet tall

C. Impatiens, 9, 14 inches tall

D. Variegated English ivy, 8, 30 feet long

E. Zonal geranium, 3, 1 to 2 feet tall

soil. Set the plants high in the planting holes so that the roots are barely covered. Water well and mulch with pine needles, shredded bark, or leaf mold.

4. Amend planting holes, then plant two hostas (B) 14 inches from edge of walkway, with a third offset behind the two, as shown.

5. Work amendments into area to be planted with impatiens and ivy, or set up a shallow raised bed and fill it with humus-rich soil that holds moisture well. Plant impatiens (C) and variegated ivy (D) and mulch.

6. Plant geraniums (E) in manger planter or wall basket, along with a few rooted pieces of variegated ivy.

7. Water thoroughly. Set furniture in place.

1. Remove plants from the woodland area where you want your enclosure. As you dig, mark natural planting holes you find between large tree roots. Prune low limbs from shade trees.

2. Define your walkway and plan placement of furniture. Add or shift topsoil as needed to create level space for furniture. Grade walkway into a slight slope, so rainwater will run off rather than form muddy puddles. Pave open area with a 2-inch layer of pebbles or gravel.

3. Plant rhododendrons (A) in planting holes that have been amended with one part peat moss to three parts

HERE'S HOW

INSTALLING A PLANTER

Wall baskets and manger planters come with burlap or moss liners to prevent loss of potting soil. While you are installing the hanging hardware for your planter, soak the liner in a bucket of water. Fit the wet liner into the planter and fill with potting soil and plants after the planter is in place.

Glossary

ACCENTS features providing focal points, shape, or shade to garden design.

ACID (ACIDIC) a soil with a pH lower than 7.0; opposite of alkaline. Also known as a sour soil. Slightly acidic soil is acceptable to most plants. A soil pH below 5.5 is too acidic for many plants.

ALKALINE a soil with a pH higher than 7.0; opposite of acidic. Also known as sweet soil.

ANALOGOUS COLORS colors that appear side by side on the color wheel, such as red and purple.

ANNUALS plants that sprout from seed, grow, flower, set seeds, and die within one growing season.

ANTITRANSPIRANT a waxy substance applied to the foliage of overwintering evergreens to prevent dieback from sudden moisture loss.

AROMATIC HERBS grown for fragrance and utility; used in cooking and herbal teas. They can also be dried for decorative purposes.

ASPARAGUS FORK a tool whose 12- to 18-inch metal shank is often used for root-pruning and for removing weeds with long taproots.

BARE-ROOT a plant without soil around its roots, usually shipped dormant. Many trees, shrubs, and perennial plants are sold this way, especially by mail-order nurseries.

BARK MULCH a material sold in bags, made from tree bark that is stripped from logs at lumber mills. The size of the bark varies between large nuggets and small chips.

BASAL CUT to prune a branch or stem at the ground or where it meets another branch or the trunk.

BASE PLAN a map of an existing site showing the location of major features, such as buildings, utilities, roads, trees, and boundaries.

BICOLOR a blossom in which petals are marked with two colors, as when pansies have dark blotches, or petunias have white petals edged with purple.

BIENNIAL a plant that produces only leafy growth during the first growing season, then flowers, sets seed, and dies after living through one winter or a certain period of cool temperatures.

BIODEGRADABLE can be decomposed by living organisms such as bacteria and fungi.

BONE MEAL finely ground white or light gray, rendered slaughterhouse bones; adds nitrogen and phosphorous to soil.

BRANCH COLLAR a series of rings or a bulge where a branch or stem meets another branch or trunk. Place where wound healing occurs.

BROAD-LEAVED EVERGREEN a nonconiferous shrub or tree that retains its green foliage year round, such as a rhododendron or holly.

BUILDER'S SAND also known as horticultural sand; has coarse, large grains that increase drainage and aeration when added to heavy soils.

BULB specifically, a compact structure composed of a central growth bud surrounded by food-storing leaves; also used as a general term to include true bulbs, corms, rhizomes, tubers, and tuberous roots.

BULB PLANTER a cylindrical, hand-held tool used to dig holes for bulbs; minimizes disturbance to nearby tree or shrub roots.

BULBIL a small, bulb-like structure that forms along a plant stem, at the joint of a leaf and the stem.

BULBLET a small bulb that develops underground, from the base of a mature bulb or from the stem produced by a mature bulb.

CANDLES soft new spring growth on pines and other conifers.

CANE stem; often used in relation to roses.

CANOPY the leafy branches of a tree or shrub.

CENTRAL LEADER the main stem of a plant from which laterals are produced, or a shoot growing from its tip.

CLAY SOIL soil composed of very small, flat particles that tend to pack tightly together. Clay soil feels sticky or slippery when wet and forms hard crust or clumps when dry; drains poorly without organic amendments.

CLIMBER a plant that produces long stems that climb up a support or another plant.

CLOSED SOCKET the attachment of a handle to a tool head, such as a spade, where the metal socket wraps around the base of the handle, covering it completely. Usually found on high-quality digging tools.

COMPOST an organic material composed of decaying plant and animal materials.

COMPOUND LEAF a branched leaf with three or more leaflets attached to the main stem.

CONIFEROUS trees or shrubs that bear cones and usually retain their needle-like evergreen foliage year round.

COOL-SEASON GRASSES lawn grasses that grow actively in the spring and fall and become semidormant in the heat of the summer. Grow best in northern climates.

CORM a bulb-like structure composed of a swollen stem surrounded by a papery tunic (covering).

COTTAGE GARDEN an informal combination of annuals, shrubs, perennials, herbs, and/or vegetables; originally a family garden of medicinal and culinary plants.

CROTCH the angle formed between a branch and trunk. Wide angles promote flowering and fruiting and strong branch attachment. Narrow angles are weak and prone to splitting.

CROWN the point where leaves emerge from a plant, just above the place where roots are joined to aboveground plant parts.

CULTIVAR a group of plants that have been chosen and propagated for a particular characteristic, such as flower color or height, and are genetically uniform. Cultivar names are always given in single quotes (as in 'Moonbeam' coreopsis).

CUTTINGS pieces of stems, leaves, or roots taken from plants for propagation.

DEADHEADING removing spent flowers before they produce seeds. Done to stimulate further bloom and conserve plant strength.

DECIDUOUS a plant that loses its leaves for part of the year, usually the fall, prior to becoming dormant.

DIEBACK death of shoot tips and leaves due to disease or damage. Also, a leafless dormant period before regrowth in regular cycle.

DIVISION the technique of separating plant clumps into several smaller parts by pulling or cutting apart crowded roots, bulbs, or corms.

DORMANT plants that are in a resting state, usually during a period of low or high temperatures. They may die down to the roots.

DOUBLE DIGGING the process of loosening the top 12 to 16 inches of soil by removing the top layer with a spade, loosening the lower layer with a spading fork, mixing in amendments, and replacing the top layer.

DOUBLE FLOWER a flower with more than the normal number of petals found in that species, usually in more than one row.

DRAINAGE the gradual flow of water through soil. Drainage depends on steepness of slope, type of soil, and factors such as compaction.

DRIPLINE the area under the outermost branch tips of a tree or plant.

EDGING a line that establishes visual interest and separation; for example, between a lawn and the foliage of a shrub or perennial border.

EROSION the movement of topsoil away from a given site by water or wind.

EVERGREEN plants that hold their foliage for more than one growing season.

FLAT a shallow tray used to hold soil or pots.

FOLIAGE PLANTS annuals or perennials grown for leaf shape, size, texture, and color; supplying contrast and interest in the garden.

FORCING providing the right combination of temperatures to encourage growth and flowering; usually used in relation to growing bulbs for indoor flowering in late winter.

FORGED STEEL metal that has undergone heat treatment to increase its strength and durability.

FORMAL in garden design, a style that is clearly structured by defined lines, and shows a high degree of symmetry and balance. The overall mood of a formal landscape is very neat and orderly. Front yards usually involve formal designs.

FOUNDATION the part of a house that rests upon the ground, or extends into the ground. The foundation is usually constructed of concrete or concrete blocks.

FRAMING definition of a landscape view by the creation of visual boundaries with plantings or structures.

FUNGICIDE a compound applied to plants or soil to kill fungi.

GRADE a term that describes the degree of slope in a given site. Level sites have zero grade. To grade a site means to reshape soil into a very slight slope that helps water drain away from the house.

GRAFT UNION a swollen area near the base of a stem, where the top of one plant has been joined to the roots of another.

GREEN MANURE cover crops such as buckwheat and annual ryegrass grown in the garden in fall and turned under in spring to enrich soil.

GROUND COVER any plants, shrubs, or materials planted or placed where grass is not desired or practical. Used to cover steep slopes or rocky terrains, for example.

GROWING SEASON the time between the last spring frost and the first fall frost.

HALF-HARDY used to describe a plant that may be damaged by cold temperatures in a particular area. Half-hardy annuals usually need to be started indoors and set out after the last spring frost; they can generally tolerate more cold once they are established. Half-hardy perennials may survive mild winters outdoors but usually need to be brought indoors or protected with mulch to survive cold temperatures.

HARDENING OFF the process of gradually exposing plants started indoors to outdoor conditions.

HARDPAN a dense, compacted layer below the soil surface.

HARDY plants in a given area that survive winter either in a dormant state or while holding green leaves. Hardiness can be affected by heat, rainfall, and other conditions.

HEADING BACK pruning a branch or a stem in order to redirect its growth or to stimulate denser branching.

HEAVY SOIL soil with a high clay content.

HOLDFASTS aerial rootlets that end in sticky pads that vines, such as Virginia creeper, use to attach themselves to vertical objects.

HUMUS decayed organic matter that is added to soil to improve its structure and ability to hold air and water. Compost, peat moss, rotted leaves, weathered straw, composted bark, and rotted sawdust are different types of humus.

HYBRID a genetically unique variety created by crossing specific parent plants. Hybrid varieties often are unusually vigorous and resistant to pests or diseases. The seeds produced by hybrid plants often show characteristics of the parent varieties rather than the unique hybrid.

INFORMAL in garden design, a style that often shows loose, curved lines rather than straight ones, makes use of plants in their natural shapes, and imparts a mood of lush exuberance. Backyards often reflect informal designs.

INSECTICIDE a compound used to kill insects.

ISLAND BEDS focal-point plantings surrounded by lawn, paths or paving. Plants are often set from tallest in center to shortest at edges for maximum visibility.

KNOT GARDEN a garden design that creates the illusion of entwined fabric or knotted rope.

LANDSCAPE DESIGN the purposeful layout of plants, shrubs, trees, structures and ornaments in outdoor areas.

LAYERING the process of treating a shoot so it will form roots while still attached to the parent plant; a common method of propagating roses.

LEACHING the loss of nutrients from the soil's top layer due to water draining through it.

LEVEL in carpentry, a board, plank, or other structural part that is perfectly horizontal. A tool called a carpenter's level is used to see if the line is perfectly horizontal.

LIGHT SOIL soil with a high sand content.

LIME a calcium compound usually applied to acidic soil to raise the pH into the normal range. The type of lime best for gardens, called agricultural or garden lime, is made from ground limestone.

LOAM a mixture of 40 percent sand, 40 percent silt, and 20 percent clay that drains and holds nutrients well. Considered ideal for growing most plants.

MICROCLIMATE an area within a larger climate in which local factors such as shade, moisture and exposure make it different from the surrounding area.

MICROORGANISMS microscopic fungi and bacteria that live in the soil where they decompose organic material into humus.

MINIATURE WETLANDS areas in any garden where water is naturally retained and can be developed to support moisture-loving plants.

MULCH any material spread over the soil surface to retain soil moisture, moderate soil temperature, and suppress the growth of weeds.

NATIVE PLANTS species occurring naturally in any region; they are commonly hardy and easy-care.

NATURALIZE to set out plants in masses to create a natural-looking effect; often used in relation to bulbs planted in grassy or woodland areas.

NEUTRAL PLANTS in garden design, neutral plants are those with gray or gray-green foliage, or sometimes plants that bear white flowers. Neutrals are used to offset potential clashes between different colors, to bridge the visual gap between textures, or to impart a feeling of spaciousness.

NODE the point where a bud or leaf (or a pair of leaves) joins a stem.

NURSERY BED a special plot set aside for growing young plants and bulbs until they are large enough to survive in the regular garden.

OPEN SOCKET the attachment of a handle to a tool head, such as a shovel, in which the base of the wooden handle is exposed. Common on digging tools of lesser quality.

ORGANIC a general term applied to mulches and other materials derived from decomposed plant or animal products; also used to describe the process of growing plants without the use of synthetic chemicals.

ORGANIC MATTER mulch or other material derived from decomposed plant or animal products.

PANICLE the plant structure that works like a flower spike in grasses. Although not true flowers, panicles produce pollen and later develop seeds.

PATHOGEN an organism that causes disease, such as a bacteria, virus, or fungus.

PAVERS special bricks or flat pieces of formed concrete used for constructing walkways. Pavers are usually not as thick as building bricks, and are made of a dense material so that they resist cracking under pressure.

PEAT MOSS a type of humus made from pulverized peat, a bog plant that grows in scattered cold climate areas. Peat moss has an acidic pH.

PERENNIALS species that can live for more than two years.

PERGOLA an arbor or trellis connected with an open roof; used to support vines.

PERLITE white granules of a treated volcanic mineral; add to potting soil to improve drainage.

PESTICIDE a substance used to kill insects, control diseases, or both. Types of pesticides include insecticides, which control only insects, and fungicides, which control fungal diseases.

pH a measure of a soil's acidity or alkalinity on a scale of 1.0 to 14.0, with 7.0 neutral; pH below 7.0 is acidic; above 7.0 is alkaline.

PHOTODEGRADABLE material that decomposes when exposed to ultraviolet radiation from sun.

PINCHING using your thumb and forefinger to remove a shoot tip, generally to encourage a plant to produce bushier growth.

PLUMB in carpentry, a post or plank that is perfectly vertical.

PRUNING the process of cutting away unwanted branches from a plant. Pruning can be done to remove damaged or diseased plant parts, to shape the plant, or to force the plant to send available energy to flowering buds.

REJUVENATE severe pruning done to remove unwanted growth and encourage new shoots.

RESEED the ability of some plants to shed seeds that successfully germinate and grow.

RHIZOME an underground shoot that produces a new plant at its tip. Many grasses and weeds spread by this method.

ROOT SUCKER a plant stem that grows up from the roots.

ROOT ZONE area around a tree, shrub, or plant where the roots grow. May extend well beyond the dripline in some plants.

ROOTBALL the mass of roots and potting soil visible when you remove a plant from its pot.

ROOTSTOCK the root system of a grafted plant.

RUNNER a horizontal, aboveground stem that produces roots at the nodes.

RUNOFF water that flows above ground, often causing erosion.

SAND a soil type made up of large, gritty soil particles. Sandy soils drain quickly and do not hold moisture well unless they are improved by the addition of humus.

SCALE overall size of a garden; helps determine the plants used in garden design.

SEED HEADS pods or clusters of seeds at the top of mature plants at the end of growing season.

SELF-SEEDING (self-sowing) an annual's ability to drop seeds that successfully germinate and grow into seedlings.

SHEARING removing the growing tips of a plant to create a uniform height or shape. Usually done with hedge clippers.

SHOOT a branch, stem, or twig.

SHRUB a bushy, woody-stemmed plant, usually with multiple stems at ground level.

SILT medium-sized soil particles with irregular shapes. Silty soil feels smooth when wet and crumbly when dry.

SIMPLE DIGGING the process of loosening the top 1 foot of soil and amending it; suitable for shallow-rooted shrubs and perennials.

SINGLE FLOWER a flower with a single row of petals, usually four to six.

SOAKER HOSES porous, rubber hoses that allow seepage for deep root watering, eliminate evaporation and keep leaves dry.

SOCKET the extension of a tool head that joins the handle. Longer sockets yield stronger tools.

SOIL COMPACTION process by which air and water spaces between soil particles are eliminated or reduced, resulting in runoff and poor plant growth. Caused by working in, or walking on, wet soil; occurs in heavy traffic areas.

SOIL HEAVING the forcing of plants, stones, or other materials to the soil surface through alternate freezing and thawing. Affects young plants in particular.

SOLARIZING heating the soil using the sun's energy, usually to kill weeds and soil-borne pathogens. Commonly done by laying black plastic over the soil and sealing the edges.

SPECIMEN PLANT one plant positioned to show off its full development and attributes; often a focal point.

SPP. classification of plants within a genus. Species have one or more common characteristics. May reproduce themselves from seeds.

SPUR short twig or shoot that bears flowers, fruit, and leaves. Found on many fruit trees and some shade trees.

STAGGERED PLANTING positioning plants so that one is not directly in front of another.

STAKING supporting tall plants with stakes to help keep them upright.

STANDARD plant trained to grow as a single, leafless stem topped with a bushy "head."

STOLON an aboveground, horizontal shoot that produces a new plant at its tip. Many ground covers, such as periwinkle, spread this way.

STUB short piece of branch or twig that extends beyond the branch collar after pruning. It slows the healing process and should be removed.

SWALE a long depression in the ground commonly used to channel water runoff. Can be man-made or a natural contour of the land.

TANG AND FERRULE system of attaching a tool head, such as a rake or hoe, to a wooden handle with a spike and a metal jacket to prevent wood from splitting. Common on inexpensive tools.

TENDER a plant susceptible to frost damage.

TERMINAL STEM growing tip on a plant.

TEXTURE the surface characteristic of a plant.

THINNING removing individual stems or whole plants to give remaining stems or plants room to develop without crowding and to allow more air and light to reach the interior of the plant.

TOP DRESSING adding compost or fertilizer to the soil surface above plant roots.

TOPIARY shrubs trained and pruned to resemble animals and geometric shapes.

TRELLISES frames of varying shapes and sizes used to support climbing vines or canes.

TUBER fleshy underground stems with "eyes" that develop into roots or leaves and flowers.

TUBEROUS ROOTS swollen, fleshy roots joined by a bud-bearing crown.

VARIEGATED LEAVES foliage with discrete markings or margins.

VARIETY a naturally occurring variant of a plant; indicated by the word "var." in a plant's name (as in *Imperata cylindrica* var. *rubra*).

VERMICULITE a lightweight, flaky material produced by exposing mica to high heat; often added to potting mix to improve water retention and drainage.

VERTICAL ACCENT any upright plant (including trees, shrubs, vines, grasses) or structure used as a contrast or focal point in the landscape.

WARM-SEASON GRASSES lawn grasses that thrive in warm-winter climates and grow vigorously in the summer. Usually not hardy in northern climates.

WATER SPROUT vigorous shoot that grows straight up from a branch often in response to extensive pruning. Usually removed.

WOUND a cut or damaged area on a plant.

Index

Time-Life Books is a division of Time Life Inc.

TIME LIFE INC.
President and CEO: Jim Nelson

TIME-LIFE TRADE PUBLISHING
Vice President and Publisher: Neil Levin
Senior Director of Acquisitions and Editorial Resources: Jennifer Pearce
Director of New Product Development: Carolyn Clark
Director of Trade Sales: Dana Coleman
Director of Marketing: Inger Forland
Director of New Product Development: Teresa Graham
Director of Custom Publishing: John Lalor
Director of Special Markets: Robert Lombardi
Director of Design: Kate L. McConnell

YARD & GARDEN PROJECTS
Managing Editor: Donia Ann Steele
Consulting Editors: Linda B. Bellamy, Kathleen Mallow
Production Manager: Carolyn Clark
Quality Assurance: James D. King, Stacy L. Eddy
Editor for Special Markets (spiral): Anna Burgard
Technical Specialist (spiral): Monika Lynde
Project Coordinator (spiral): Jennifer L. Ward
Production Manager (spiral): Vanessa Hunnibell

PRODUCED BY STOREY COMMUNICATIONS, INC.
POWNAL, VERMONT
President: M. John Storey
Executive Vice President: Martha M. Storey
Director of Custom Publishing: Amanda Haar
Custom Acquisitions Director: Deirdre Lynch
Custom Managing Editor: Catherine Gee Graney
Project Manager: Vivienne Jaffe, Robert Pini
Book Design: Jonathon Nix/Verso Design
Design and Layout: Jennifer Jepson, Betty Kodela, Jen Rork, Stephanie Saunders, Mark Tomasi
Editing: Joan Burns, Vivienne Jaffe
Authors: Nancy Ondra, Barbara Pleasant, Luanne Urfer, Ann Turner Whitman
Primary Photography: A. Blake Gardner, David Goldberg, Kevin Kennefick
Photo Styling: Derek Fell, Pam Peirce

Additional photography: Cathy Wilkinson Barash; Linda Bellamy; Patricia J. Bruno/Positive Images; ©Crandall & Crandall; R. Todd Davis; ©Alan and Linda Detrick; Derek Fell; Peggy Fisher; Roger Foley; A. Blake Gardner; David Goldberg; Harry Haralambou/Positive Images; Margaret Hensel/Positive Images; Jerry Howard/Positive Images; Kevin Kennefick; Peter Lindtner; Charles Mann; J. Paul Moore; Kathlene Persoff; Jerry Pavia; Paul Rocheleau; Richard Shiell; Pam Spaulding/Positive Images; Patricia Taylor; Michael S. Thompson; Robert Walch; judywhite

Pre Press Services, Time-Life Imaging Center
Printed in U.S.A.
10 9 8 7 6 5 4 3 2

TIME-LIFE is a trademark of Time Warner Inc., and affiliated companies.
Time-Life How-To is a trademark of Time-Life Books.

Library of Congress Cataloging-in-Publication Data
Yard & garden projects : easy, step-by-step plans and designs for beautiful outdoor spaces / by the editors of Time-Life Books.
   p. cm.
   Includes index.
   ISBN 0-7835-5329-3 (comb binding)
   ISBN 0-7370-0604-8 (deluxe spiral binding)
   1. Gardens--Design. 2. Landscape gardening. 3. Plants, Ornamental. I. Time-Life Books.
SB473.Y28 1998   97-46418
635.9--dc21   CIP

Books produced by Time-Life Trade Publishing are available at special bulk discount for promotional and premium use. Custom adaptations can also be created to meet your specific marketing goals. Call 1-800-323-5255.

Zone Map

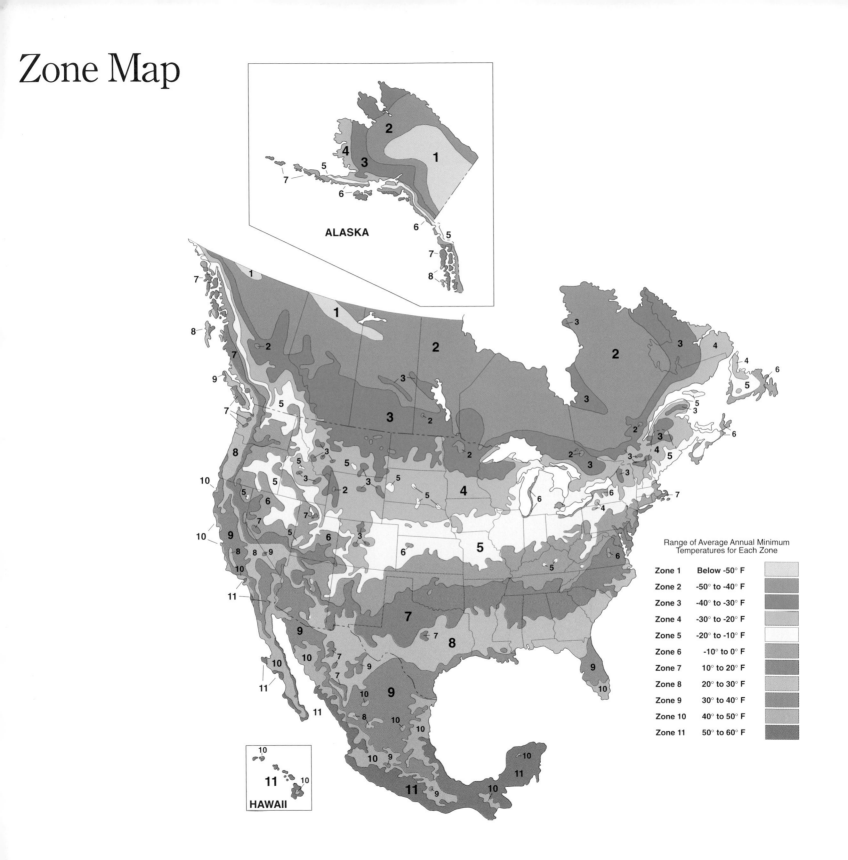

ALASKA

HAWAII

Range of Average Annual Minimum
Temperatures for Each Zone

Zone 1	Below -50° F
Zone 2	-50° to -40° F
Zone 3	-40° to -30° F
Zone 4	-30° to -20° F
Zone 5	-20° to -10° F
Zone 6	-10° to 0° F
Zone 7	10° to 20° F
Zone 8	20° to 30° F
Zone 9	30° to 40° F
Zone 10	40° to 50° F
Zone 11	50° to 60° F